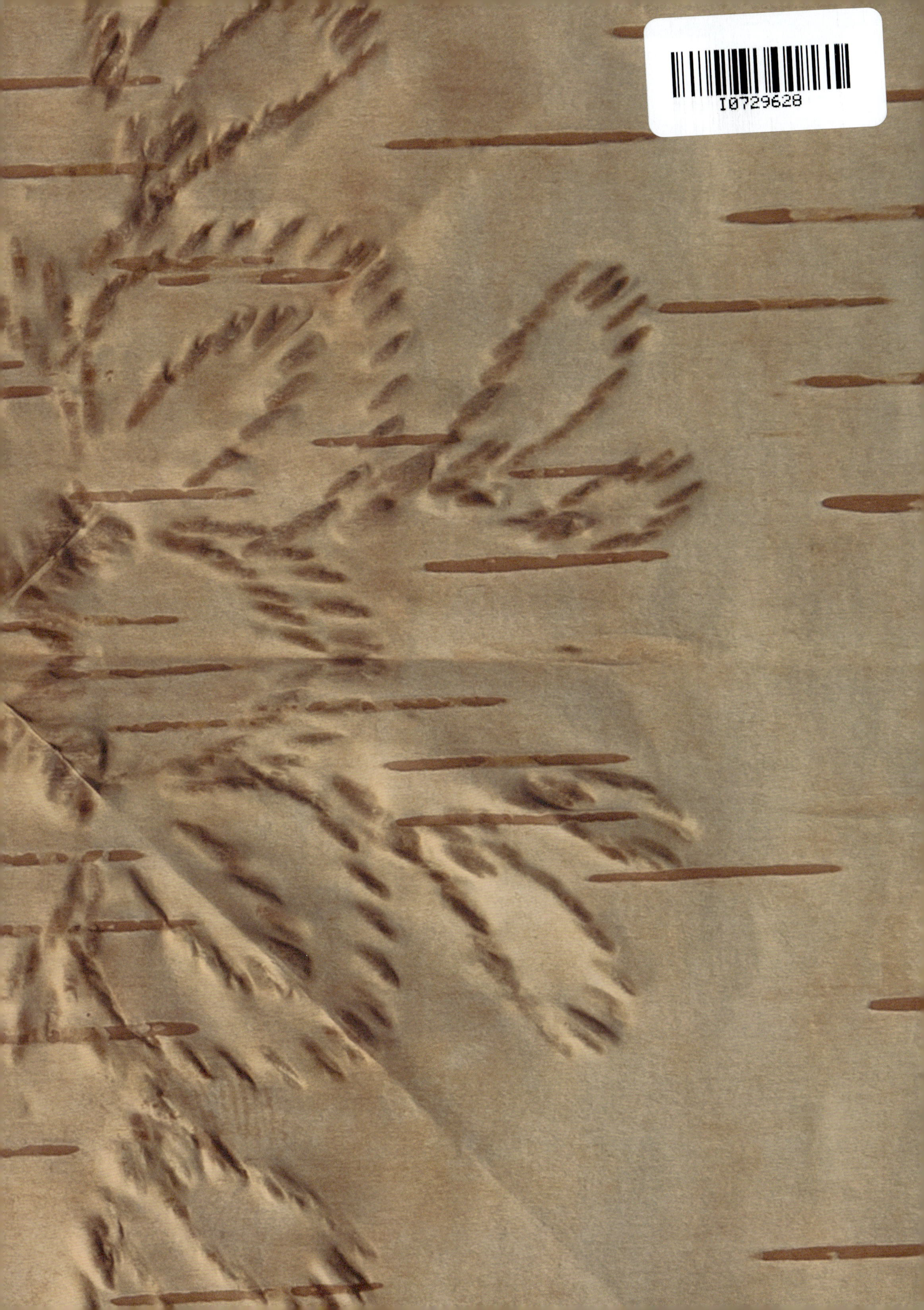

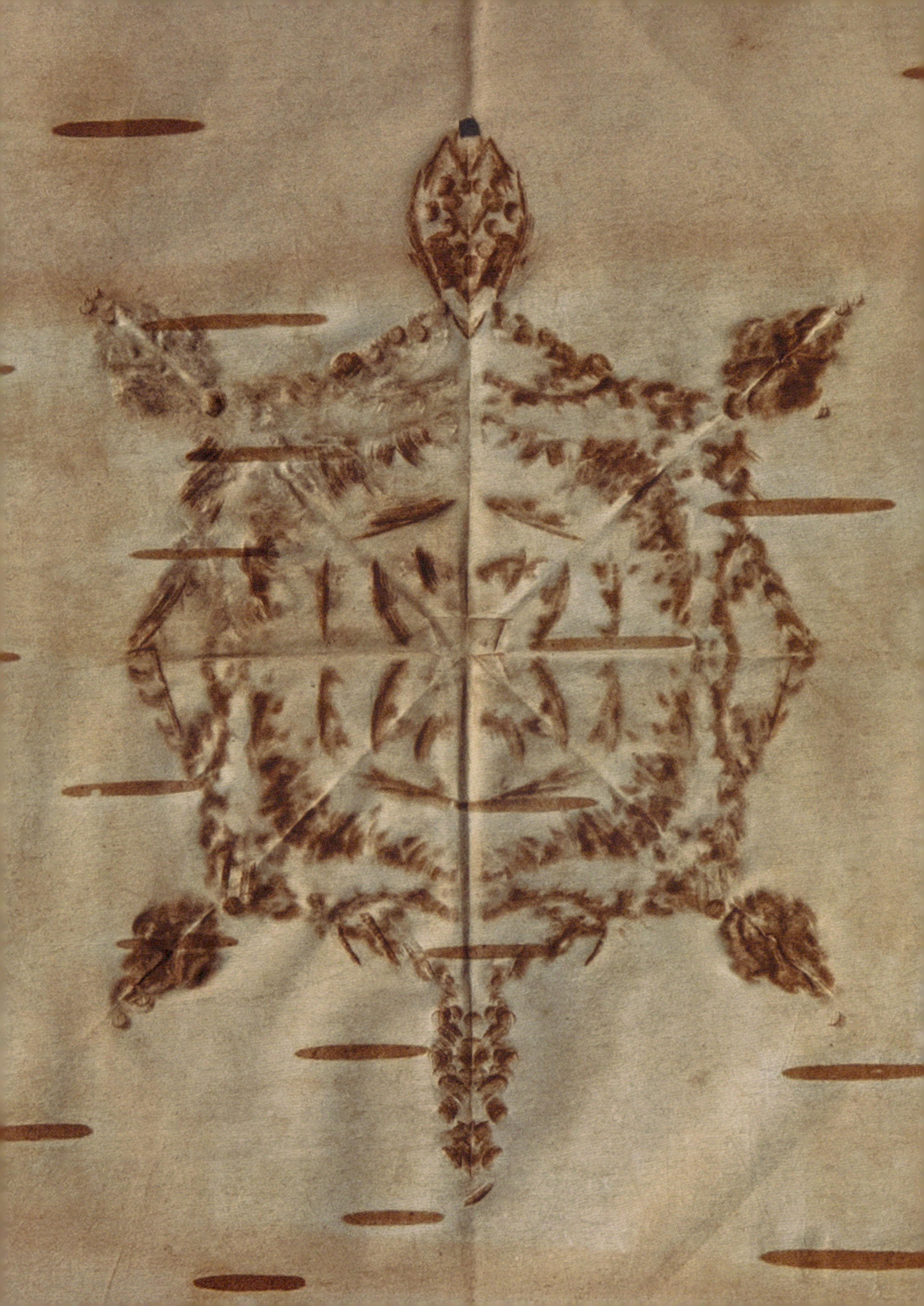

Woven Being

Edited by Kathleen Bickford Berzock, Janet Dees, and Jordan Poorman Cocker

Contributions by Marisa Cruz Branco, Denise Lajimodiere, Jacqueline Lopez, John Low, Blaire Morseau, and Anne Terry Straus

Published by the Mary and Leigh Block Museum of Art, Northwestern University, Evanston, Illinois

Woven Being

Art for Zhegagoynak/Chicagoland

Director's Foreword

Entering Northwestern University's Segal Visitors Center, one is greeted by the work of master canoe builder Wayne Valliere (Lac du Flambeau Ojibwe). Created during an artist residency hosted by the university's Center for Native American and Indigenous Research (CNAIR), Valliere's birchbark *jiimaan* carries with it the past, as represented by the boat's stern, *ishkweyaang-jiimaan*, and points us toward the future, as represented by its bow, *niigaan-jiimaan*.[1] With the exhibition *Woven Being: Art for Zhegagoynak/Chicagoland* and this accompanying book, we hope to do the same.

The Block Museum of Art supports Northwestern University's commitment to strengthening its relationships with Native American and Indigenous nations, communities, and organizations. We realize this commitment by amplifying the voices of Indigenous artists, scholars, museum colleagues, and knowledge sharers across all aspects of our work—from exhibitions and acquisitions to public programs and cinema screenings. The Block's new strategic plan prioritizes building a lasting relationship with CNAIR, which has made visual arts programming, including artist residencies, a centerpiece of its identity. CNAIR's work with artists, whether through the work of its affiliates, its Artist and Elder in Residence program, or its support of external organizations, embodies the way in which creative practices intertwine with research, offering important means of knowing and understanding the world. The Block recently reframed its own mission to focus on art's power as a form of insight, research, and knowledge creation that makes human experience visible and material. We have much to learn from Indigenous communities that have understood this to be the role of art since time immemorial.

The work of developing *Woven Being: Art for Zhegagoynak/ Chicagoland* has deepened our commitment through the embrace of Indigenous-informed methodologies. This publication reflects this process and the perspectives of those with whom we have engaged. Guest co-curator Jordan Poorman Cocker (Kiowa), Curator of Indigenous Art at the Crystal Bridges Museum of American Art, joined The Block's *Woven Being* team—Kathleen Bickford Berzock, Associate Director of Curatorial Affairs; Janet Dees, former Steven and Lisa Munster Tananbaum Curator of Modern and Contemporary Art; Erin Northington, Susan and Stephen Wilson Associate Director of Campus and Community Education and Engagement; and Dan Silverstein, Associate Director of Collections and Exhibition Management—at the outset. Jordan has served as both colleague and mentor. Among her first recommendations to the *Woven Being* team was to examine The Block's positionality in relation to Indigenous people. This critically important contribution, which focused on our role as a museum, as part of Northwestern, and in Evanston and the Chicagoland region, has left a lasting impression on The Block's staff. We will be forever grateful to Jordan for her trust in us as we embarked on an extraordinary journey of learning.

The final shape of the exhibition was developed in collaboration with artists Andrea Carlson (Grand Portage Ojibwe/European descent), Kelly Church (Match-E-Be-Nash-She-Wish Band of Pottawatomi/Ottawa), Nora Moore Lloyd (Lac Courte Oreilles Band of Lake Superior Ojibwe), and Jason Wesaw (Pokagon Band of Potawatomi). Their perspectives breathed meaning into the exhibition title, and their approach has embodied a spirit of generosity and care. Lois Taylor Biggs (Cherokee Nation/White Earth Ojibwe), former Terra Foundation Curatorial Research Fellow at The Block, played a significant role in the early phase of the project, conducting invaluable research that informed the positionality statement, exhibition approach, and selection of collaborating artists. Current Terra Foundation Curatorial Research Fellow Marisa Cruz Branco (Isleta Pueblo/Portuguese) and Terra Foundation Engagement Fellow Teagan Harris (Cherokee Nation) have deftly supported the implementation phase of the project.

Our work on this project would not have been possible without the counsel and support of Native American and Indigenous colleagues and organizations on and off campus, who have helped us understand the context in which this exhibition is being presented, specifically the actions and events that have shaped our region and Northwestern University. Programs such as Northwestern's "30 Days of Indigenous" and the Native American and Indigenous Student Alliance's annual Pow Wow have been important campus touch points for the Block team to connect to the past and reflect on what it means for us now. The many individuals and organizations that have contributed to this project are thanked in the acknowledgments; however, I would like to offer my gratitude in particular to CNAIR and its director, Megan Bang (Ojibwe/Italian descent), Professor of Learning Sciences; Jasmine Gurneau (Oneida Nation/Menominee Tribe of Wisconsin), Director of Native American and Indigenous Affairs in the Office of Institutional Diversity and Inclusion; Aaron Golding (Seneca Nation), Senior Program Administrator in the School of Education and Social Policy; Bryan Brayboy (Lumbee), Dean of the School of Education and Social Policy and Carlos Montezuma Professor of Education and Social Policy; and Kim Vigue (Menominee), Executive Director of the Gichigamiin Indigenous Nations Museum and Block Museum board member.

At The Block, we continually ask ourselves what it means to be doing our work now and from here. We believe that we can deepen the resonance of what we do by making decisions grounded in our time and place. We think about "place" in all its richness and complexity: within Northwestern, within the context of our region, and as part of the global community. We think about our place on Indigenous lands, the traditional homelands of the people of the Council of Three Fires—the Ojibwe, the Potawatomi, and the Odawa—as well as the Menominee, Miami, and Ho-Chunk Nations. We also remember our connection to another site, in southeastern Colorado, Sand Creek, that is woven into the identity of our university. Northwestern was founded by John Evans, who served as second governor of the Territory of Colorado and superintendent of Indian affairs when the Sand Creek Massacre took place in 1864. During the development of this exhibition, members of the Block team visited the Sand Creek

Massacre National Historic Site to better understand the connection between Northwestern's history and what occurred there.

In undertaking *Woven Being*, The Block is enacting our commitment to Native American and Indigenous artists and histories. I wish to thank our funders, lenders, artists, and contributors for their support. We owe special recognition to the Terra Foundation for American Art for their crucial funding of this project from inception to presentation through their Art Design Chicago initiative, and for their encouragement and openness to the exhibition's methodologies.

Finally, we wish to acknowledge the Northwestern University Office of the Provost and Michael Schill, President of Northwestern University, for making the arts a priority. At his 2023 investiture, President Schill exchanged gifts with representatives of Northwestern's Indigenous campus community. Gifts were offered to the president four times before he accepted, symbolizing his careful consideration of obligations to Indigenous faculty, students, staff, and community within our region.

A similar kind of careful consideration has imbued our efforts at The Block as we work to more fully realize our responsibilities as a museum in relationship to our Indigenous campus community members, artists, and knowledge sharers. *Woven Being* is one manifestation of our deepening commitment to these responsibilities, grounded in the values of generosity and reciprocity. Its creation has been an experience of profound learning and growth for those of us who have had a hand in it, and has built a strong foundation for our future work.

Lisa Graziose Corrin
Ellen Philips Katz Executive Director
The Block Museum of Art, Northwestern University

1 For an explanation of the parts of the canoe, see the website "These Canoes Carry Culture," cnair-canoe.github.io/canoe/index.html.

Acknowledgments

Our sincere gratitude extends first to the land, the lakefill, and the water that surrounds us in Zhegagoynak, the Chicagoland region. The Block, Northwestern University's art museum, stands on the shore of Lake Michigan, and we begin these acknowledgments by thanking the land and water that give life and provide the place and site for this work. Past, present, and future generations are sustained by you, the land. We are grateful to the ancestors of the artists and writers engaged in this project, whose resilience and love carried art forms from one generation to the next. We know this exhibition is but one step on the path paved by generations of Indigenous artists, scholars, activists, advocates, and allies, whose life's work toward sovereignty and social equity transforms this place into a home. We hope this single step contributes to a better collective future.

We thank the artists whose work is shown in the exhibition and featured in this publication: Artist Once Known (Anishinaabe), Josef Albers (American, born Germany), Rick Bartow (Mad River Band of Wiyot Indians), Frank Big Bear (White Earth Ojibwe), Roy Boney (Cherokee Nation), Avis Charley (Spirit Lake Dakota/Diné), Woodrow Wilson Crumbo (Citizen Potawatomi), Nancy Fisher Cyrette (Grand Portage Ojibwe), Jim Denomie (Lac Courte Oreilles Band of Ojibwe), Heid E. Erdrich (Turtle Mountain Band of Ojibwe), Jeffrey Gibson (Mississippi Band of Choctaw Indians/Cherokee), Teri Greeves (Kiowa), Denise Lajimodiere (Turtle Mountain Band of Ojibwe), Mark LaRoque (White Earth Ojibwe), Jeanne LaTraille (Oneida), Courtney M. Leonard (Shinnecock), Agnes Martin (American, born Canada), Wanesia Misquadace (Minnesota Lake Superior Chippewa Tribe, Fond du Lac Band), George Morrison (Grand Portage Ojibwe), Barnett Newman (American), Daphne Odjig (Odawa/Potawatomi), Virgil Ortiz (Cochiti Pueblo), Chris Pappan (Kaw [Kanza]/Osage/Lakota), Cherish Parrish (Match-E-Be-Nash-She-Wish Band of Pottawatomi/Ottawa), John Pigeon (Pokagon Band of Potawatomi), Simon Pokagon (Pokagon Band of Potawatomi), Jason Quigno (Saginaw Chippewa), Monica Rickert-Bolter (Prairie Band Potawatomi/Black), Jane Johnston Schoolcraft (Ojibwe), Sharon Skolnick (Fort Sill Apache/Lakota), Rhiannon Skye Tafoya (Eastern Band Cherokee/Santa Clara Pueblo), Lisa Telford (Haida), Mary Person Topash (Pokagon Band of Potawatomi), Thomas Topash (Pokagon Band of Potawatomi), Mark Turcotte (Turtle Mountain Band of Ojibwe), Joe Yazzie (Navajo), and Debra Yepa-Pappan (Jemez Pueblo/Korean).

We are grateful to our collaborating artists, Andrea Carlson (Grand Portage Ojibwe/European descent), Kelly Church (Match-E-Be-Nash-She-Wish Band of Pottawatomi/Ottawa), Nora Moore Lloyd (Lac Courte Oreilles Band of Lake Superior Ojibwe), and Jason Wesaw (Pokagon Band of Potawatomi), who have generously given their time and their creativity to shaping this exhibition. They have participated with kindness and modeled reciprocity in collaboration. *Woven Being: Art for Zhegagoynak/Chicagoland* also benefited from the intellectual contributions and daily partnership of Lois Taylor Biggs (Cherokee Nation/White Earth Ojibwe), Terra Foundation

Curatorial Research Fellow and Assistant Curator at The Block, during the two-year research and development phase of the project (2021–23).

We extend our gratitude to the private and institutional lenders who have so generously made works available for exhibition: Kelly Church, Elaine and Peter Liebesman, Jason Wesaw, the Art Institute of Chicago, Blue Rain Gallery, the Denver Art Museum, the Eiteljorg Museum of American Indians and Western Art, Forge Project, the Gochman Family Collection, the Indian Arts Research Center at the School for Advanced Research, the J.W. Wiggins Native American Art Collection at the University of Arkansas at Little Rock, the Minneapolis Institute of Art, the Newberry Library, the Sequoyah National Research Center at the University of Arkansas at Little Rock, the Smart Museum of Art at the University of Chicago, the Vanderbilt University Museum of Art, and the Walker Art Center.

We are indebted to authors Denise Lajimodiere (Turtle Mountain Band of Ojibwe), John Low (Pokagon Band of Potawatomi), Blaire Morseau (Pokagon Band of Potawatomi), and Anne Terry Straus for their thoughtful contributions. They have deftly integrated their areas of expertise and experience with their personal connections to the artists they write about, weaving stories that deepen our sense of how each artist has approached this project. Additionally, Jacqueline Lopez's resource guide to the Indigenous artists and art spaces of Chicago from the 1950s to today is a significant contribution to research and provides important context for the other chapters. We warmly thank Marisa Cruz Branco (Isleta Pueblo/Portuguese), who has fearlessly managed the image captions throughout the book and contributed her thoughts to the Plates section. We are also grateful to Forrest Bruce (Fond du Lac Ojibwe), Bmejwen Kyle Malott (Pokagon Band of Potawatomi), and Isadore Toulouse (Wiikwemkoong First Nation) for their skill and sensitivity in translating the book and chapter titles and portions of text.

Staff, faculty, students, and offices at Northwestern University have been our stalwart partners, collaborators, and mentors throughout this project. In particular, we thank Megan Bang (Ojibwe/Italian descent), Patty Loew (Bad River Band of Lake Superior Ojibwe), Michaela Marchi (Isleta Pueblo/Filipina/Italian), Pamala Silas (Menominee Tribe of Wisconsin/descendant of the Oneida Nation), and Katherine Castillo Valentin at the Center for Native American and Indigenous Research; Bryan Brayboy (Lumbee) and Aaron Golding (Seneca Nation), School of Education and Social Policy; Jasmine Gurneau (Oneida Nation/Menominee Tribe of Wisconsin), Office of Institutional Diversity and Inclusion; Doug Kiel (Oneida Nation), Department of History; Eli Suzukovich III (Little Shell Band of Chippewa-Cree/Krajina Serb), Program in Environmental Policy and Culture; Kelly Wisecup, Department of English; and members of the Indigenous Graduate Student Collective and the Native American and Indigenous Student Alliance.

Woven Being: Art for Zhegagoynak/Chicagoland was imagined through dialogue with participants in two external visioning sessions.

We express deep appreciation to the following individuals for their foundational insights that have helped to shape the direction of the project: Forrest Bruce, Andrea Carlson, Kelly Church, Aaron Golding, Kendra Greendeer (Ho-Chunk), Josh Honn, River Kerstetter (Oneida), John Low, Jennifer Michals (Citizen Potawatomi/Lac Courte Oreilles Ojibwe/Kickapoo), Blaire Morseau, Chris Pappan, Margaret Pearce (Citizen Potawatomi), Pamala Silas, Dave Spencer (Mississippi Chata/Diné), Isabel St. Arnold (Keweenaw Bay Ojibwe), Jane Stevens, Eli Suzukovich III, Dorene Wiese (White Earth Ojibwe), and Debra Yepa-Pappan.

We are grateful to the organizations that undertake the necessary work of supporting, sharing, and amplifying the stories and experiences of Indigenous communities in Zhegagoynak. We have learned from and thank the Chicago American Indian Community Collaborative, the Center for Native Futures, the Gichigamiin Indigenous Nations Museum, the American Indian Center of Chicago, the Field Museum, and the D'Arcy McNickle Center for American Indian and Indigenous Studies at the Newberry Library.

Beyond Chicago, we are thankful to the following individuals who generously gave their time and shared insights with us: heather ahtone (Chickasaw), Keri Ataumbi (Kiowa), Kalyn Fay Barnoski (Cherokee Nation/Muskogee Creek descent), Madalene Big Bear (Pokagon Band of Potawatomi), Otto Braided Hair (Northern Cheyenne), Christina Burke, Candice Byrd (Cherokee Nation), Joe Tali Byrd (Cherokee Nation/Quapaw Nation), Raquel Byrd, Teri Greeves, John Hamilton (Kiowa/Caddo/Cheyenne), Adrienne Lalli Hills (Wyandotte Nation), Nicole Holloway (Pokagon Band of Potawatomi), Dakota Hoska (Oglála Lakȟóta), Miranda Lash, John Lukavic, Leilani Lynch, Krystan Moser (Cherokee Nation), Maryann Parker (Kiowa), Jeff Strand, and Jill Ahlberg Yohe.

Woven Being is part of Art Design Chicago, a citywide collaboration initiated by the Terra Foundation for American Art that highlights the city's artistic heritage and creative communities. We thank the Terra Foundation for American Art for its lead support of this project, as well as the Art Design Chicago learning community for their support and insights throughout the project's development. We are appreciative of the major support provided by the Andy Warhol Foundation for the Visual Arts, the National Endowment for the Arts, The Joyce Foundation, and a grant from the Illinois Arts Council. Additional generous support was provided by the Sandra L. Riggs Publication Fund and the Alumnae of Northwestern University.

Sébastien Aubin (Opaskwayak Cree Nation) inspired us with his design for this book and other elements of the exhibition's graphic identity. We are grateful for his creative engagement with the project. We also thank Allen's Cruz and the staff at the design studio OTAMI. Marquand Books brought us together with OTAMI, and we warmly thank Gina Broze, Ryan Polich, Kestrel Rundle, and the staff at Marquand for this and for so confidently leading the process of book production. We extend appreciation to the entire Marquand staff for their support and expertise. We also thank copy editor Kristin Kearns for her collaborative spirit and careful and thoughtful work on this manuscript over many months, and Carrie Wicks, who proofread the manuscript with alacrity and a keen eye for detail.

Finally, we are grateful to Lisa Graziose Corrin, Ellen Philips Katz Executive Director of The Block Museum of Art, who has been a steadfast and enthusiastic advocate and partner throughout the development of this exhibition and publication. We also thank Marisa Cruz Branco, Terra Foundation Curatorial Research Fellow, and Teagan Harris (Cherokee Nation), Terra Foundation Engagement Fellow, who joined our team in summer 2024 and brought their ideas and energy to the project's implementation. We extend deep appreciation to present and former staff and students at The Block, without whom the realization of *Woven Being: Art for Zhegagoynak/ Chicagoland* would not have been possible: Lindsay Bosch, Kristina Bottomley, Christiana Castillo, Aaron Chatman, Ben Creech, Christopher Forrester, Iliana Garner, Madeleine Giaconia, Corinne Granof, Malia Haines-Stewart, Isabella Ko, Mark Leonhart, Kirsten Lopez, Brad Martin, Michael Metzger, Rocio Olasimbo, Elisa Miller Quinlan, Essi Rönkkö, Liz Rudnick, Joe Scott, Rita Shorts, Jeff Smith, Warren Smith, James Stauber, Melanie Garcia Sympson, Vincent Taylor, Kate Hadley Toftness, Bobby Yalam, and the Block Museum Student Associates and our community of student colleagues, who enrich and enliven our work. The Block Museum is, in turn, supported in its work by Northwestern University Provost Kathleen Hagerty and Jake Julia, her Chief of Staff, as well as a dedicated board of advisors, led by Co-Chairs Cheryl Johnson-Odim and Stuart H. Bohart. Our gratitude goes out to them for their belief in what we do.

Signed:

Kathleen Bickford Berzock, Associate Director of Curatorial Affairs

Jordan Poorman Cocker (Kiowa), Terra Foundation Guest Co-Curator

Janet Dees, former Steven and Lisa Munster Tananbaum Curator of Modern and Contemporary Art at The Block

Erin Northington, Susan and Stephen Wilson Associate Director of Campus and Community Education and Engagement

Dan Silverstein, Associate Director of Collections and Exhibition Management

Note to the Reader

The *Woven Being* project honors the multiplicity of Indigenous voices. Following this value, the book embraces the variety and diversity of Indigenous languages. In editorial decision-making, we have referenced the *First American Art Magazine* (FAAM) Style Guide, available at firstamericanartmagazine.com/submissions/faam-style-guide.

As the FAAM guidelines advise, we strike "a balance between accuracy, brevity, consistency, and personal choice." For capitalization, tribal and cultural affiliations, and other matters that reflect Indigenous perspectives, we have largely followed the FAAM guidelines; however, where a choice has been necessary, we have prioritized the personal preference of the Indigenous artist or author over style guidelines.

Anishinaabemowin, the dominant Indigenous language of the Great Lakes region, comprises many dialects, each with its own preferred transliterations into the Roman alphabet. We use the preferred spelling of each tribe—for example, Pokagon Band of Potawatomi; Match-E-Be-Nash-She-Wish Band of Pottawatomi. When representing titles of chapters focused on or artworks by a specific artist, we use the preferred language of the artist.

The terms "Indigenous," "Native," and "American Indian" are at times used interchangeably by the book's contributors, and we have maintained author preference in these instances.

Zhegagoynak is the Potawatomi word for the Chicago region.

Curatorial Statements

JORDAN POORMAN COCKER (KIOWA)

As a Kiowa woman raised in Oklahoma, I root my curatorial practice in Indigenous sovereignty, the land, and intergenerational futures. The late N. Scott Momaday's words resonate: "I am interested in the way that we look at a given landscape and take possession of it in our blood and brain. None of us lives apart from the land entirely; such an isolation is unimaginable. If we are to realize and maintain our humanity, we must come to a moral comprehension of earth and air as it is perceived in the long turn of seasons and of years."[1] I inherited all my relations through my (maternal) great-grandmother, Alice Poorman Paddlety Toyebo, a renowned Kiowa bead worker;[2] my great-grandfather Charles "Charlie" Toyebo, who taught Kiowa language classes throughout his life; and my mother, Deborah Àu:híñ:bàumà (Cedar Tree Woman) Cocker. Our Keintaddle descendant allotments are located in Redstone, Oklahoma, and our Toyebo family allotment encompasses Rainy Mountain, including the Rainy Mountain Baptist Church, built on our family's allotment land selected by my ancestor Gotebo upon his conversion in 1893.[3] Atah, my ancestor through our Toyebo family and the last Kiowa woman to ride on a war party, was an iconic bead worker and cradle-board maker.[4] Both of our family allotments are located on the Kiowa Comanche Apache reservation in southwest Oklahoma.[5] My father's people are the Cocker Kāinga, descending through Vilifākātāhā Tupau Fā from the Kingdom of Tonga; my paternal grandparents moved to Aotearoa (New Zealand) after World War II. I carry these territories, waterways, and bloodlines with me wherever I go: I am accountable to my Kiowa mother, Àu:híñ:bàumà; our Toyebo family from Rainy Mountain; our Keintaddle kinfolk from Redstone; and the land, who raised me.

Woven Being: Art for Zhegagoynak/Chicagoland embraces Indigenous curatorial approaches and methodologies. The Kiowa concept of carrying an intrinsic kinship to the land, to place, and a profound responsibility to the earth is synthesized in the phrase *Daum Yì:dop*, which roughly translates to "touching the earth."[6] Although *Daum Yì:dop* is a Kiowa phrase and cultural practice, in this context the process functions as a lens that incorporates a broader worldview or responsibility referred to in many Indigenous languages—that is, the tangible, intangible, and embodied relationships between people and place.

Indigenous ways of knowing and doing, Indigenous matriarchies and feminisms, oral history methodologies,[7] and other forms of sovereignty sustain my curatorial approach, informing decision-making processes and practices. Research methodologies intentionally created to Indigenize specific research fields of study—such as Talanoa, which re-centers artistic discourses through "our own words and on our terms," modeling a *refusal* of Indigenous artistic discourses as monolithic[8]—provide an intellectual form of kinship toward data sovereignty.[9] I have deep gratitude for the genealogical and intellectual kinship systems that continue to inform me—elders, aunties, and community members. From my perspective, *Woven Being* represents an important step toward strengthening The Block's institutional responsibilities and commitments to Indigenous art and artists by both serving as a curatorial model and holding space for broader collective visions of better futures for Indigenous art.

JANET DEES

I came to The Block Museum of Art in 2015, after seven years spent living and working in Santa Fe. As an African American curator who had moved to New Mexico from the Northeast, I became alerted to the lapses in my knowledge as a contemporary art curator and historian of American art when it came to the work of contemporary Indigenous artists. I had to confront these gaps and think about the structural ways in which my education and networks of circulation had limited my contact with the ongoing work of Indigenous artists, curators, and scholars. Through the work of Kanien'kehá:ka curator Ryan Rice at the Institute of American Indian Arts' Museum of Contemporary Native Arts and others who worked in and visited New Mexico, I began my process of reeducation through "showing up," learning by being present in Indigenous-directed spaces.[10]

My curatorial practice has increasingly become more explicitly grounded in Black feminist values. Black Canadian art historian Joana Joachim productively articulates how aspects of intersectional Black feminist values and commitments manifest themselves in curatorial practice.[11] These manifestations include "opening discussion between communities about topics that are difficult to unpack, yet necessary for our collective well-being"; championing the work of underrecognized artists; productive self-interrogation to alert oneself to one's blind spots; and valuing "embodied knowledge and everyday individual experience" as "crucial places of knowing that allow for important insights and transformative justice work."[12] I have also been influenced by the concept of "radical friendship" as theorized by Kate Johnson. Based on the Buddhist concept of *Kalyana Mitta*, or "spiritual friendship," and informed by the work of Black feminists, Johnson proposes radical friendship as an alternative to allyship, which she views as potentially locked within existing systems of privilege, whereas friendship is a reciprocal practice. Johnson writes, "Friends feed each other, check in on each other, cheer each other up, and let each other be. We help when help is needed and wanted. We do our very best to protect each other from harm. We support each other in accountability when we fail to live up to our values and agreements. We begin again."[13] For me, these values influence the "what" and "how" of my curatorial work, as well as "for whom" and "with whom" I work. This includes supporting the efforts of Indigenous arts professionals on their own terms.

I acknowledge and am grateful to the Indigenous colleagues and friends—artists, curators, and scholars—who have been interlocutors, collaborators, and informal mentors over the last fifteen years and to whom I hold myself accountable.[14] For me, then, *Woven Being* is not just a part of The Block's ongoing institutional commitment to Indigenous art and artists. It is also a part of a personal and intellectual commitment to Black feminist values and "radical friendship," which in this case means being led by the generative Indigenous methodologies offered by Jordan Poorman Cocker, our advisors, and colleagues in the field.

KATHLEEN BICKFORD BERZOCK

I joined The Block Museum of Art in 2014, my hire coinciding with a cluster of actions and initiatives at Northwestern University that set a new course for its Indigenous commitments. That year, in response to the activism of Northwestern's Native American and Indigenous Student Alliance, the university released the report of the John Evans Study Committee, a first step toward public recognition of the culpability of Northwestern's founder in the 1864 massacre of over two hundred Cheyenne and Arapaho people at Sand Creek, in present-day Colorado.[15] It was soon followed by the first report of the Native American Outreach and Inclusion Task Force, formed to respond to the Evans report.[16] The two reports included recommendations for faculty and staff to build relationships with Indigenous organizations and communities and to support learning about Indigenous culture, history, and sovereignty. Their publication was followed by the opening of Northwestern's Center for Native American and Indigenous Research (CNAIR) in 2016.

In light of these events, as a settler scholar working in a museum without Indigenous staff, I began to reflect on how I could join with other Block Museum colleagues to respond to the calls to action that were coming from Indigenous students, faculty, and staff. Our response has been gradual and iterative and has included purchasing works of art by contemporary Indigenous artists, featuring Indigenous artists in several exhibitions, and presenting public lectures and cinema programs that have offered Indigenous points of view. We have also connected with colleagues at CNAIR and other Indigenous-led offices on campus, and with Indigenous-led organizations in the Chicagoland region. Each of these steps has been important, but they are also transient. Within an institution like The Block, which at this time does not have permanent staff members who are Indigenous, this commitment requires continuous mindful effort to make sure Indigenous perspectives inform our thinking and are incorporated into our work.

In 2020, Janet Dees, The Block's curator of modern and contemporary art, and I proposed a collaborative process that would engage Indigenous peers to create an exhibition using Indigenous-informed curatorial methodologies. This proposal became the *Woven Being* project. Among my personal goals for this project was to engage in a curatorial process in which I consciously decentered my role, bolstered listening, practiced consultative decision-making, and

supported others. I am beholden to previous experiences that prepared me to step into this style of work. The partnership model of the
exhibition *Benin—Kings and Rituals: Court Arts from Nigeria*, which I
presented at the Art Institute of Chicago in 2008, provided me with
the experience of working with cultural knowledge holders from the
Court of Benin and the Nigerian National Commission for Museums
and Monuments (NCMM).[17] The exhibition *Caravans of Gold, Frag-
ments in Time: Art, Culture, and Exchange across Medieval Saha-
ran Africa* (2019), which I organized at The Block Museum of Art,
involved multiyear dialogues and relationship building with museum
professionals and scholars in Mali, Morocco, and Nigeria. Through
these projects, I built relationships with many individuals who have
influenced my curatorial practice by modeling generous collaboration
and openness to different perspectives and ways of doing. I especially
want to acknowledge Edith Ekunke, retired director of museums
at the Nigerian NCMM, and Abdallah Fili, professor of history and
archaeology at Chouaib Doukkali University in El Jadida, Morocco,
each of whom has offered generous mentorship and friendship that
has adapted and lasted over time. I wish to thank them here for their
continuing support and belief in me.

It is an honor to continue my learning through collaboration with
the extended circle of specialists involved in *Woven Being*, including curators Jordan Poorman Cocker and Janet Dees; collaborating
artists Andrea Carlson (Grand Portage Ojibwe/European descent),
Kelly Church (Match-E-Be-Nash-She-Wish Band of Pottawatomi/
Ottawa), Nora Moore Lloyd (Lac Courte Oreilles Band of Lake Superior Ojibwe), and Jason Wesaw (Pokagon Band of Potawatomi); book
contributors Denise Lajimodiere (Turtle Mountain Band of Ojibwe),
Jacqueline Lopez, John Low (Pokagon Band of Potawatomi), Blaire
Morseau (Pokagon Band of Potawatomi), and Anne Terry Straus; and
the artists, poets, and other knowledge sharers who have contributed
to the exhibition and book. The project has also connected me more
deeply to Indigenous colleagues at Northwestern, in Evanston and
Chicago, and in the Zhegagoynak/Chicagoland region. I'm grateful
for this opportunity to expand my learning and broaden my perspectives by following in their footsteps.

1   N. Scott Momaday, "An American Land Ethic," in *The Man Made of Words* (New York: St. Martin's Press, 1997), 42.

2   Further reading on Alice Poorman Paddlety's family legacy of Kiowa bead-work artistry inspired by Keintaddle (1849–1938) can be found in Barbara A. Hail, ed., *Gifts of Pride and Love: Kiowa and Comanche Cradles* (Norman: University of Oklahoma Press, 2001), 89–99.

3   William C. Meadows and Kenny Harragarra, "The Kiowa Drawings of Gotebo (1847–1927): A Self-Portrait of Cultural and Religious Transition," *Plains Anthropologist* 52, no. 202 (2007): 229–44.

4   Further reading on Atah (1855–1947) and her husband Toyebo's historic contributions to the Kiowa Tribe and artistic legacy can be found in Hays, "Gifts of Pride and Love," 71–75.

5   Paul W. Gates, "Indian Allotments Preceding the Dawes Act," in *The Frontier Challenge: Responses to the Trans-Mississippi West*, ed. John G. Clark (Lawrence: University Press of Kansas, 2021), 141–70.

6   See Jordan Poorman Cocker, "*Daum Yi:dop* (Touching the Earth): Researching Gilcrease Museum's Indigenous Paintings," Gilcrease Museum, June 14, 2022, web.

7   On Indigenous matriarchy, see Kathleen Whitaker, "Gifts of Pride and Love: The Cultural Significance of Kiowa and Comanche Lattice Cradles," *American Anthropologist* 103, no. 3 (2001): 803–8. On Indigenous feminisms, see Lisa Kahaleole Hall, "Navigating Our Own 'Sea of Islands': Remapping a Theoretical Space for Hawaiian Women and Indigenous Feminism," *Wicazo Sa Review* 24, no. 2 (2009): 15–38. For oral histories, see Hall, 18.

8   Timote M. Vaioleti, "Talanoa Research Methodology: A Developing Position on Pacific Research," *Waikato Journal of Education* 12 (2006): 21–34; Linda Tuhiwai Smith, *Decolonizing Methodologies: Research and Indigenous Peoples* (London: Zed Books, 2021).

9   Teresia Teaiwa, "The Ancestors We Get to Choose: White Influences I Won't Deny," in *Theorizing Native Studies*, ed. Andrea Smith (Durham, NC: Duke University Press, 2014), 43–55.

10   Currently the executive director and curator of Indigenous art at Ontario College of Art and Design's Onsite Gallery, Rice was chief curator of the Museum of Contemporary Native Arts from 2009 to 2014.

11   Joana Joachim, "'Embodiment and Subjectivity': Intersectional Black Feminist Curatorial Practices in Canada," *RACAR* 43 (2018): 34–47.

12   Joachim, "'Embodiment and Subjectivity,'" 44–45 and 36–37.

13   Kate Johnson, *Radical Friendship: Seven Ways to Love Yourself and Find Your People in an Unjust World* (Boulder, CO: Shambhala, 2021), 34.

14   See, for example, Janet Dees and Ryan Rice, "A Questionnaire on Decolonization: 35 Responses," *October* 174 (Fall 2020): 31–38; Janet Dees et al., eds., *Unsettled Landscapes* (Santa Fe: SITE Santa Fe, 2014); and Janet Dees, "Home Is Where the Heart Is," in the brochure for the exhibition *C. Maxx Stevens: House of Memory*, curated by Kathleen Ash-Milby, at the Smithsonian National Museum of the American Indian, New York, 2012, web.

15   *Report of the John Evans Study Committee*, Northwestern University, 2014, web. The report has been criticized for not going far enough in holding Evans accountable for violence against Native people of the region when he was territorial governor of Colorado; see, for instance, "Reassessing Culpability: Departures from the Northwestern Report," *Report of the John Evans Study Committee*, University of Denver, November 2014, 88–94, web.

16   For more on the Native American Outreach and Inclusion Task Force, see northwestern.edu/native-american-and-indigenous-peoples/history/native-american-outreach-and-inclusion-task-force.

17   The exhibition, which was curated by Barbara Plankensteiner and organized by the Kunsthistorisches Museum, Vienna, was developed in close partnership with the Court of Benin and the Nigerian NCMM.

Janet Dees, Jordan Poorman Cocker (Kiowa), and Kathleen Bickford Berzock

Building a Foundation for *Woven Being* at The Block

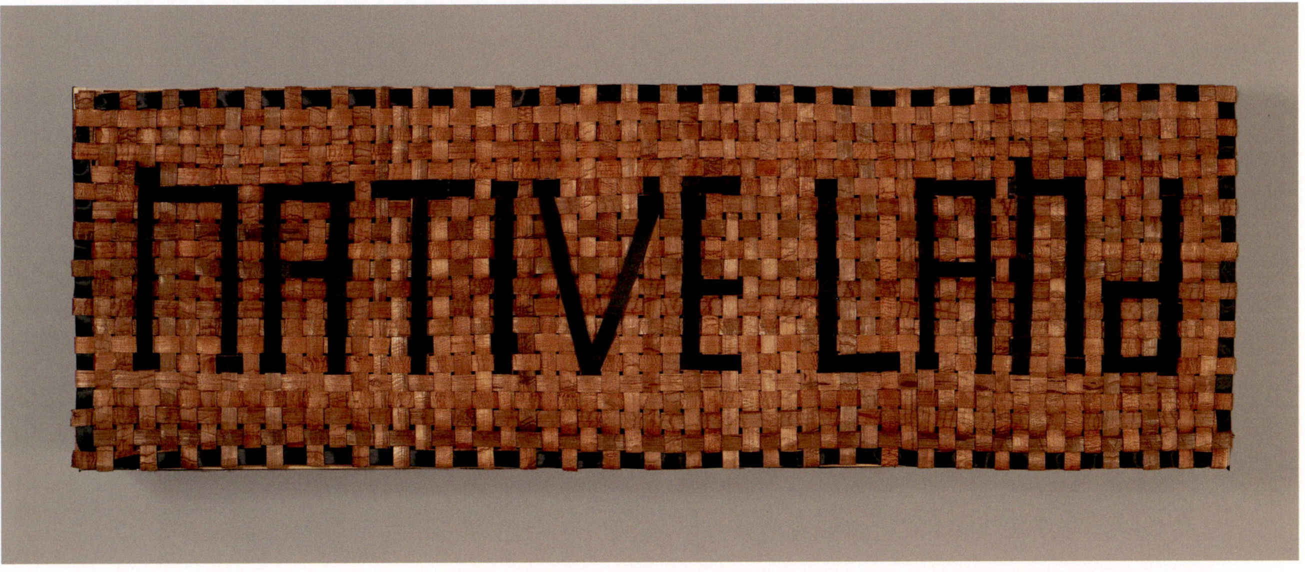

Fig. 1.1

Fig. 1.1 Kelly Church (Match-E-Be-Nash-She-Wish Band of Pottawatomi/Ottawa, born 1967), *Native Land*, 2024. White cedar bark, black ash, ribbon, wood, and laminated black construction paper, 13½ × 41¼ × 6 inches. Collection of the artist. Photograph by Holly Trevan.

Māori scholar Linda Tuhiwai Smith calls decolonization "an urgent, necessary, challenging yet hopeful journey beyond colonialism: Decolonising is only partly about dismantling colonialism. It is also partly about restorative processes for addressing and healing the past. It is partly about the reclamation of Indigenous sovereignty. These things then create new spaces for imagining a different future."[1] The work of imagining a different future in the context of The Block Museum of Art began with an institutional awareness of positionality, or an understanding of institutional responsibilities to place, the land, and the site-specific context of historical and ongoing colonialism, with special attention paid to institutional commitments and responsibilities as forms of reparation and restitution.[2]

The prompt to begin the research phase of *Woven Being* with a consideration of The Block's place-based positionality, encompassing the museum's relationships and responsibilities to Indigenous lands and people, came from guest co-curator Jordan Poorman Cocker. This was especially important because at The Block we are committed to deepening our relationships to contemporary Indigenous art and artists, and this starting point would provide a strong foundation for our work. We focused on three areas of our institutional identity: The Block's historical and ongoing relationship to place, beginning with site-specific understandings, including relationships to land and US treaties with sovereign Indigenous nations; The Block's relationship to Northwestern University; and its responsibilities as a museum.[3] We explored many narratives across these facets of The Block's positionality and researched how they are connected through the use of Indigenous-informed research methodologies including oral histories and polyvocality. We also considered them through Indigenous conceptions of time that weave together past, present, and future.[4] Northwestern University's land acknowledgment recognizes that the ancestral and treaty territories of Zhegagoynak—the Chicagoland region—are the homelands of the Council of Three Fires, comprising the Ojibwe, Potawatomi, and Odawa; and of the Menominee, Miami,

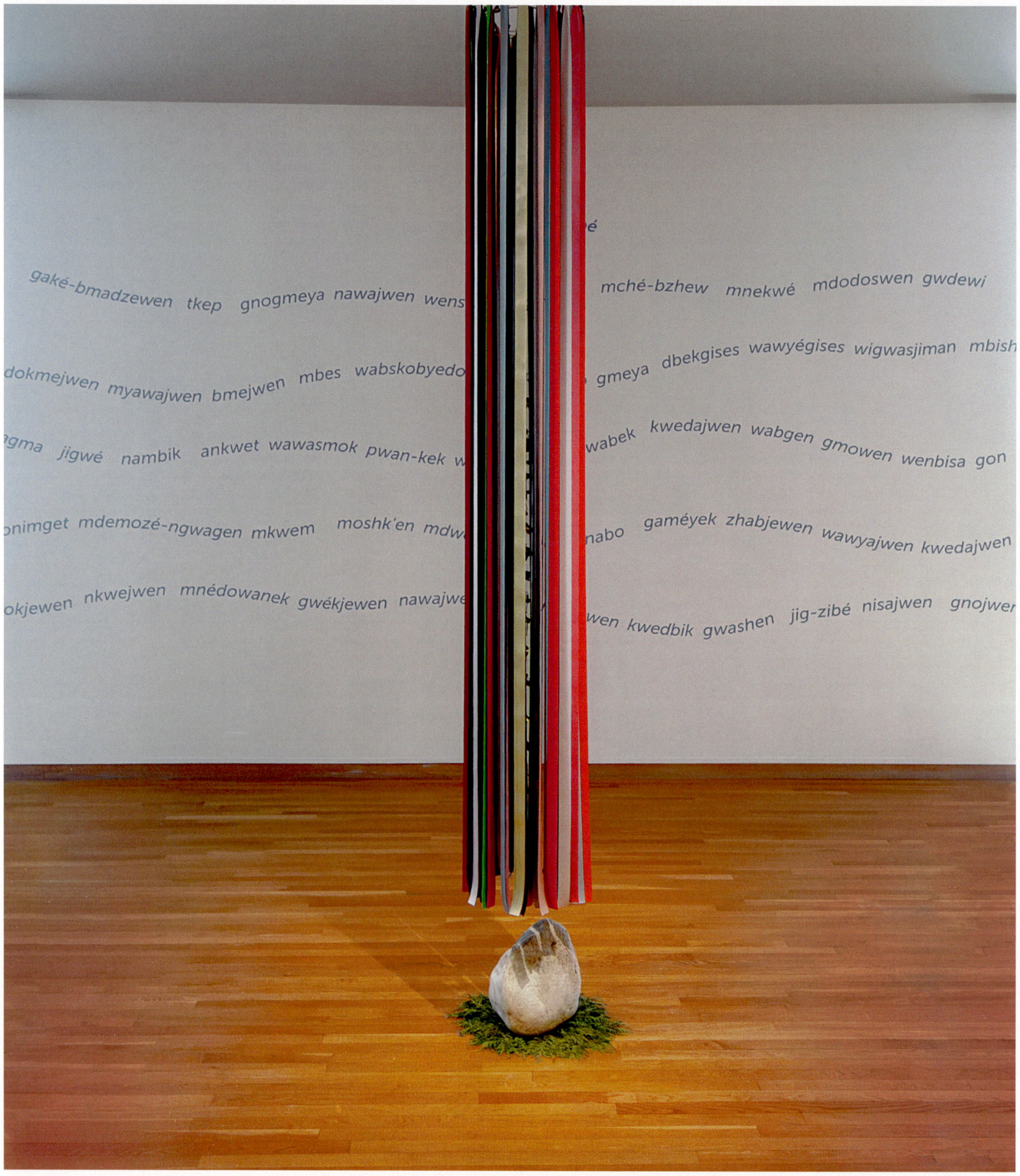

Fig. 1.2

Fig. 1.2 Jason Wesaw (Pokagon Band of Potawatomi, born 1974), *Wabshkya Sen*, 2023 (installation view, South Bend Museum of Art, Indiana). Polyester ribbon, cotton cloth, artificial sinew, tobacco, cedar, and stone, dimensions variable. Collection of the artist.

JANET DEES, JORDAN POORMAN COCKER, AND KATHLEEN BICKFORD BERZOCK

and Ho-Chunk Nations and many other nations whose ancestors were the original stewards of this land. Zhegagoynak was a site of gathering for over a dozen other nations, and Illinois is currently home to over one hundred thousand tribal members from different communities. This has been Indigenous land since time immemorial. Through our positionality research, we see how the location of The Block is connected to the violence of settler colonial histories, including forced removal and the forced ceding of lands to the US government through the 1821 and 1833 Treaties of Chicago. Opened in 1980, The Block is built on a Lake Michigan landfill that was constructed in the 1960s on unceded territory. Indeed, in 1914, the Pokagon Band of Potawatomi sued for the return of Chicago's landfill in a case that went all the way to the Supreme Court.[5] Northwestern University and The Block also are linked to the Cheyenne and Arapaho people through the actions of Northwestern's founder, John Evans. As territorial governor of Colorado, Evans established policies and issued orders that led to the 1864 Sand Creek Massacre, in which over two hundred Cheyenne and Arapaho people were murdered by US soldiers.[6] Starting in 2012, Northwestern's Native American and Indigenous Student Alliance (NAISA) began to advocate for acknowledgment of Evans's culpability in the Sand Creek Massacre and increased structures of support and visibility in a campus environment characterized by Native absence.[7] The Block's commitment to Indigenous art and artists stems from those efforts.

At The Block, we are mindful of the ways in which museums have historically harmed and continue to harm Indigenous artists and communities by perpetuating a mindset that relegates Indigenous life to the past, flattens Indigenous experiences, and justifies keeping Indigenous objects separated from their communities of origin, among other forms of colonialism. The Block's efforts are focused on engaging with contemporary Indigenous art and artists. The Block does not have historical cultural belongings in its collection. Its earliest work by an Indigenous artist is currently a print by Aaron Leonard Freeland (Diné) made circa 1989. *Woven Being* uses Indigenous research methodologies to center Indigenous voices in telling stories through art. This is just one step The Block is taking to strengthen our support of Indigenous art and artists. We also act on this commitment by building relationships with Indigenous colleagues, peers, artists, and communities in our region; acquiring artwork by contemporary Indigenous artists for The Block's collection; including work by Indigenous artists in exhibitions; presenting programs that highlight Indigenous artists and other knowledge sharers; using Indigenous-informed methodologies; aligning with and supporting the strategic initiatives of Indigenous-led efforts on campus; and supporting the work of arts and cultural initiatives developed by Indigenous organizations. Our positionality research led to the definition and refinement of the scope of *Woven Being*, couched in a situational context, along with a deeper institution-wide understanding of Indigenous relationships to place through the lens of tribal sovereignty across ancestral and treaty territories [fig. 1.1].

Building on our work to better understand our positionality and our unique responsibilities to Indigenous communities and artists, we conducted a series of community forums, which we framed as "visioning sessions": meetings with Indigenous knowledge sharers and non-Indigenous allies designed to imagine together the possibilities for the project. We also undertook one-on-one conversations and studio visits with artists, visits to museums, and conversations with museum colleagues as part of our research [fig. 1.2].[8] The focus of this research was to understand what stories The Block was best situated to tell and what approaches would be best suited to an exhibition about Indigenous art in Chicagoland. The visioning sessions were intended to engage community members in a way that was specifically defined: starting with Indigenous Northwestern faculty, students, and staff and expanding to include a selection of Chicago-based or displaced Indigenous arts and culture practitioners, scholars, and other knowledge keepers. In addition to imagining together what would make a successful exhibition, we presented and tested the emergent themes of landways and waterways, material kinship, and Indigenous time as potential organizing principles for the exhibition.

Multiple measures of success for the exhibition were identified in these meetings. Participants expressed the desire for an exhibition that was intergenerational in its content and welcoming to visitors of all ages, including through the offering of food. Participants envisioned an exhibition that sparked joy, laughter, and engagement and noted the importance of visitors hearing and seeing Indigenous languages throughout. Participants also envisioned a museum

Fig. 1.3 Andrea Carlson (Grand Portage Ojibwe/European descent, born 1979), *The Indifference of Fire* (detail), 2023. Oil, acrylic, gouache, ink, colored pencil, and graphite on paper, twenty-four panels: 11½ × 30 inches each, overall: 46 × 182 inches. Gochman Family Collection, New York.

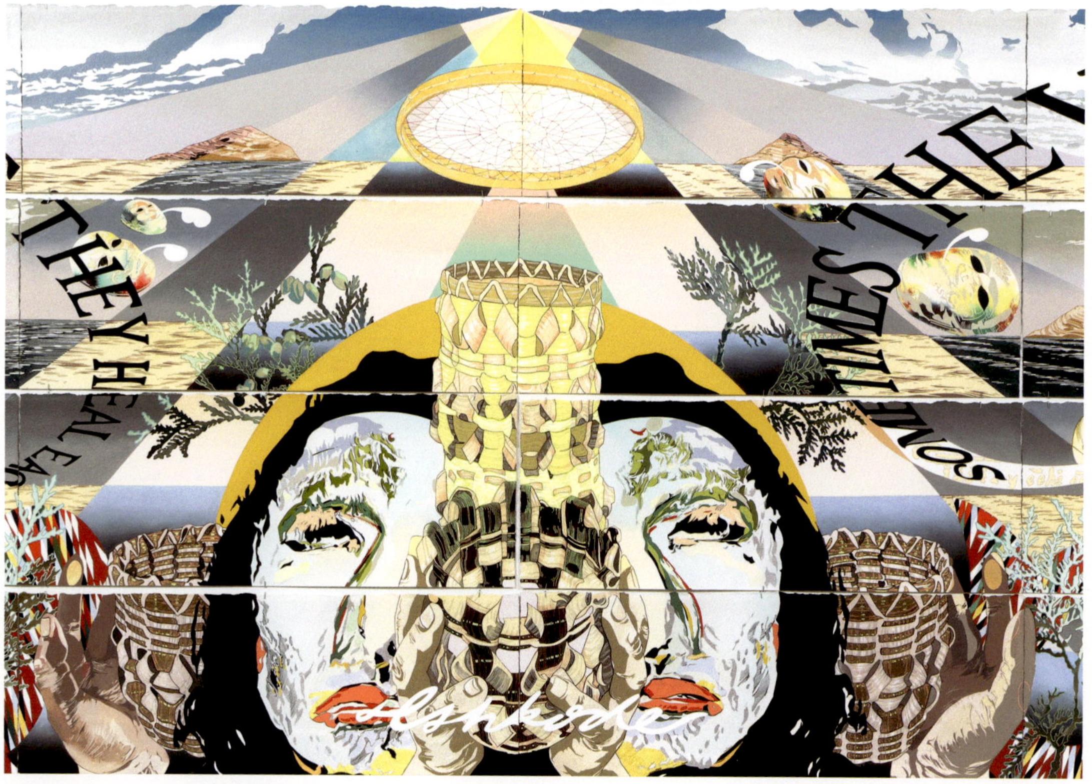

Fig. 1.3

JANET DEES, JORDAN POORMAN COCKER, AND KATHLEEN BICKFORD BERZOCK

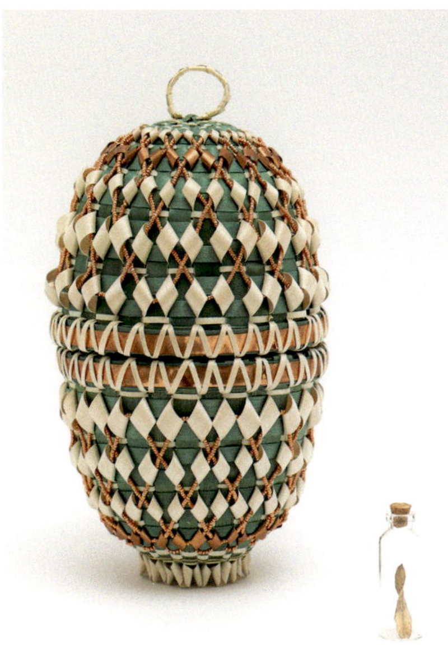

Fig. 1.4

Fig. 1.4 Kelly Church (Match-E-Be-Nash-She-Wish Band of Pottawatomi/Ottawa, born 1967), *You Can't Drink Oil*, 2024. Black ash, Rit dye, silver beads, sinew, fine silver strips, black velvet, vial containing Lake Michigan water, and vial containing containing oil mixed with Lake Michigan water, 9 × 4¾ inches. Collection of the artist. Photograph by Holly Trevan.

permeated with the sounds of the natural world, including Lake Michigan, and the smells of sweetgrass, cedar, sage, and tobacco. Additionally, the exhibition should be of benefit to Chicagoland's urban Indigenous communities and to descendants of the Council of Three Fires and other communities who have called this place home. The exhibition should reinforce feelings of pride and resilience and evoke memories. Finally, through its presentation of contemporary art, the exhibition should connect to the past and present and envision futures, challenging people to think differently.

The themes of landways and waterways, material kinship, and Indigenous concepts of time are currents, rather than strict organizing principles, that flow through *Woven Being*, connecting the artworks and stories included in the exhibition. These currents emerged early in our research and became refined throughout our consultative process. Starting with the land, as discussed above, it was important to ground the project in the specificity of place. This took the form of recognizing the Indigenous peoples who occupied and continue to occupy this place through engagement with our land acknowledgment, treaty histories, and the diverse urban Indigenous community that has more recently developed over the last hundred-plus years in the Chicagoland area.[9] We reflected on how the regional waterways, particularly the lakes and rivers, have linked and continue to link this region to many others, making Zhegagoynak a place of confluence and connection. This theme is also about "ways"—that is, how Indigenous people have related to and continue to relate to the land and water of this region. For example, these streams of thought are poetically engaged within the installation piece *Water Carries Memory*, by Jason Wesaw (Pokagon Band of Potawatomi, born 1974), which invokes Lake Michigan and its shores within the space of the gallery [pls. 7, 8]. Blaire Morseau discusses the multiple resonances of this work in her chapter in this volume [pp. 44–47].

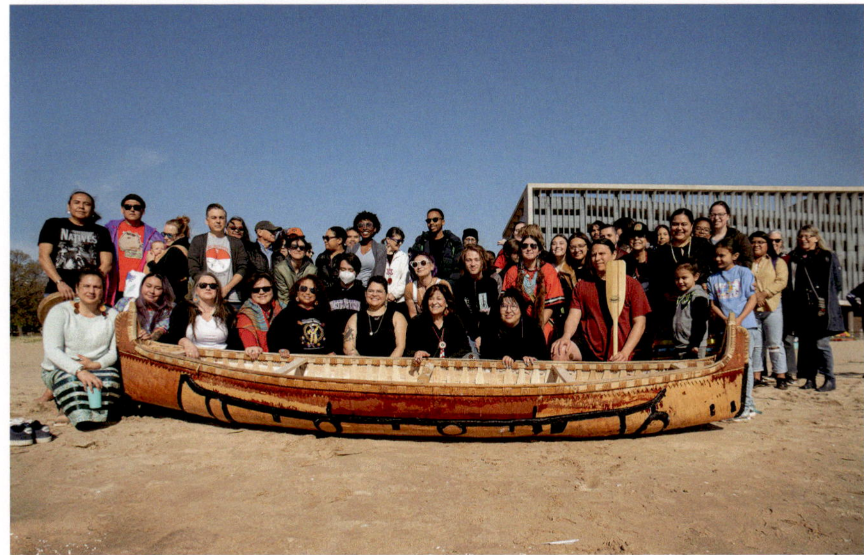

Fig. 1.5 Community members pose with the birchbark canoe built with CNAIR 2021–22 artist in residence Wayne Valliere (Lac du Flambeau Ojibwe), 2021. Photograph by Anthony McCray/Northwestern University.

Fig. 1.5

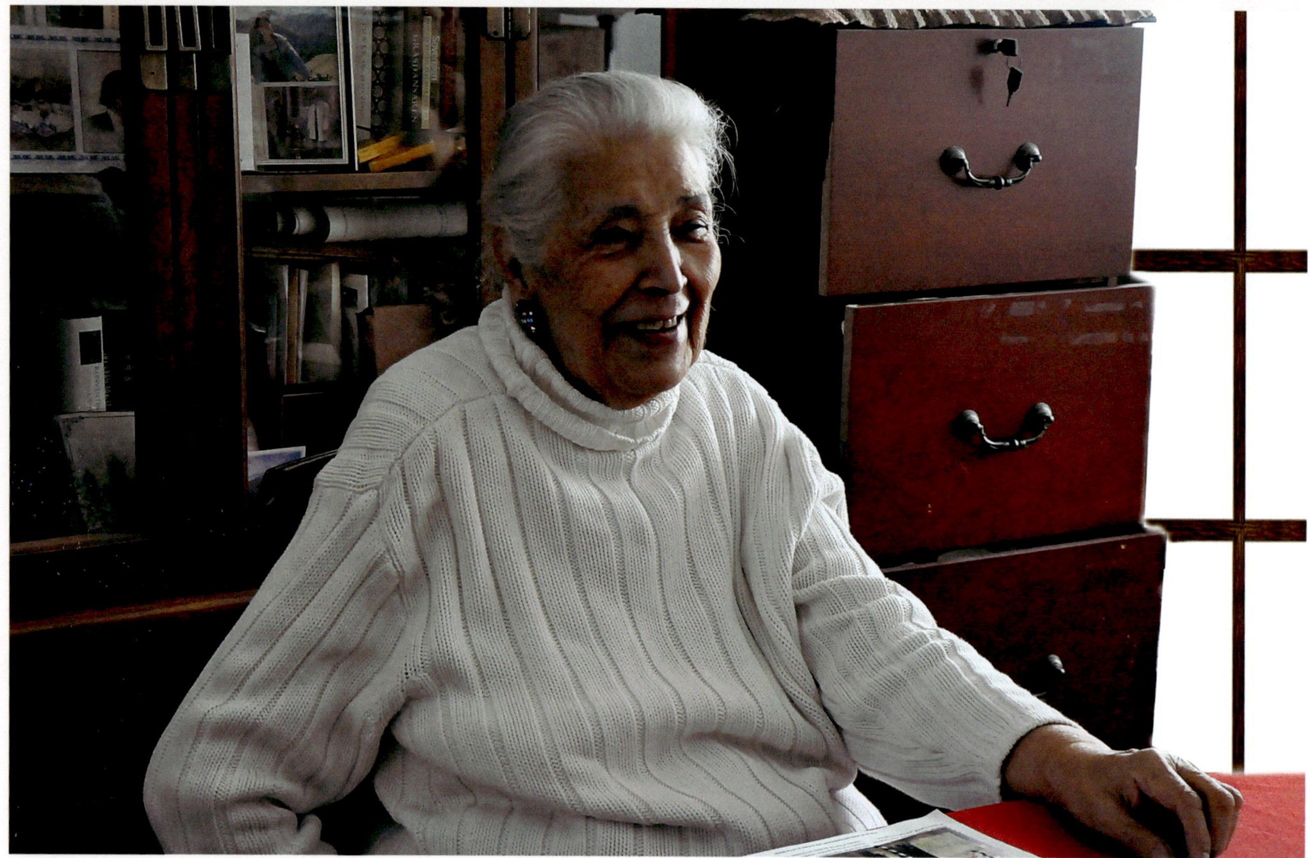

Fig. 1.6

The theme of material kinship illuminates the complex and inter-woven relationships between the materials used to create works of art rooted in plant and animal life, the environments from which they are drawn, related cultural practices, and the artists as creators. This is reflected in Kelly Church's (Match-E-Be-Nash-She-Wish Band of Pottawatomi/Ottawa, born 1967) black ash baskets, made from bark that the artist ethically and consciously harvests from black ash trees, and the stories these baskets contain about the environmental threat caused by the invasive emerald ash borer beetle [fig. 1.4]. It is also reflected in the reference to one of Kelly's baskets by Andrea Carlson (Grand Portage Ojibwe/European descent, born 1979) in her large-scale drawing *The Indifference of Fire*, which also pays homage to several other artists Andrea views as aesthetic relatives [fig. 1.3; see also fig. 4.8 and pl. 9].

The perspective on Indigenous time that has informed *Woven Being* is influenced by the writing of Abenaki scholar Lisa Brooks, who asks us to consider whether "time also operates like a spiral" as a way to free us from the colonial mindset of linear time,[10] as well as the work of settler scholar Mark Rifkin and the teachings of birchbark canoe maker Wayne Valliere (Lac du Flambeau Ojibwe). Rifkin's notion of temporal sovereignty reinforces the reconfiguration of chronological or linear timelines in Indigenous concepts of time,

Fig. 1.6 Nora Moore Lloyd (Lac Courte Oreilles Band of Lake Superior Ojibwe, born 1947), *Susan Kelly Power (Yanktonai Dakota)*, from the series "Chicago's Native American Community: Our Elders Look Back," 1998–ongoing. Archival digital photograph from original 35 mm negative, 8 × 10 inches. Collection of the artist.

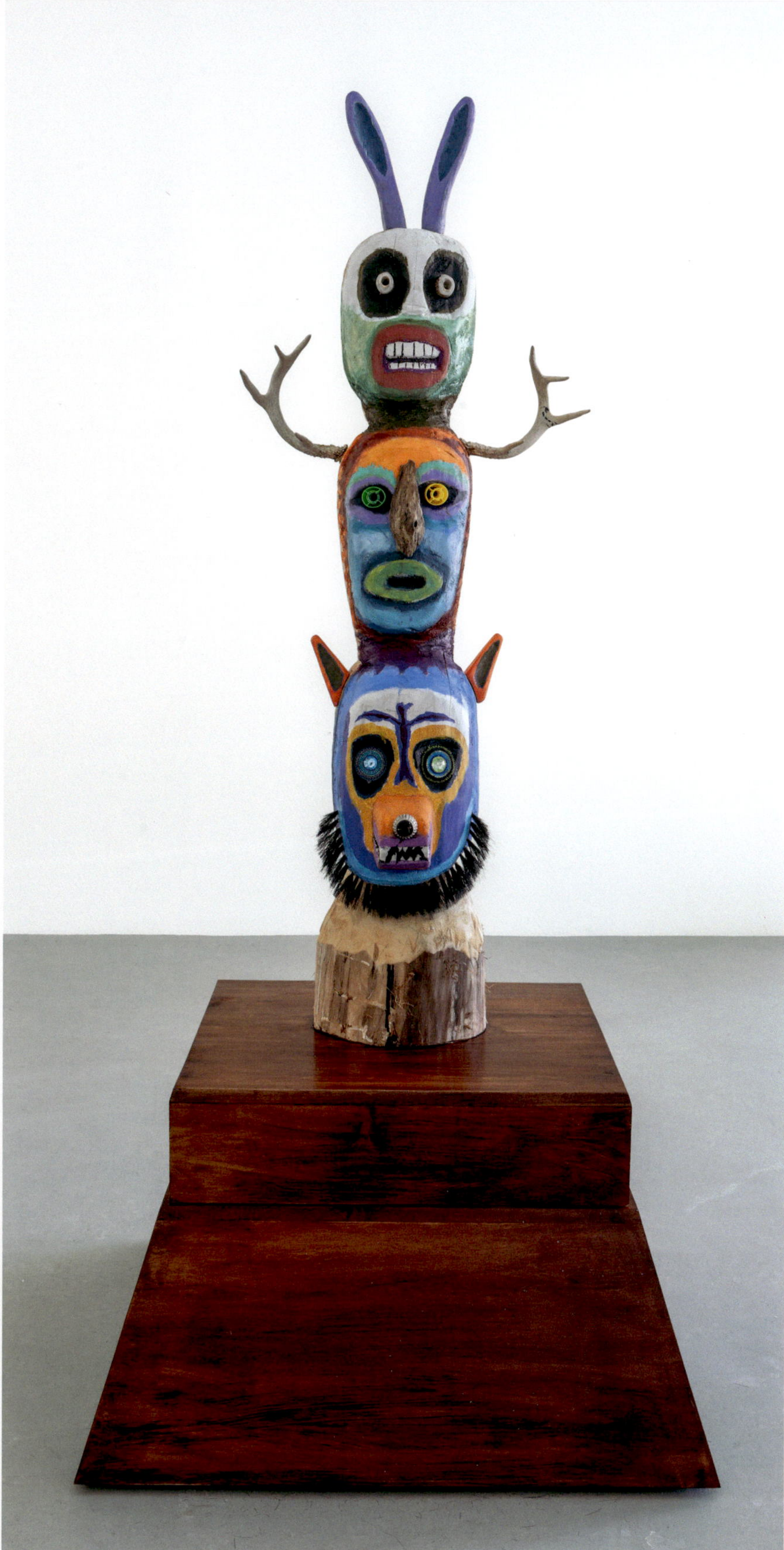

Fig. 1.7 Jim Denomie (Lac Courte Oreilles Band of Ojibwe, 1955–2022), *Totem, Animal Spirits*, 2021. Wood, oil, paint, deer antlers, horsehair, and found objects, 78 × 32 × 32 inches. Forge Project Collection, traditional lands of the Moh-He-Con-Nuck. © Jim Denomie Estate. Courtesy of the Jim Denomie Estate and Bockley Gallery, Minneapolis.

Fig. 1.7

land-based knowledge, tribal sovereignty, and oral histories. This is located, for instance, in the contextualizing of kinship or the relational webs housed within Indigenous art forms.[11] During an artist residency hosted by Northwestern's Center for Native American and Indigenous Research in 2021, Valliere shared that in Anishinaabemowin, the word for a canoe's bow, *niigaan-jiimaan,* translates to "future," and the word for stern, *ishkweyaang-jiimaan,* to "past," reflecting how multiple temporalities are embodied in the same object and in the same moment [fig. 1.5].[12] These multidirectional relationships to time are evident in the exhibition layout, which resists a linear historical narrative, and are latent in many of the included artworks. The exhibition also emphasizes relationality over chronology, recognizing artistic and intellectual kinship across time.[13]

Woven Being has been developed through an in-depth collaboration with and between four artists: Andrea Carlson, Kelly Church, Nora Moore Lloyd (Lac Courte Oreilles Band of Ojibwe, born 1947), and Jason Wesaw. These artists have worked with the project team to develop an exhibition that centers their perspectives without centering themselves. Works by these artists are placed in dialogue with works by other artists, exploring kinship in a capacious sense. The artworks and artists in *Woven Being* are linked by aesthetics and material interests, as well as by community and familial connections.

This curatorial framework relies on Indigenous research methodologies and the vital relationships between Indigenous sovereignty, artists, and art. Collaboration with these artists developed out of existing relationships and new relationships forged through referrals and studio visits. This culminated into a curatorial approach that sought to eliminate traditional hierarchical structures by redistributing the power of decision-making throughout a team of artists and curators. This artist-centered methodology was developed out of feedback we received through the visioning sessions and conversations with colleagues who have been developing best practices in the field. Visioning session participants advocated for a process that foregrounded artists, their voices, and their agency in shaping the context in which their work is presented. They warned against a flattening approach that puts art at the service of an overarching historical narrative. Jordan, in particular, was inspired by Kiowa artist Teri Greeves (born 1970), who co-curated the exhibition *Hearts of Our People: Native Women Artists* with Jill Ahlberg Yohe.[14] During a panel moderated by Anya Montiel (Mestiza/Tohono O'odham descent) and devoted to the exhibition, Greeves shared the importance of having protocols that honor sovereignty and inviting Indigenous artists to "speak for themselves" through artist-led dialogues and their inclusion in curatorial decision-making processes beyond advisory roles, moving toward a collaborative curatorial model.[15] In the same conversation, Ahlberg Yohe emphasized the importance of upending colonial museum practices that traditionally grant expertise and power over decision-making to a single (often non-Native) curator. Accordingly, *Hearts of Our People* distributed expertise through collaborative decision-making processes. As more curators who

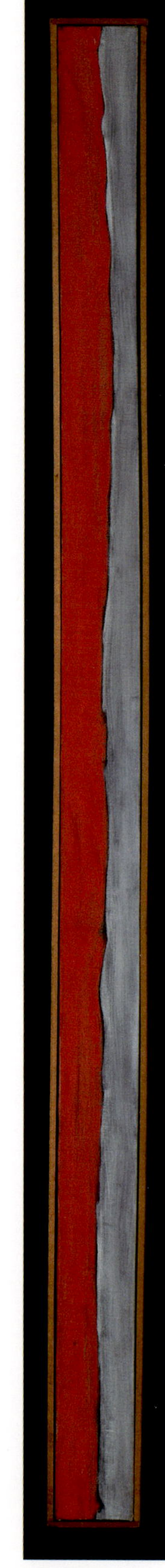

Fig. 1.8

are Indigenous, Black, and/or people of color enter the field, new curatorial frameworks will continue to emerge to better meet the needs of Indigenous artists and communities.

In addition to the previously articulated themes of landways and waterways, material kinship, and time, Andrea, Jason, Kelly, and Nora identified other themes that are integral to their own work and the work of others. For Nora, it was important to honor elder artists within Chicago's urban community. She was particularly inspired by the work of Chicago-based artists Sharon Skolnick (Fort Sill Apache/Lakota, born 1946) and Joe Yazzie (Navajo, born 1942) [figs. 3.5–3.7 and pl. 11]. (Anne Terry Straus's chapter in this volume goes into detail about these artists' importance within the Chicago community [pp. 68–69].) Moreover, Nora's series "Chicago Native American Community: Our Elders Look Back" features portraits of twelve elder community members [fig. 1.6; see also fig. 3.4 and pl. 10]. Andrea depicts a dream catcher created by her relative Raymond Duhaime (Grand Portage Ojibwe, 1909–1986) at the pinnacle of her work *The Indifference of Fire* [fig. 1.3 and pl. 9], and, along with Jason, she selected a work by her friend and mentor Jim Denomie (Lac Courte Oreilles Band of Ojibwe, 1955–2022) for inclusion in the exhibition [fig. 1.7 and pl. 10].

The inclusion of work by Barnett Newman (American, 1905–1970) and Josef Albers (American, born Germany, 1888–1976) reflects Jason Wesaw's interest in exploring a dialogue between American modernist abstraction and abstraction in Indigenous art forms, highlighting, from an Indigenous perspective, how Indigenous art and American art influence each other [fig. 1.8]. Jason draws inspiration from artists whose work encompasses a range of media, including Woodrow Wilson "Woody" Crumbo (Citizen Potawatomi, 1912–1989), Jeffrey Gibson (Mississippi Band of Choctaw Indians/Cherokee, born 1972), and Daphne Odjig (Odawa/Potawatomi, 1919–2016) [figs. 2.4, 2.5, 2.11 and pl. 11]. Among its multiple themes, Kelly's constellation draws upon relocation histories to and from Chicago. The city is and was a place of connection and confluence for many Indigenous communities as a result of removal, relocation, and other processes. Kelly chose to signal this sense of movement by including works like Teri Greeves's *My Family's Tennis Shoes* [fig. 5.6 and pl. 12].

In this companion publication to the exhibition *Woven Being*, Denise Lajimodiere, John Low, Blaire Morseau, and Anne Terry Straus introduce and expand on the collaborating artists' contributions from their own disciplinary and artistic vantage points. Their chapters are interspersed with eight selections of poetry and prose from the late nineteenth century to the present day, which were chosen in dialogue with the artists to expand their narratives. Following these chapters, a resource guide by Jacqueline Lopez, a PhD candidate in history at Northwestern University, sheds light on the underrecognized work of Chicago-based Indigenous artists and institutions from the mid-twentieth century to the present. Based on primary source research Jacqueline undertook across the city, the guide opens with brief summaries of key Chicago organizations and initiatives that

Fig. 1.8 Barnett Newman (American, 1905–1970), *Untitled 3*, 1950. Oil on canvas, 56 × 3 inches. Art Institute of Chicago, through prior gift of Mr. and Mrs. Carter H. Harrison, 1989.3. © 2024 The Barnett Newman Foundation / Artists Rights Society (ARS), New York.

have supported the work of Indigenous artists, beginning with the American Indian Center, which opened in 1953 [fig. 6.1]. This is followed by a timeline of select exhibitions highlighting the varied work of Chicago's Indigenous artists and a list of secondary sources of use to researchers.

The collaborative working process between the artists Andrea Carlson, Kelly Church, Nora Moore Lloyd, and Jason Wesaw, and between the artists and the *Woven Being* curatorial team, resulted in a unique exhibition. In addition to loans of existing work by artists whose careers span the period from the mid-twentieth century to the present, the installation included many new works in a range of media, some by the collaborating artists and some by artists they invited into the project. Large-scale works and installations conceived specifically for the project provided anchors around which groupings of more intimately scaled works were clustered. This book includes photographs documenting the installation of *Woven Being: Art for Zhegagoynak/Chicagoland* at The Block, which join with the chapters to recount a story of the project. We are grateful for the knowledge generously shared during and throughout this process.

1   Linda Tuhiwai Smith, "Decolonising Cultural Institutions: An Urgent, Necessary, Challenging yet Hopeful Journey beyond Colonialism," in *Uneven Bodies (Reader)*, ed. Ruth Buchanan et al. (Ngāmotu New Plymouth: Govett-Brewster Art Gallery, 2021), 7. For more on Smith's work on decolonizing, see her book *Decolonizing Methodologies: Research and Indigenous Peoples* (London: Zed Books, 2021).

2   Our understanding of the concept of positionality derives from the work of scholar Marisa Duarte (Xixanz/Pascua Yaqui Tribe), who describes it as a methodology that "requires researchers to identify their own degrees of privilege through factors of race, class, educational attainment, income, ability, gender, and citizenship, among others." She continues, "Before researchers can reframe a social problem and diagnose an intervention, they must see themselves and their conceptual universe in relation to the nature of the problem." Marisa Elena Duarte, *Network Sovereignty: Building the Internet across Indian Country* (Seattle: University of Washington Press, 2017), 135.

3   Positionality research at The Block was undertaken in part by Lois Taylor Biggs (Cherokee Nation/White Earth Ojibwe) during her tenure as Terra Foundation Curatorial Research Fellow for *Woven Being* in 2021–23.

4   For Indigenous-informed concepts of time, see, for instance, Lisa Brooks, "The Primacy of the Present, the Primacy of Place: Navigating the Spiral of History in the Digital World," *PMLA* 127, no. 2 (2012): 308–16; and Robin Wall Kimmerer, *Braiding Sweetgrass* (Minneapolis: Milkweed Editions, 2012).

5   The court found against the Pokagon Band of Potawatomi. For more on the history of these land claims, see John Low, *Imprints: The Pokagon Band of Potawatomi Indians and the City of Chicago* (East Lansing: Michigan State University Press, 2016), 67–94.

6   See, for instance, the *Report of the John Evans Study Committee*, University of Denver, November 2014, web; and the exhibition *The Sand Creek Massacre: The Betrayal That Changed Cheyenne and Arapaho People Forever*, which opened at the History Colorado Center, Denver, in November 2022.

7   NAISA efforts led to the drafting of Northwestern University's 2014 *Report of the John Evans Study Committee*, and to the reports of the Native American Outreach and Inclusion Task Force (2014, 2015, 2017, 2018, and 2019), web.

8   We visited the following institutions over the course of project development: Cherokee National History Museum, Denver Art Museum, First Americans Museum, Grand Rapids Public Museum, Greenwood Rising, History Colorado, Minneapolis Institute of Art, Museum of Contemporary Art Denver, Museum of Wisconsin Art, Oklahoma Contemporary, Osage Nation Museum, Philbrook Museum of Art, Pokagon Center of History and Culture,

JANET DEES, JORDAN POORMAN COCKER, AND KATHLEEN BICKFORD BERZOCK

Pokagon Court and Peacemaking Center, Sand Creek Massacre National Historic Site, Sand Creek Massacre Visitor and Education Center, South Bend Museum of Art, Tia Foundation, University of Michigan Museum of Art, and Ziibiwing Center.

9 See, for example, Rosalyn LaPier and David R. M. Beck, *City Indian: Native American Activism in Chicago, 1893–1934* (Lincoln: University of Nebraska Press, 2015); and James B. LaGrand, *Indian Metropolis: Native Americans in Chicago, 1945–1975* (Champaign: University of Illinois Press, 2002).

10 See Brooks, "The Primacy of the Present, the Primacy of Place," 310.

11 Mark Rifkin, *Beyond Settler Time: Temporal Sovereignty and Indigenous Self-Determination* (Durham, NC: Duke University Press, 2017).

12 See "These Canoes Carry Culture," a website developed by students in Dr. Patricia Loew's Northwestern University undergraduate class Native American Environmental Issues and the Media, cnair-canoe.github.io/canoe/index.html.

13 For the concept of intellectual kinship, see Teresia Teaiwa, "The Ancestors We Get to Choose: White Influences I Won't Deny," in *Theorizing Native Studies*, ed. Audra Simpson and Andrea Smith (Durham, NC: Duke University Press, 2014), 43–55, web.

14 *Hearts of Our People*, curated by Jill Ahlberg Yohe and Teri Greeves, traveled to three subsequent museums after opening at the Minneapolis Institute of Art: the Frist Art Museum, Nashville (September 27, 2019–January 12, 2020); the Renwick Gallery of the Smithsonian American Art Museum, Washington, DC (February 21–August 2, 2020); and the Philbrook Museum of Art, Tulsa (October 7, 2020–January 3, 2021). See Jill Ahlberg Yohe and Teri Greeves, eds., *Hearts of Our People: Native Women Artists* (Minneapolis: Minneapolis Institute of Art; Seattle: University of Washington Press, 2019).

15 "Hearts of Our People: Curator and Artist Conversation," Smithsonian American Art Museum, October 1, 2020, web.

Blaire Morseau
(Pokagon Band of Potawatomi)

Gdankobthëgnenanêk é zhë denwémdëygo

Kinship, Place, and Time in the Artwork of Jason Wesaw

Everything else is tertiary. My family and my bundle.
That's the direction I go.
—Jason Wesaw[1]

NDENWÉMAGNÊK (MY RELATIVES)

Jason Wesaw (Pokagon Band of Potawatomi, born 1974), one of four collaborating Indigenous artists in the exhibition *Woven Being: Art for Zhegagoynak/Chicagoland*, is clear about his priorities. He is a father, nephew, peacemaker, and ceremonial leader, among many other kinship relationships and titles, both formal and informal. The bundle he mentions in the epigraph is an important part of ceremonial life for Neshnabé peoples.[2] In these bundles, we carry our medicines and sacred items.

   Jason might grimace at my calling him a ceremonial leader. He's humble that way. Indeed, most traditional people in the Pokagon Band of Potawatomi community are reluctant to claim a title like that, lest it sound boastful or arrogant. Some of us—the younger generation[3]—are transitioning into a season of life in which we're asked to take on more ceremonial roles. This is due in large part to the inevitable passing of our elders—a journey that takes them across the Milky Way, or what we call *thibékanêk*, "spirit path." Community is not external to personhood. Like our relationships with other humans, our connections to land, water, and skies are also seen in light of *ndenwémagnêk* (my relatives, literally "those who sound like me"). Jason says, "Much of my work has to do with connection to the natural world and how it teaches us about healthy relationships, reciprocity, and abundance. The Land is our first teacher."[4]

   Understanding our community context is central to understanding our art, as Jason's work makes clear. Amid life's seemingly endless beckoning for our attention to a variety of matters, some urgent and some that just seem urgent, when elders in our community walk on,[5] tradition calls for us to stop what we may have intended to prioritize and visit with relatives, help with preparations, and be there for extended kin, whether biologically related or not. Recently, when an important teacher to Jason walked on, the artist went straight to work on the ceremonial responsibilities that guide our relatives into the spirit world. This emphasis on relationships, with both the human and the other-than-human world, is reflected in Jason's art [fig. 2.1 and pl. 2].

   Kinship exists at all levels of Indigenous creative processes. We carry our community with us everywhere we go, similar to the way we carry our bundles. While some of our art may be "abstract" in style,[6] it is not *abstracted* or alienated from our communities and ways of knowing [fig. 2.2]. Reflecting this reality, *Woven Being* departs from the desultory, and all too common, curatorial practice in which artworks are disassociated from their original cultural contexts, infused with the exhibiting institution's perspectives and values rather than those of the artists or their cultural sensibilities.[7] With this approach, artists often feel a lack of agency in the curatorial process. Reflecting on past experiences with museums, Jason says, "I do believe in my stories and the things that I want to share with the outside world, but I move real carefully as I get older in the places I go because I've realized a lot of times that projects and people aren't necessarily worth my time. And in years past I said yes to things that really didn't pan out in the right way."[8] This issue is particularly poignant for Indigenous artists, who are already underrepresented as creators. Responding to the ubiquitous loss of control experienced by Native artists in the framing of their work after a museum acquires it, the unique structure of *Woven Being*, through what are called "constellations," allows the works of many artists to speak to one another in ever-expanding dialogues of meaning and interpretation. The works featured in each constellation date from the early twentieth century to the present day and are by artists with diverse cultural backgrounds, almost all of them indigenous to North America [figs. 2.3–2.7, 2.11 and pl. 11].[9]

Constellations are pictures made by drawing imaginary lines between stars in the sky, and for many traditional societies, they serve as symbols of sophisticated stories embedded in specific cultural contexts.[10] Socially significant narratives guide human societies spiritually, politically, and even creatively to ensure our communities survive and thrive. Thus, the conversations between works of art in the constellations created by Jason Wesaw and the artists Andrea Carlson (Grand Portage Ojibwe/European descent, born 1979), Kelly Church (Match-E-Be-Nash-She-Wish Band of Pottawatomi/Ottawa, born 1967), and Nora Moore Lloyd (Lac Courte Oreilles Band of Lake Superior Ojibwe, born 1947) in *Woven Being* are like nebulae, birthing new asterisms of significance through which museumgoers can discover and experience modes of symbolic reading. In addition to creating works expressly for this exhibition, Jason, Andrea, Kelly, and Nora selected other artists' work to showcase, and the new and previously existing works are woven together in thematic, stylistic, and spiritual wefts, so much so that the constellations themselves are no longer distinguishable. Like Potawatomi traditional black ash baskets made from elaborately woven splints, these curatorial choices parallel Indigenous modes of relation [fig. 2.7]. For example, the Potawatomi word for "our ancestors" is *gdankobthëgnenanêk*.[11] Interestingly, the same word is used for "great-grandchildren." This is because *gdankobthëgnenanêk* more accurately translates to "the ones we are tied to through generations." Whether tied or woven, Indigenous relationality is intimate and expands through generational time. Neshnabé conceptions of kinship are woven together and bound by specific Indigenous spaces on the land and in the waters, and they spiral through time in all directions.

In addition to giving artists more agency in how their work is exhibited, the constellation format sheds light on another component that is fundamental to Indigenous artists: our communities. On one hand, anthropology and natural history museums have attempted to contextualize their "artifacts" almost to a fault.[12] On the other hand, art museums are known for their white walls, sanitized spaces, and

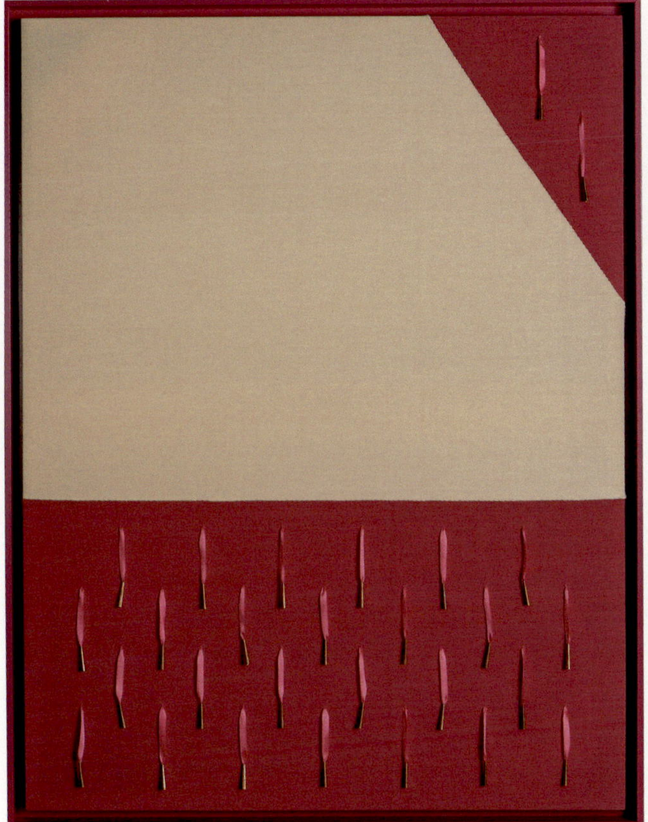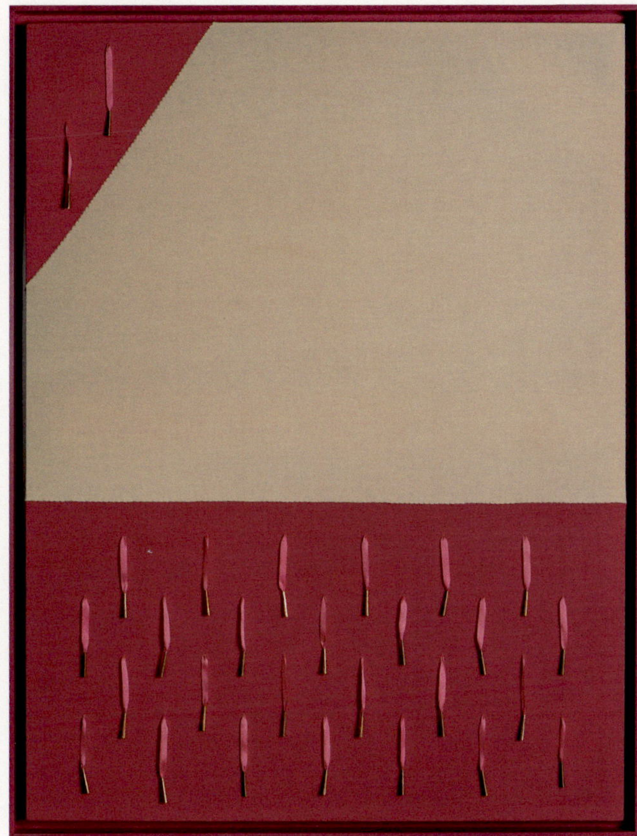

Fig. 2.1

Fig. 2.1 Jason Wesaw (Pokagon Band of Potawatomi, born 1974), *Neon Sunrise*, 2023. Hand-sewn muslin hand-dyed with sassafras bark and Rit dyes, polyester ribbon, copper cones, and artificial sinew, in custom-constructed and painted frame, two frames: 42 × 32 inches each. Collection of the artist. Photograph by Holly Trevan.

decontextualized exhibits with simple, unobstructive labeling. Lest art enthusiasts become distracted or feel forced to interpret art in a way that doesn't suit them, art museums invite visitors to dwell, intellectually engage, and dream with the works, with few or no texts telling us how we *should* feel or see through didactic curatorial strategies. However, in creating these minimal spaces, they have often separated the works from the important cultural contexts in which they were produced—autochthonous contexts that amplify their meaning. In fact, the art museum's "white box" is itself a curatorial strategy that assumes neutrality, masking the processes of recontextualization it creates while obstructing certain kinds of interpretation in favor of others.

Like constellations that lose their form when connecting lines are removed, we lose key elements of Indigenous art when the threads that bind them to socially important places, specific ceremonies, cultural practices, and stories are severed. While societies around the world have their own unique stories archived in sky-bound pictures, constellations as a whole symbolize unity, storytelling, and culturally significant patterns. They represent the human process of finding meaning or understanding in seemingly unrelated events. In *Woven Being*, works are arranged so as to encourage our imaginations to identify dialogues between them—for instance, how Jason relates to the way George Morrison (Grand Portage Ojibwe, 1919–2000) represents water and the duality between our physical

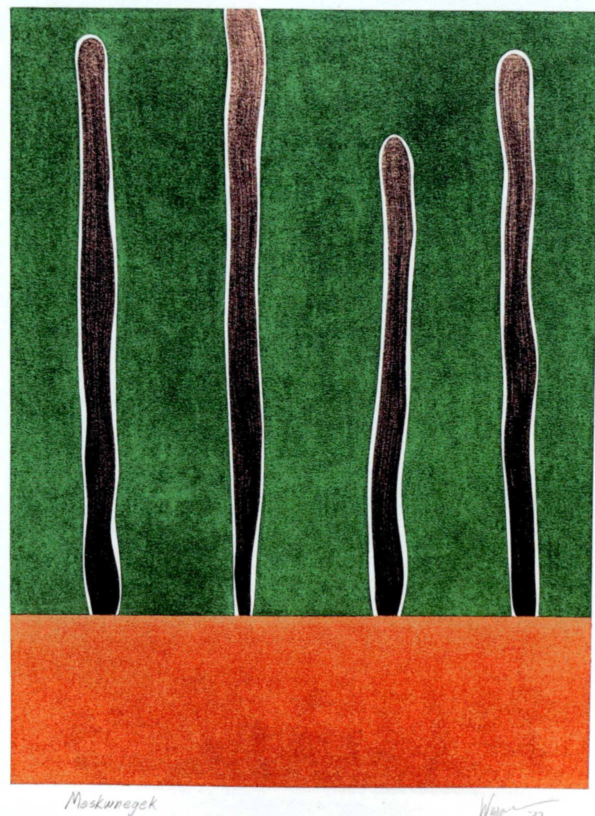

Fig. 2.2

and spiritual selves [fig. 2.3], and how Jeffrey Gibson (Mississippi Band of Choctaw Indians/Cherokee, born 1972) includes people of different identities within his practice.[13] The constellation approach to curation echoes the allegories and metaphors in stories that take on new meanings with each retelling. More than merely trying to re-create the cultural environs in which Indigenous art is embedded, the constellation framework of *Woven Being* is generative in its approach to fostering new intellectual and interpretive insights.

Another foundation of Native North American art is the exploitative history that is still palpable in regional pockets of the United States, epitomized by places like "Indian trading posts" and in the references made to our work as "crafts," to name just two pejorative examples.[14] Despite these unequal relationships of power, for Indigenous peoples—both traditional and contemporary—the creation of art has always held a special kind of agency. One of the first ways in which Native peoples in North America participated in market economies after the seventeenth- and eighteenth-century fur trade was through the selling of their handiwork, including beadwork, moccasins, bandolier bags, and birch bark "curios." Later, in the eighteenth and nineteenth centuries, Native communities were forcefully removed from their homelands to make way for white settlers.[15] This made way in part for professional anthropologists and museum curators who took an interest in the things we made, but not so much in the continuity or survival of our communities. Meanwhile, amateur collectors took

Fig. 2.2 Jason Wesaw (Pokagon Band of Potawatomi, born 1974), *Mswekengek (Sassafras)*, 2022. Oil pastel on incised paper with copper leaf, 24 × 20 inches. Private collection, Bristol, UK.

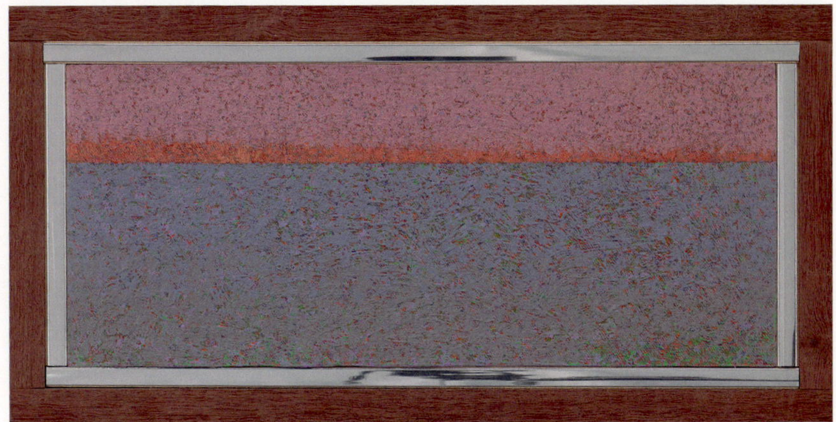

Fig. 2.3

little interest in Native peoples at all beyond the consumption of Indian-made souvenirs.[16] Jason says, "It's like they didn't want us, or they didn't want us to have the freedoms that other people had, but they've often wanted the goods that we made."[17] Here, he is making a connection between the market, which disassociated Indigenous artists from their works, and the community contexts that gave the works significance.

Unlike amateur collectors and tourists, anthropologists and folklorists did engage with Native peoples, albeit in a somewhat longer-term extractive relationship (longer, that is, than a passing commercial transaction). Due to a belief, widely held in the nineteenth and early twentieth centuries, that American Indians would soon disappear, stories, songs, artworks, and even human remains were collected, bought, and stolen to "preserve" Native cultures in exhibit cases and storage rooms at new, well-funded museums and universities in major cities like New York, Berkeley, and Chicago.[18] While academics buttressed their careers through the procurement of Indian goods and intellectual property, higher education and cultural institutions benefited from the Native-made materials they hoarded.[19] And finally, local communities benefited from having access to the stolen Indian land upon which they lived and worked, as well as from the well-funded educational resources, many supported by the sale of that land, all while American Indians weren't even naturalized as US citizens.[20] At the same time, after the establishment of the railroad infrastructure that opened the American "frontier" in the nineteenth century, travelers—mostly white—to popular tourist destinations ranging from the lakeshore of Michigan to the deserts of the Southwest would purchase Indian handicrafts and "curios" for their own use and as gifts for friends and family back home [fig. 2.9].

Fig. 2.3 George Morrison (Grand Portage Ojibwe, 1919–2000), *Far Echo, Red Rock Variation: Lake Superior*, 1993. Acrylic on canvas board, 6 × 14 inches. Minneapolis Institute of Art, gift of Charlotte Karlen, 93.52.1. Photograph by Minneapolis Institute of Art, © George Morrison Estate. Courtesy of Bockley Gallery, Minneapolis.

KĖ MINĖ ĖTHĖ BMETHWÊK (LAND AND WATERWAYS)

When it's said that Indigenous artwork is embedded in specific community contexts, this refers, of course, to the people, the family and

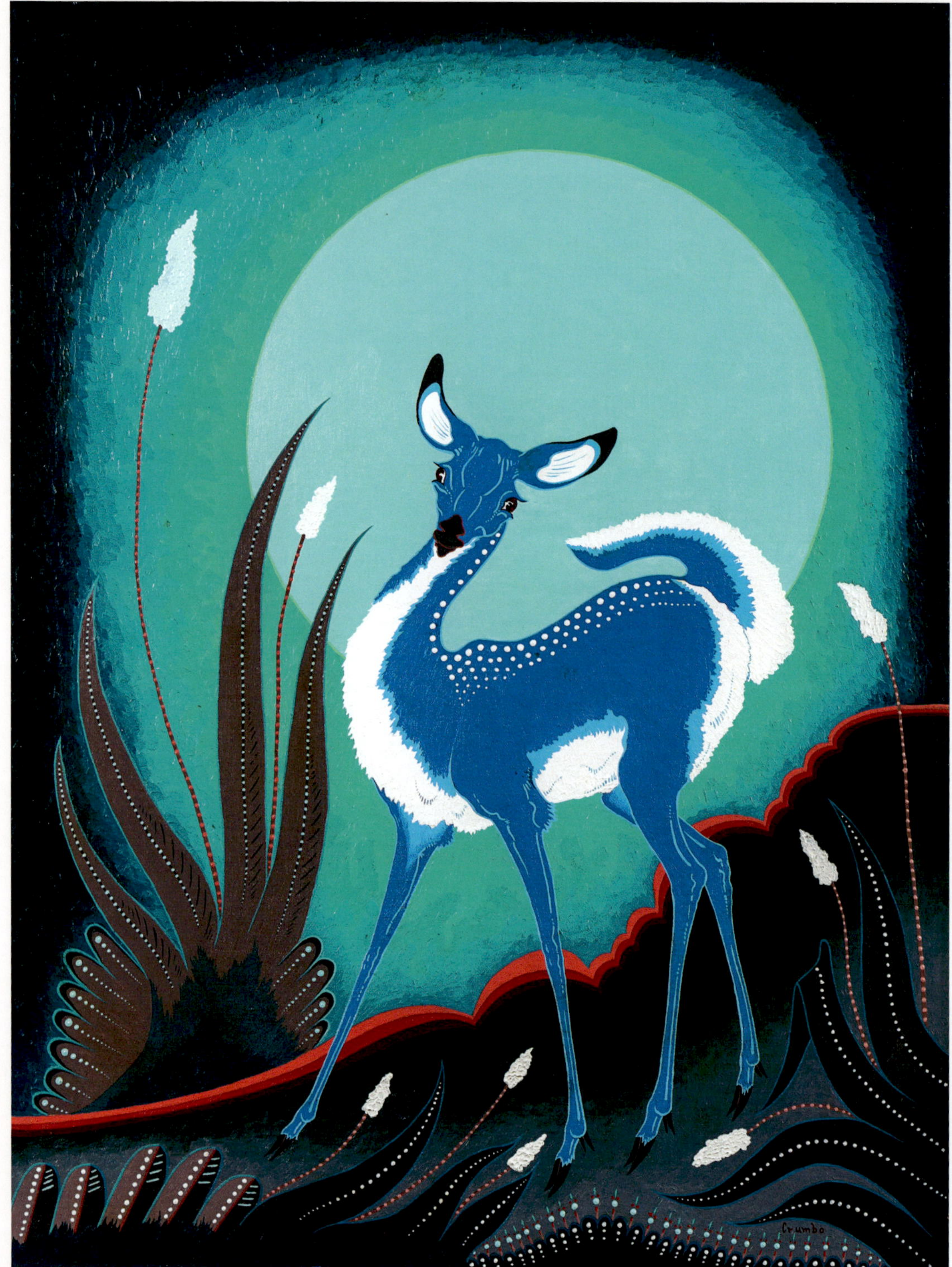

Fig. 2.4

Fig. 2.4 Woodrow Wilson Crumbo
(Citizen Potawatomi, 1912–1989), *Deer
and the Moon*, 1945. Oil on canvas board,
30 × 22 inches. Eiteljorg Museum of
American Indians and Western Art,
Indianapolis, 1998.15.1.

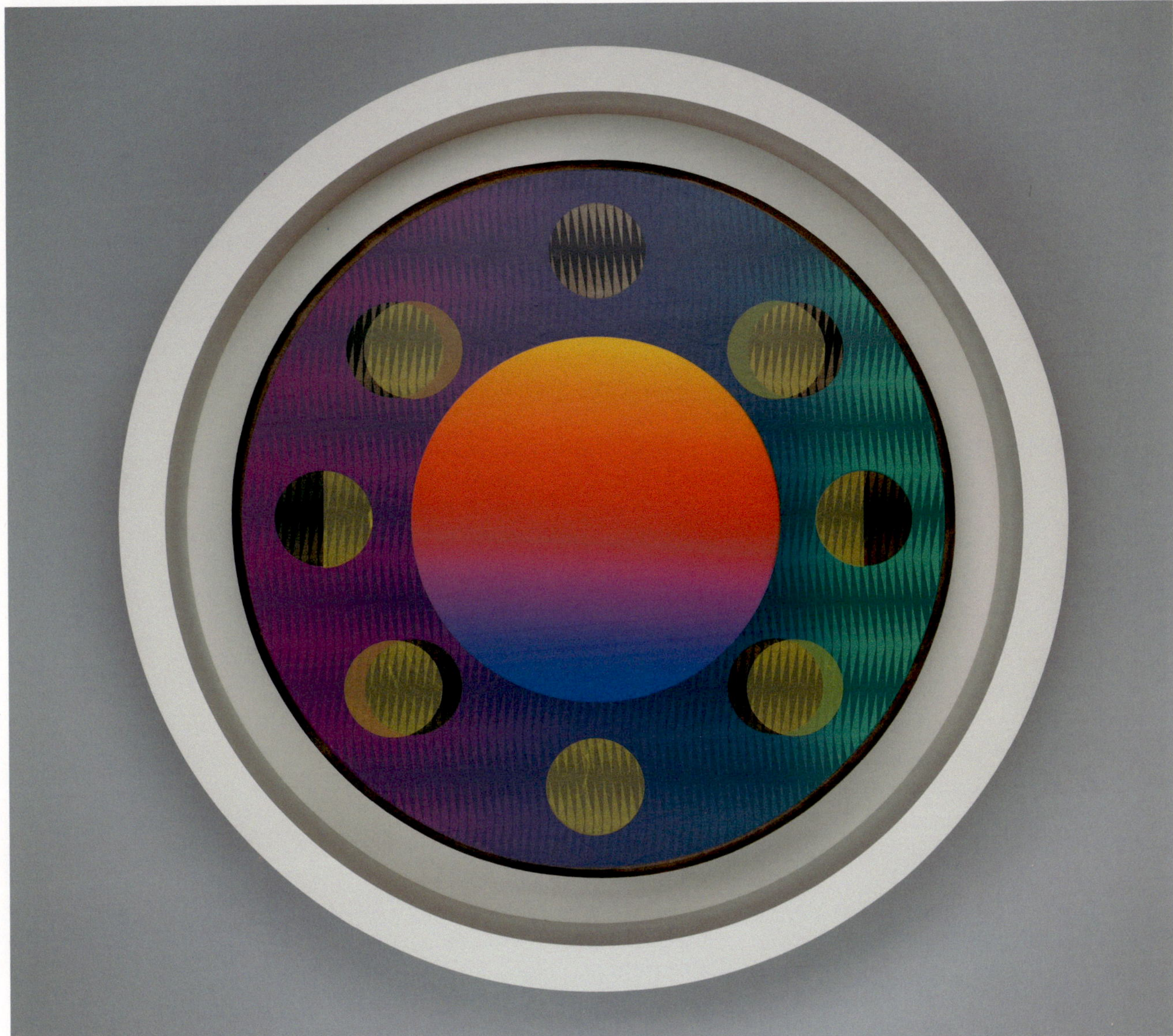

Fig. 2.5

Fig. 2.5 Jeffrey Gibson (Mississippi Band
of Choctaw Indians/Cherokee, born 1972),
A Time for Change, 2020. Acrylic matte
primer, screenprint, and acrylic gloss
varnish on handmade elk hide drum, 19⅞ ×
19⅞ × 3¼ inches. Varied edition of 21.
Vanderbilt University Museum of Art,
Nashville, Hamilton Hazlehurst Memorial
Fund Purchase, with additional support
provided by Dr. and Mrs. E. Williams
Ewers Gift for Fine Arts Fund, 2021.001.
© Vanderbilt University Museum of Art.

clan designs that are used, and the stories connected to those clans
[figs. 2.6a, 2.6b]. But it also refers to the environment in which our
ancestors have lived for generations, the sacred sites that serve as
archives of our traditional knowledge and where we hold our ceremonies. And finally, it refers to the lands where we mobilize our tribal
sovereignty today. For Neshnabék peoples—that is, Potawatomi,
Odawa, and Ojibwe—the ribbonwork and appliqué on our regalia
index both our creative traditions that are thousands of years old and
the more recent history Native peoples have with the French in the
Great Lakes region [fig. 2.10]. The French Revolution left a surplus
of silk fabrics and ribbons with no one to purchase them, and traders
capitalized on this by shipping out materials to trade and sell to the
Native folks with whom they already had relationships via the Great
Lakes fur trade. Indigenous peoples took to these new commodities

and indigenized their use with elaborate sewing techniques, making some patterns that were floral and rounded and others that were geometric and sharp.

While the materials they were using were indeed of European origin, contemporary Indigenous artists can see a tangible connection between the new forms of clothing and styles of ribbonwork being produced at that time and more "traditional" Neshnabé designs found on birch bark containers, quillworked items, tattoos, and other media [fig. 2.8]. The intricate etching of birch bark items is indicative of the northern environments in which the tree grows and the seasons in which it can be harvested. For instance, the birch's winter bark is darker than its summer bark, with tannins that can be scraped off to create ornamented designs through use of negative space. Contemporary Indigenous artists continue to innovate by building on their knowledge of these materials while dialectically linking them to Neshnabé insights about our connections to the natural world. Explaining his use of ribbons, Jason says they "represent that flowing and ethereal nature water has."[21] Elsewhere, he has said, "No matter how we try to shift and change and contain it, the spirit of the Water is forever flowing, finding a way around or through the misdeeds of humans."[22]

The ribbons suspended from the ceiling in Jason's installation *Water Carries Memory*, made for *Woven Being*, not only index the history and contemporary uses of the material in Neshnabé communities but also reference the land upon which museumgoers stand while at The Block, as well as the nearby waters that send cool breezes along Chicago's shores [see pls. 7, 8]. In their delicate rippling, they invite us to join the artist in the calm, meditative observation of nature. "I want to offer a place of peace and contemplation for the viewer while they are in the gallery space, a feeling much like if they were sitting on the shore with the waves rippling and the breeze flowing," says Jason.[23] He achieves this viewer experience in part through the materials he uses in the work:

> We are bringing in sand from the shoreline just footsteps away from The Block Museum, and it will act as the foundation for the installation. Importantly, the sand that was brought into Evanston to actually form the lakeshore around [Northwestern University] was harvested from the area at Indiana Dunes.[24] My relative, old Chief Wesaw, had a village of around three hundred people, and our winter camp was within the boundaries of what is now known as the Indiana Dunes National Park. That land, and indeed this very sand, is ancestral to me personally and many other Bodéwadmi people; the water ensures that it remembers where it came from. The piece will . . . hopefully not just capture the viewers' attention but cause them to reflect more sensitively about these beautiful spaces they now call "home."[25]

In encouraging this awareness, Jason wishes to move individuals from a sense of estrangement from the natural surroundings of

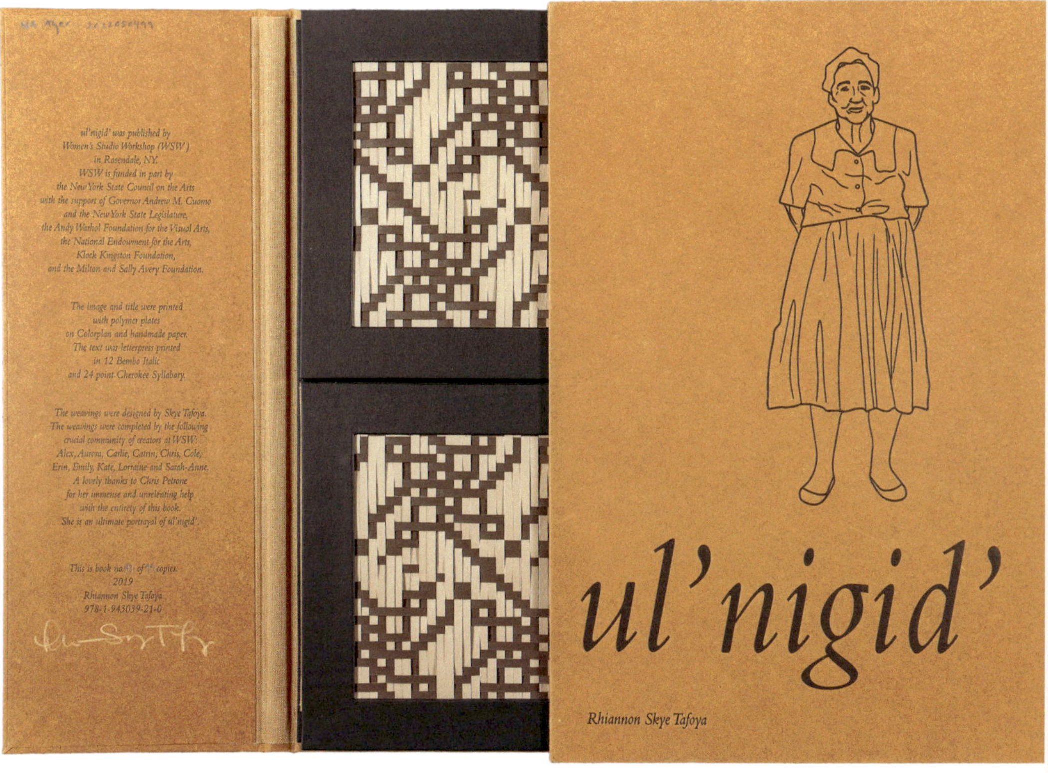

Fig. 2.6a

Figs. 2.6a and 2.6b
Rhiannon Skye
Tafoya (Eastern
Band Cherokee/
Santa Clara
Pueblo, born 1989),
Ul'nigid', 2020.
Accordion-fold,
letterpress-printed
booklet bound in a
portfolio composed
of woven panels,
11 × 11¼ inches
closed; 11¼ ×
23½ × 5⅝ inches
assembled. Edition
of 44. Published
at the Women's
Studio Workshop,
Rosendale, NY.
The Newberry
Library, Chicago.

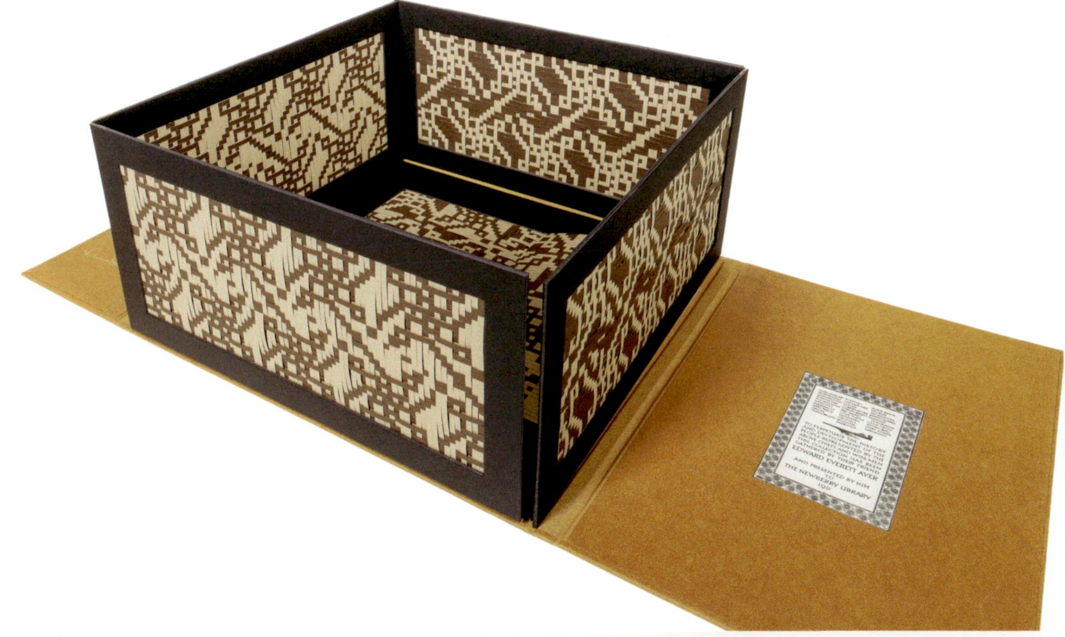

Fig. 2.6b

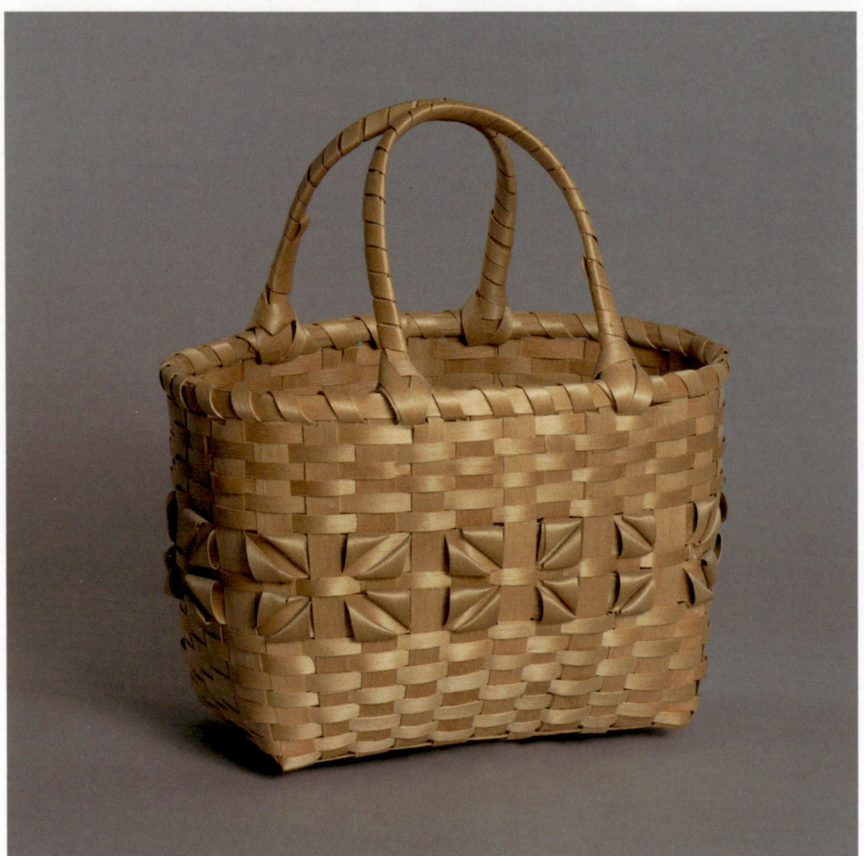

Fig. 2.7

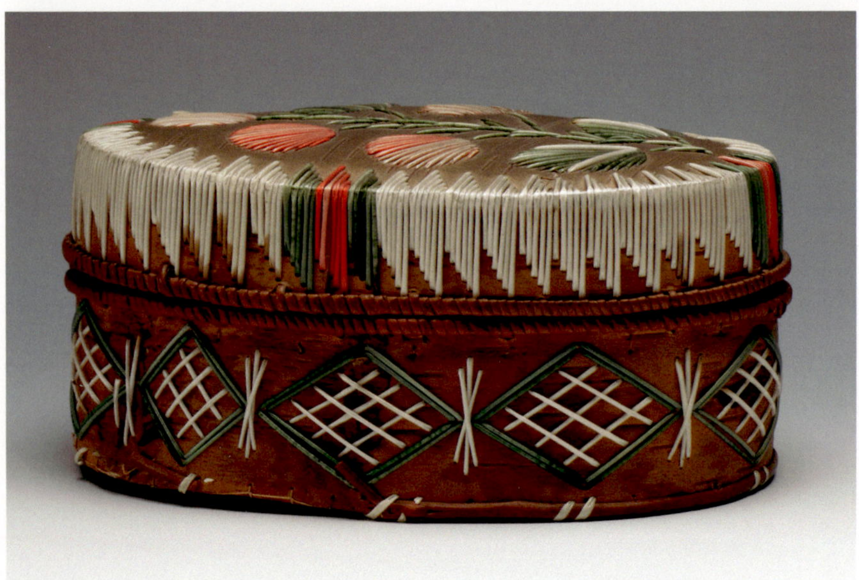

Fig. 2.8

Fig. 2.7 John Pigeon (Pokagon Band of Potawatomi, born 1957), *Purse Basket*, 2005. Black ash, 11½ × 7 × 13 inches. Collection of Jason Wesaw, Michigan. Photograph by Holly Trevan.

Fig. 2.8 Artist once known (Anishinaabe), *Oblong Birch Bark Basket with Lid*, ca. 1900. Birch bark, spruce root, wood, porcupine quills, thread, and dye, 3⅛ × 4⅛ × 6⁷⁄₁₆ inches. Hood Museum of Art, Dartmouth, bequest of Frank C. and Clara G. Churchill, 47.17.9562.

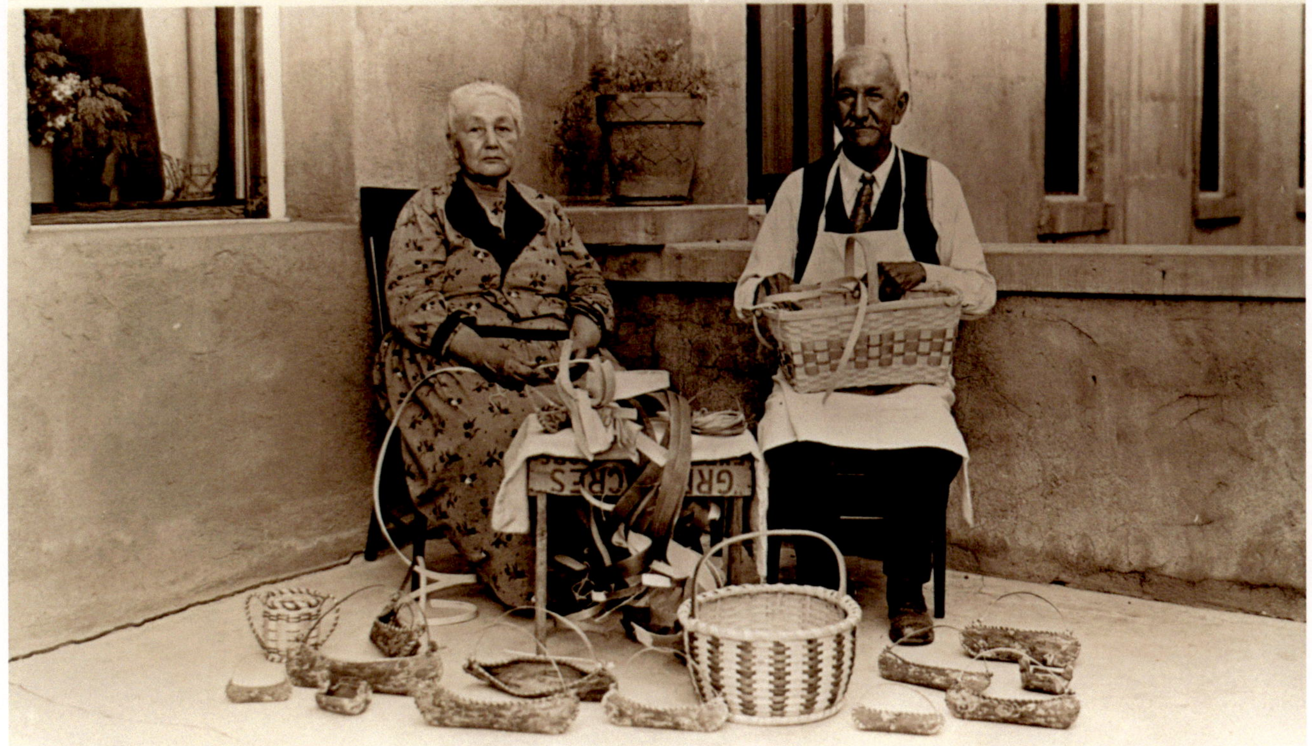

Fig. 2.9

Fig. 2.9 Photographer once known, *Thomas Topash and Mary Person Topash with Baskets*, early twentieth century. Center of History and Culture, Pokagon Band of Potawatomi Archives, Dowagiac, MI, 2020.8.13.

the places they call home to a sense of kinship and, perhaps more importantly, a sense of responsibility. This sense of responsibility ideally moves us to actualize our work while thinking about our actions seven generations into the future.[26] Are we living as sustainably as we can? Are we holding our political leaders as accountable as we could be? Generational thinking is Indigenous thinking; and this is an ethical shift Jason plans to share with the rest of the world, altering our conceptions of time by allowing us to see ourselves in relation to the future as well as the past and present.

NESHNABÉ DBË'GÉWEN (INDIGENOUS CONCEPTS OF TIME)

The Neshnabék, like many Indigenous communities, conceptualize time in a circle, rather than linearly. In fact, Potawatomi peoples traditionally measure the year in thirteen phases of the moon, or *gizes*,[27] codified on the back of a painted turtle (*Chrysemys picta*), a species indigenous to North America. On the shell of the turtle are thirteen segments representing the different moons; these are surrounded by twenty-eight smaller segments representing the number of days in each month. Our calendar is literally a circle. Each month is associated with significant cultural doings, such as sugar bush season, or maple syrup season, which takes place during *zisbakwtoké gizes* (making sugar moon), and ricing, which takes place during *mnomnëké gizes* (wild rice harvesting moon), as well as what our other-than-human relatives are up to, as in *wzawbëgya gizes* (leaves turning

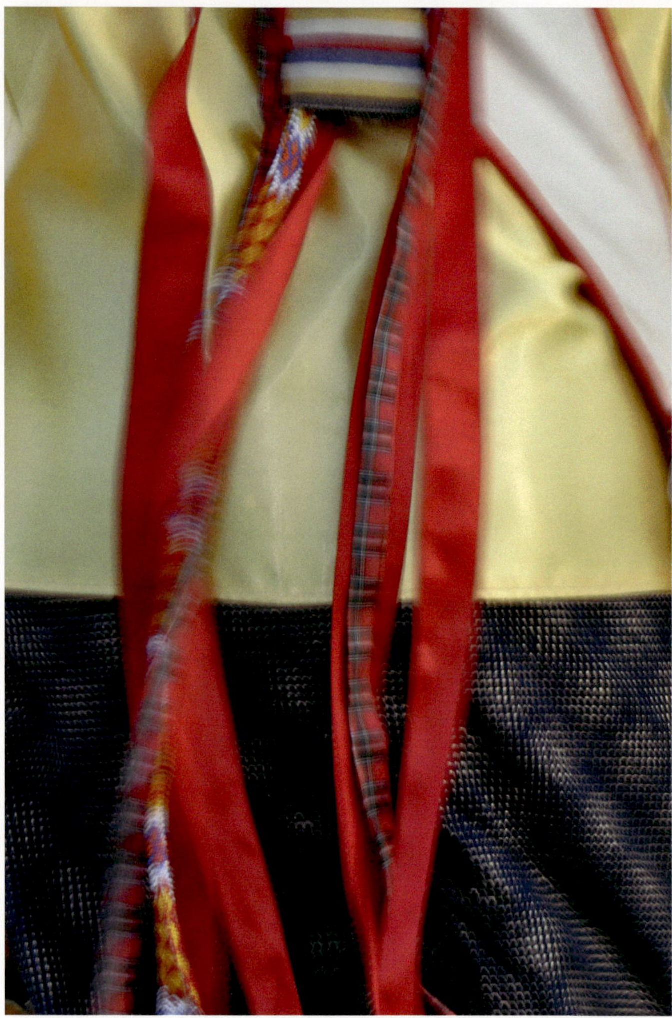

Fig. 2.10

yellow moon) and *ktthe mko gizes* (big bear moon). As previously explained, the Potawatomi word for "ancestor," *ankobthëgën*,[28] means both "great-grandparent" and "great-grandchild" and translates literally to "the one we are tied to through generations." A similar kinship term, *ndenwémagnêk*, translates to "my relatives" or "those who sound like me." The phrase gestures to the profound importance of language in how we interpret and assign value to the world and the cosmos. "Our elders have told us the more that we learn of our language, the more we will think in our language, the more we'll dream in our language."[29] What registers of Indigenous art will be dreamt in light of the generative dialogues presented in this exhibition remains to be seen.

Whether tied or woven, Indigenous relationality is intimate and extends both forward and backward in time; *ankobthëgën*, our term for "ancestor," encapsulates this truth. Neshnabé conceptions of kinship are also woven together by sound, as epitomized by *ndenwémagën*, our term for "my relative." Like slipstreams that disrupt normative (Western) concepts of linear time, Jason's work

Fig. 2.10 Jason Wesaw (Pokagon Band of Potawatomi, born 1974), *She Gives Life*, 2014. Digital photograph, dimensions variable. Collection of the artist.

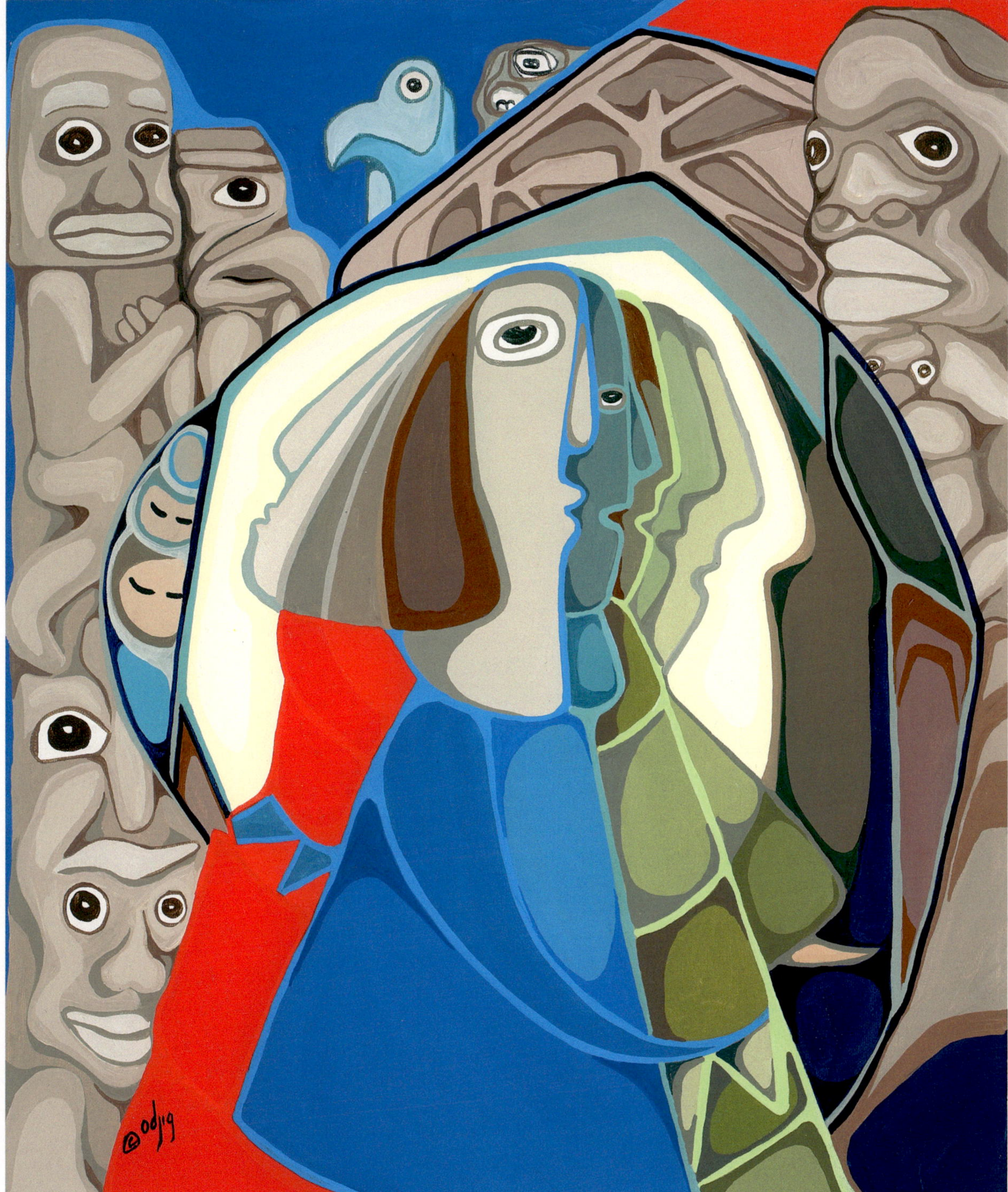

Fig. 2.11

Fig. 2.11 Daphne Odjig (Odawa/Potawatomi, 1919–2016), *Entrance to the Lodge*, 1984. Acrylic on canvas, 24 × 20 inches. J.W. Wiggins Native American Art Collection, Sequoyah National Research Center, University of Arkansas at Little Rock.

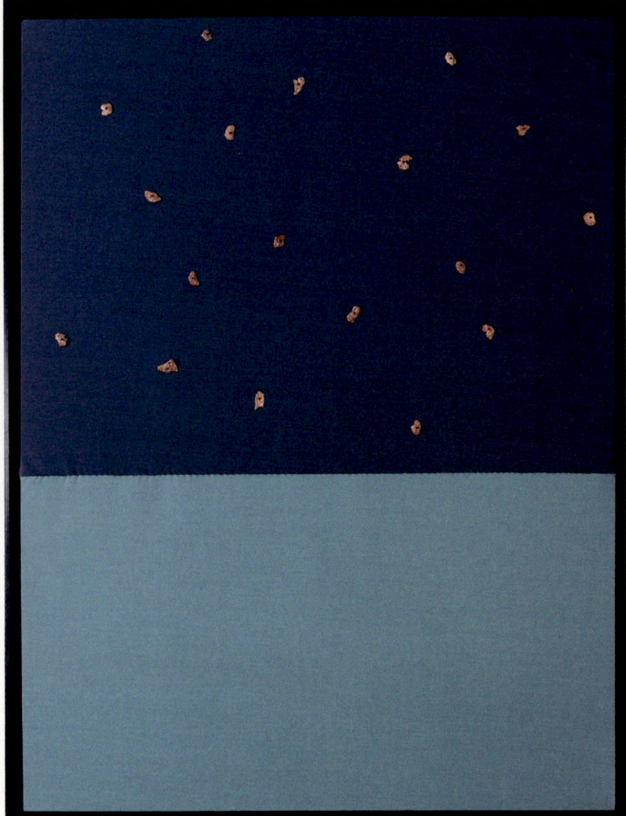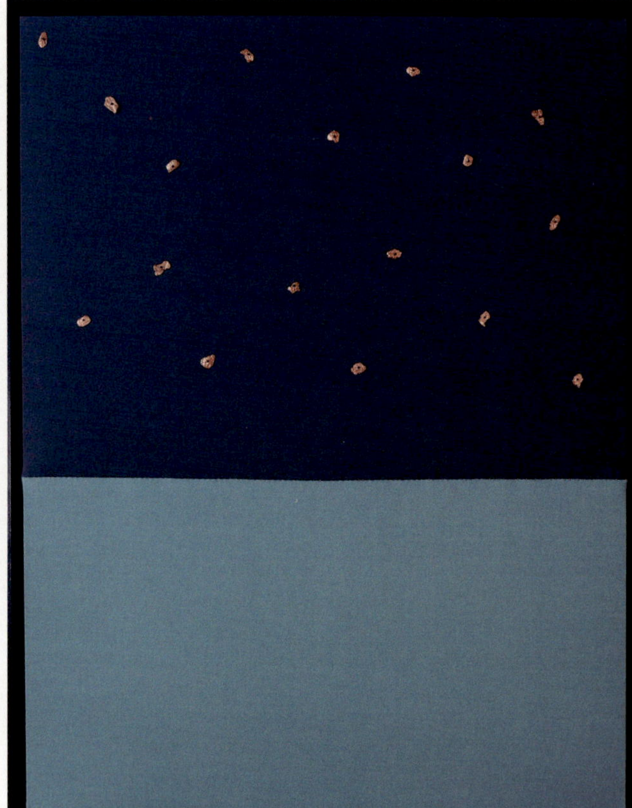

Fig. 2.12

in conversation with the other art in the exhibition's constellations is "a continuation of these old stories and cultural lifeways that we still practice within the community" [fig. 2.11].[30]

Constellations, the patterns humans create in the sky, not only hold stories but also act as wayfinding tools and methods of orienting us to the time of year. Stars on their own are also significant; they are the literal memories of the Creator [fig. 2.12]. One of our traditional stories explains how the universe was created through the emergence of sound when *gzhémnedo* cast out their thoughts in all directions of the vast, empty universe, only to receive no response from the black void.[31] Once called back, those thoughts left twinkling spots in the inky sky. There is even a traditional name related to this story, Bamewawagezhik, which means "the sound the stars make rushing through the sky."[32] As you, reader or museumgoer, consider your experience with *Woven Being: Art for Zhegagoynak/Chicagoland*, I ask, Have you ever reflected on what sound the stars make as they rush through the sky? What might an awareness of such environmental and cosmological phenomena do for our current society and the ways we relate to one another or, rather, fail to?

Fig. 2.12 Jason Wesaw (Pokagon Band of Potawatomi, born 1974), *Negos Gkéndaswen* (*Star Knowledge*), 2023. Hand-sewn muslin hand-dyed with indigo and Rit dyes, float copper, vintage glass beads, and artificial sinew, in custom-constructed and painted frame, two frames: 42 × 32 inches each. Collection of the artist. Photograph by Holly Trevan.

The literal translation of *Gdankobthëgnenanêk ë zhë denwémdëygo*, the Potawatomi title for this chapter, is "Our Ancestors and How We Relate to Each Other." Potawatomi translations throughout this chapter have been provided by Bmejwen Kyle Malott (Pokagon Band of Potawatomi).

1   Jason Wesaw, recorded interview by Kathleen Bickford Berzock and Jordan Poorman Cocker, July 24, 2023.

2   *Neshnabé* (*Neshnabék*, plural) is the Potawatomi spelling for "the true humans" or "the original people," while *Anishinaabé* is the more common Ojibwe spelling. Both versions include particles that reference a state of being low. Some relate this to stories about the original Native peoples being lowered down from the sky world, while others interpret it as referring to the humble position of human beings as the least important animal on Earth.

3   "Younger" is a relative term. For me, it means anyone who isn't an elder.

4   Jason Wesaw, email communication to author, April 3, 2024.

5   When someone passes, we refer to that process as "walking on," referencing the journey that is made to the spirit world.

6   "Abstract" is one way to describe the artistic genre Jason most often works in when painting.

7   Amy Lonetree, *Decolonizing Museums: Representing Native America in National and Tribal Museums*, ill. ed. (Chapel Hill: University of North Carolina Press, 2012).

8   Jason Wesaw, recorded interview by Kathleen Bickford Berzock and Jordan Poorman Cocker, November 27, 2023.

9   Jason's constellation also includes works by the non-Indigenous artists Josef Albers (American, born Germany, 1888–1976), Agnes Martin (American, born Canada, 1912–2004), and Barnett Newman (American, 1905–1970), whose color field works speak to his own use of color.

10 Indeed, the Pokagon Potawatomi have our own constellations that depart from the hegemonic Greco-Roman constellations most astronomers use.

11 *Ankobthëgnanêk* is the plural form of the noun *ankobthëgën*, meaning "ancestor." The addition of the prefix "gda-" and the suffix "-nanêk" in *gdankobthëgnenanêk* changes the meaning to "our ancestors."

12 I'm thinking, of course, of the anthropological exhibit archetype: the problematic dioramas that surround ill-gotten and often stolen Indigenous artwork, grave goods, and sacred items exhibited in Eurocentric registers of "savagery" and primitiveness. Amy Lonetree addresses the damaging impact of this style of display in the introduction to her seminal 2012 book, *Decolonizing Museums: Representing Native America in National and Tribal Museums*.

13 Jason Wesaw, recorded interview by Kathleen Bickford Berzock and Jordan Poorman Cocker, May 1, 2023.

14 The same can be said for other societies that have experiences with colonialism, from Africa and New Zealand to Latin America and everywhere in between.

15 The Removal Era in the United States began around 1830, formalized by President Andrew Jackson's Indian Removal Act of that year, though less formal removals happened before the act's passage, facilitated by settler violence and military aggression. American Indian tribes experienced further dispossession after the passage of the Homestead Act in 1862, which encouraged European immigrants (mostly from Germany) to encroach and establish homesteads on Indian land in the Midwest. Another major policy that adversely affected tribes while diminishing their land base resulted from the Dawes Act of 1887, under which reservation land was forcefully parceled and "excesses" transferred, first to the federal government and then to settlers. Today, territorial dispossession continues to occur in many forms, often resulting from natural resource extraction by corporations that participate in mining, hydraulic fracturing, and other practices that damage the environment, threaten livelihoods, and make local people sick from contamination.

16 For more information regarding the history of tourism specific to Indigenous peoples in the United States, see Pieter Hovens and Mette van der Hooft, eds., *Indian Detours: Tourism in Native North America* (Havertown, PA: Sidestone Press, 2016).

17 Wesaw, recorded interview, July 24, 2023.

18 These institutions were well funded at least at their inception. Many present-day museum professionals could certainly claim a lack of resources and support, especially for departments working in repatriation or the humanities more generally.

19 What are often referred to as "land-grab universities" also received federal support and investments in the form of endowments established from stolen Indian land by way of the Morrill Act of 1862. For information about the digital humanities project that mapped out the land parcels connected to American university financial ledgers as well as the history of land-grab universities, see Robert Lee, "Morrill Act of 1862 Indigenous Land Parcels Database," *High Country News*, March 2020, web.

20 Naturalization didn't occur until 1924, with the Indian Citizenship Act, which encompassed all American Indians, investing them with American citizenship upon birth (whether tribes who saw themselves as sovereign nations wanted it or not).

21 Wesaw, recorded interview by Kathleen Bickford Berzock and Jordan Poorman Cocker, November 7, 2023.

22 Wesaw, email communication to author.

23 Wesaw, recorded interview, November 7, 2023.

24 Honoring the cultural protocol of reciprocity, Jason says, "we have already offered *séma* (tobacco) and collected a small amount of sand as a group of artists, curators, and NU Native community members." Wesaw, email communication to author.

25 Wesaw, recorded interview, November 7, 2023.

26 References to the seventh generation or the seventh fire as both a prophecy and a philosophical tenet are ubiquitous across Native North America. Interpretations of this seven-generational thinking are diverse, but it is often used to describe strategies of ecological stewardship intended to ensure that our current generation's actions will have positive effects on our descendants for at least seven generations into the future.

27 *Gizes* means "month" or "moon." Depending on the context, it can also mean "sun," translating more accurately to "he or she is rising."

28 See note 11 in this essay.

29 Wesaw, recorded interview, November 7, 2023.

30 Wesaw, recorded interview, November 7, 2023.

31 *Gzhémnedo* translates to "the creating spirit," from *gzhé*, meaning "creating," and *mnedo*, meaning "spirit" (one that has never lived as a human—in other words, not a ghost). I use the pronoun "their" in reference to *gzhémnedo* because, while the use of the masculine pronoun is very common when relaying this story in English, traditional uses of the Neshnabé term for God tend not to have a gender.

32 Bamewawagezhikaquay, or "Woman of the Sound [the Stars Make] Rushing through the Sky," is the Ojibwe name of nineteenth-century author Jane Johnston Schoolcraft, whose poem "To the Pine Tree" is included in this volume [pp. 54–55].

Jane Johnston Schoolcraft, also known as Bamewawagezhikaquay (Ojibwe, 1800–1842)

"To the Pine Tree"

*on first seeing it
on returning from Europe*

This translation appears in *The Sound the Stars Make Rushing through the Sky: The Writings of Jane Johnston Schoolcraft*, ed. Robert Dale Parker (Philadelphia: University of Pennsylvania Press, 2007), 89.

Shing wauk! Shing wauk! nin ge ik id,
Waish kee wau bum ug, shing wauk
Tuh quish in aun nau aub, ain dak nuk i yuan.
Shing wauk, shing wauk No sa
Shi e gwuh ke do dis au naun
Kau gega way zhau co zid.

Mes ah nah, shi egwah tah gwish en aung
Sin da mik ke aum baun
Kag ait suh, ne meen wain dum
Me nah wau, wau bun dah maun
Gi yut wi au, wau bun dah maun een
Shing wauk, shing wauk nosa
Shi e gwuh ke do dis au naun.

Ka ween ga go, kau wau bun duh e yun
Tib isht co, izz henau gooz ze no an
Shing wauk wah zhau wish co zid
Ween Ait ah kwanaudj e we we
Kau ge gay wa zhau soush ko zid.

Translation

The pine! the pine! I eager cried,
The pine, my father! see it stand,
As first that cherished tree I spied,
Returning to my native land.
The pine! the pine! oh lovely scene!
The pine, that is forever green.

Ah beauteous tree! ah happy sight!
That greets me on my native strand
And hails me, with a friend's delight,
To my own dear bright mother land
Oh 'tis to me a heart-sweet scene,
The pine—the pine! that's ever green.

Not all the trees of England bright,
Not Erin's lawns of green and light,
Are half so sweet to memory's eye,
As this dear type of northern sky
Oh 'tis to me a heart-sweet scene,
The pine—the pine! that ever green.

Simon Pokagon (Pokagon Band
of Potawatomi, 1830–1899)

Excerpts from *The Red Man's Rebuke*

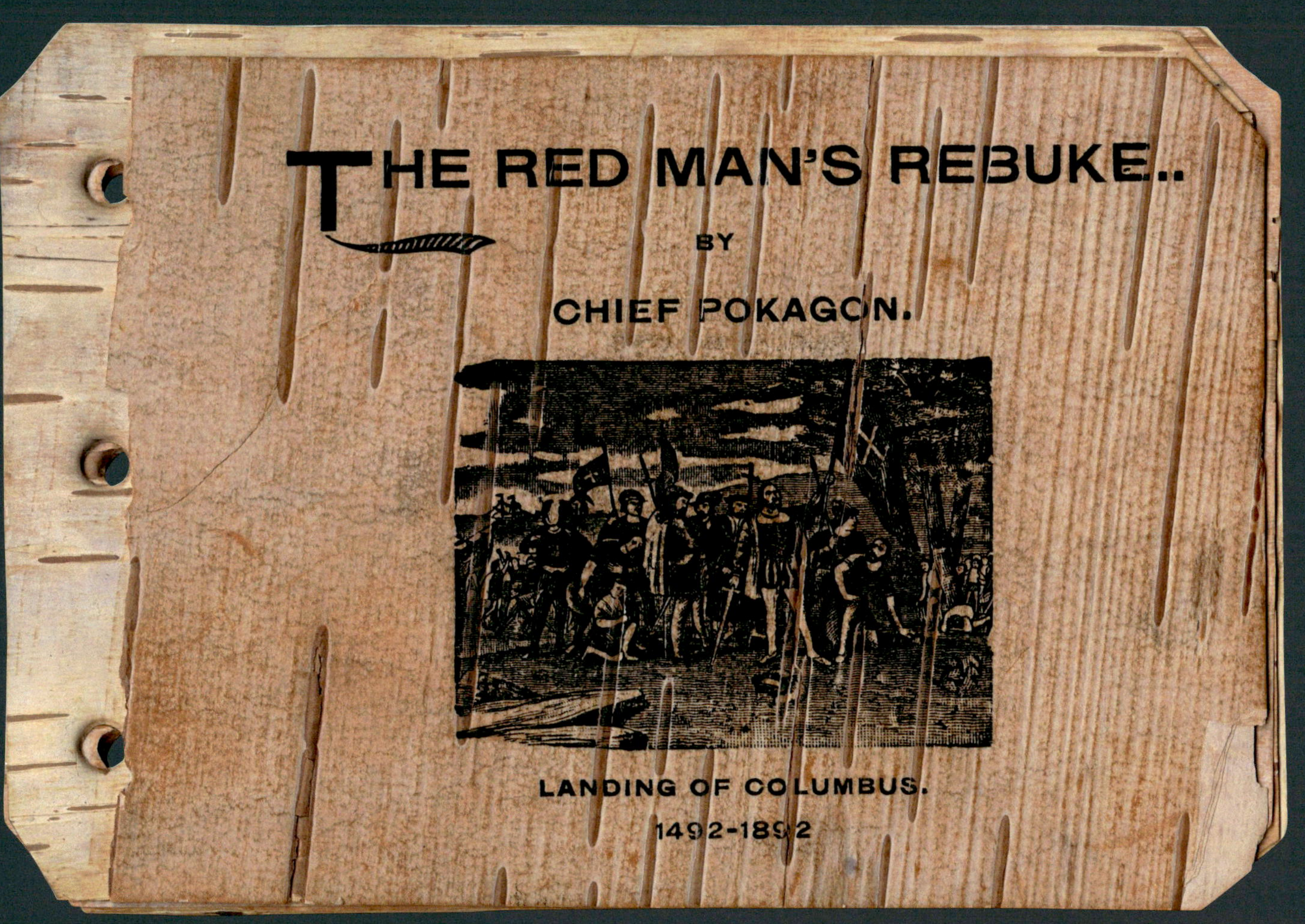

Simon Pokagon, *The Red Man's Rebuke*
(Hartford, MI: C. H. Engle, 1893), cover

By The Author.

My object in publishing the "Red Men's Rebuke" on the bark of the white birch tree, is out of loyalty to my own people, and gratitude to the Great Spirit, who in his wisdom provided for our use for untold generations, this most remarkable tree with manifold bark used by us instead of paper, being of greater value to us as it could not be injured by sun or water.

Out of the bark of this wonderful tree were made hats, caps and dishes for domestic use, while our maidens tied with it the knot that sealed their marriage vow; wigwams were made of it, as well as large canoes that outrode the violent storms on lake and sea; it was also used for light and fuel at our war councils and spirit dances. Originally the shores of our northern lakes and streams were fringed with it and evergreen, and the white charmingly contrasted with the green mirrored from the water was indeed beautiful, but like the red man this tree is vanishing from our forests.

"Alas for us; our day is o'er
Our fires are out from shore to shore;
No more for us the wild deer bounds—
The plow is on our hunting grounds.
The pale man's ax rings through our woods,
The pale man's sail skims o'er floods;
Our pleasant springs are dry.
Our children—look by power oppressed,
Beyond the mountains of the west—
Our childern go—to die."

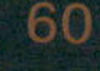

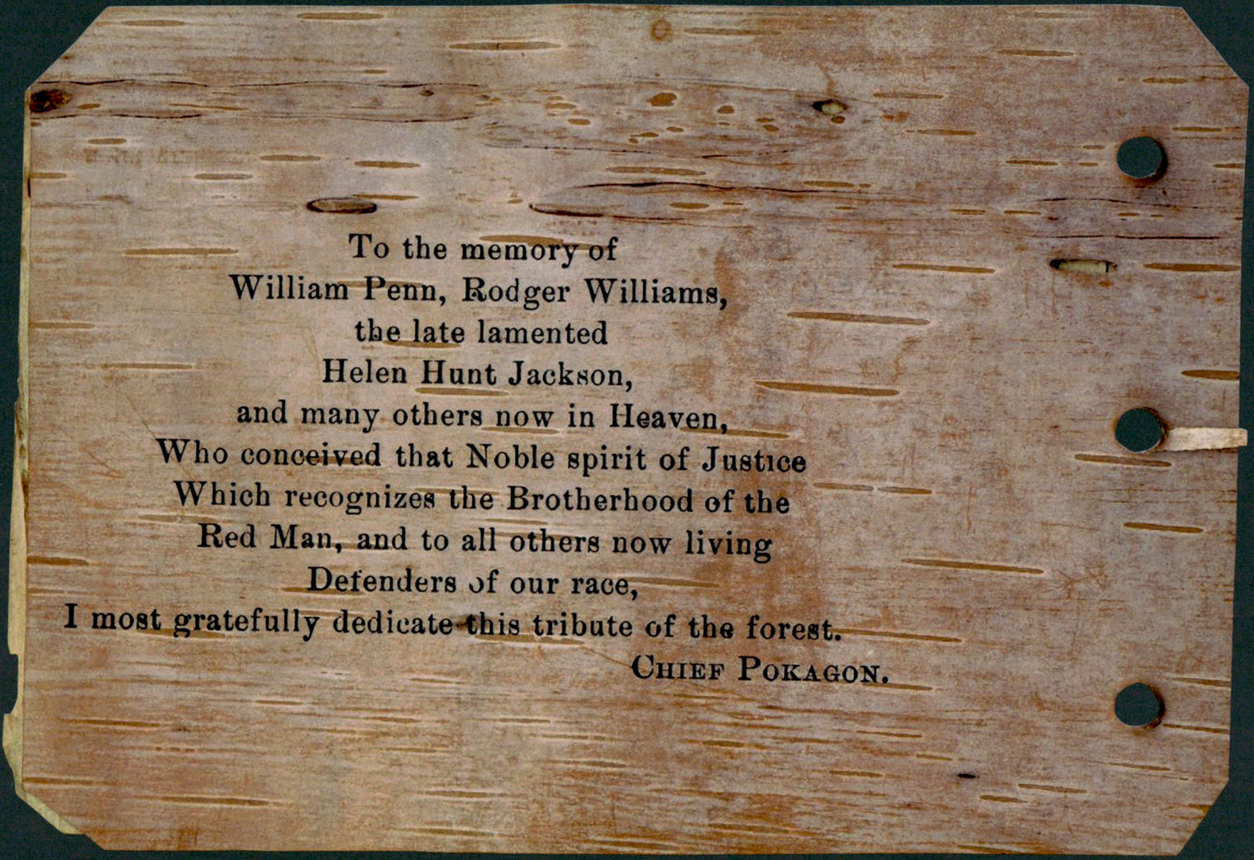

To the memory of
William Penn, Rodger Williams,
the late lamented
Helen Hunt Jackson,
and many others now in Heaven,
Who conceived that Noble spirit of Justice
Which recognizes the Brotherhood of the
Red Man, and to all others now living
Defenders of our race,
I most gratefully dedicate this tribute of the forest.
CHIEF POKAGON.

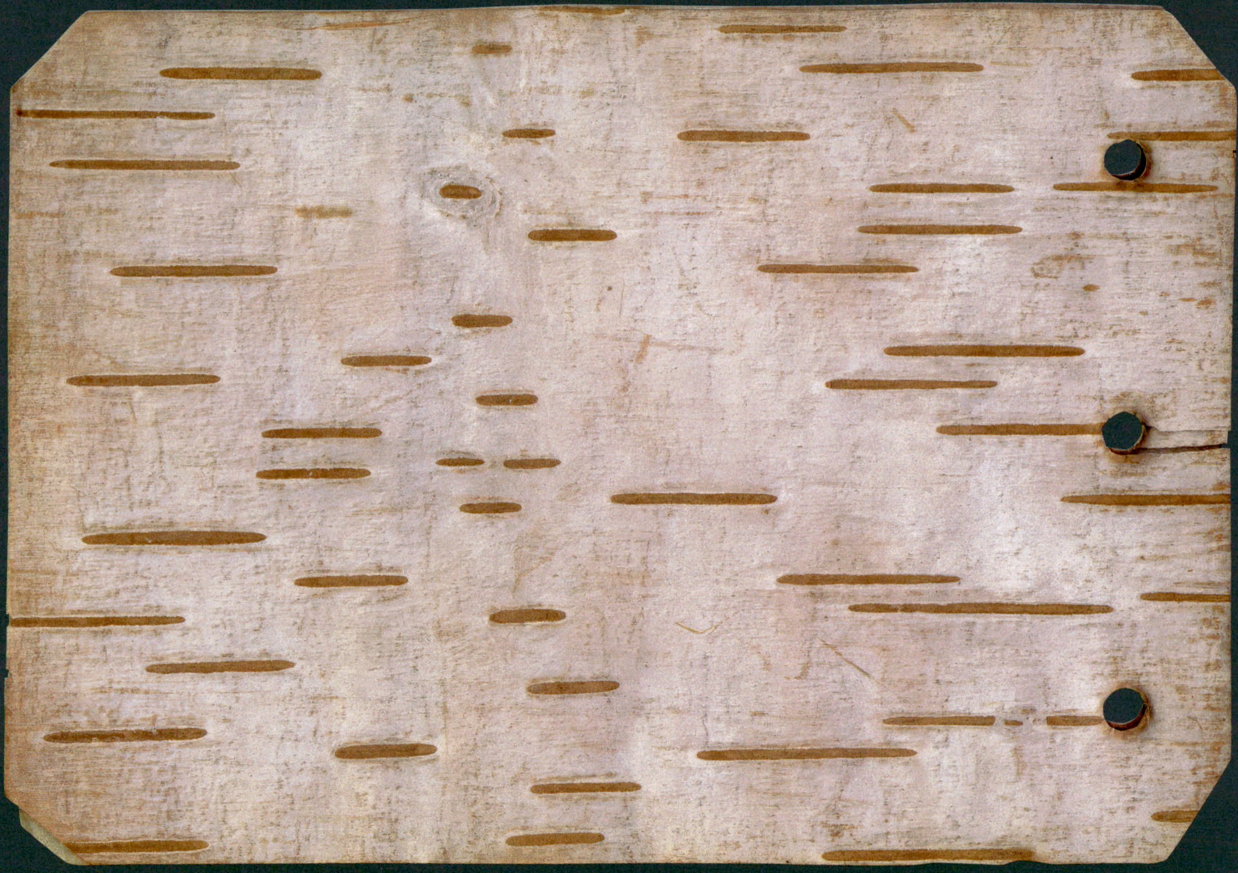

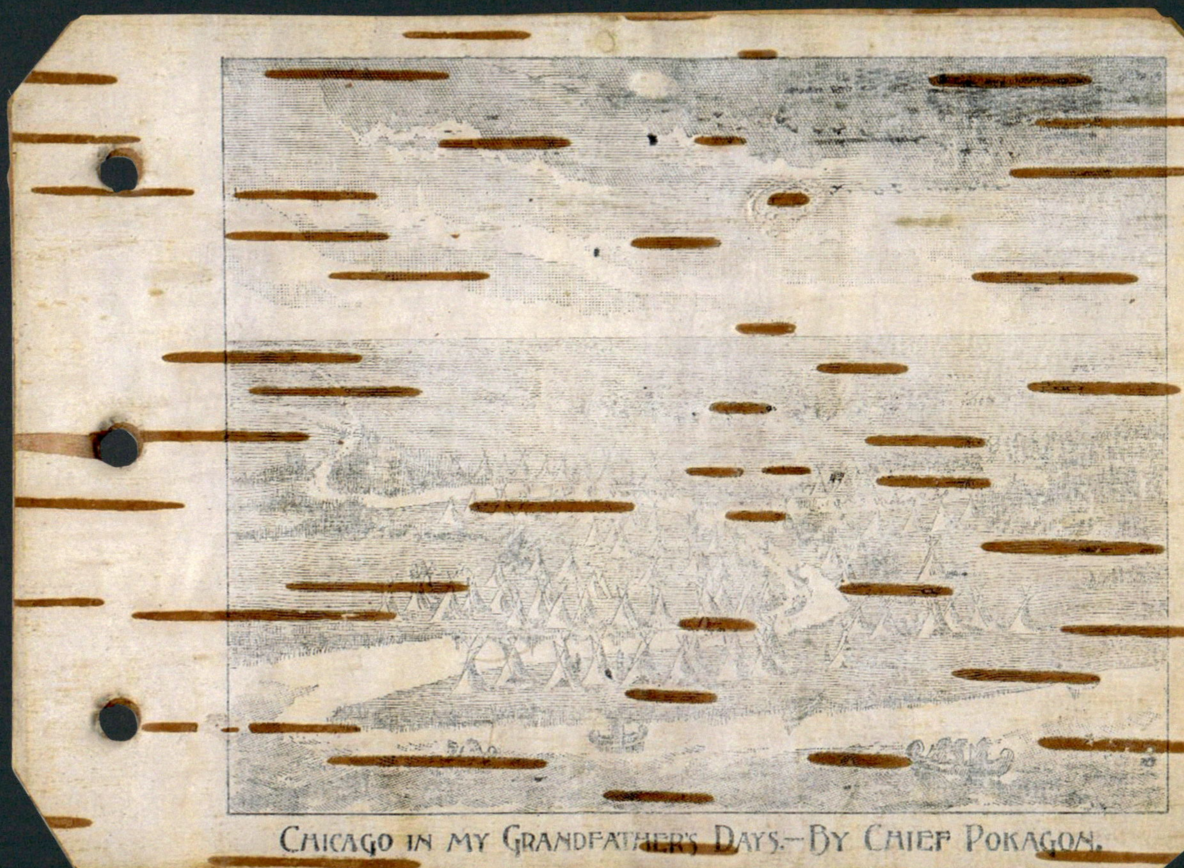

CHICAGO IN MY GRANDFATHER'S DAYS.—BY CHIEF POKAGON.

BY SIMON POKAGON

Pottawattamie Chief.

"Shall not one line lament our forest race,
For you struck out from wild creation's face?
Freedom — the selfsame freedom you adore,
Bade us defend our violated shore."

In behalf of my people, the American Indians, I hereby declare to you, the pale-faced race that has usurped our lands and homes, that we have no spirit to celebrate with you the great Columbian Fair now being held in this Chicago city, the wonder of the world.

No; sooner would we hold high joy-day over the graves of our departed fathers, than to celebrate our own funeral, the discovery of America. And while you who are strangers, and you who live here, bring the offerings of the

Anne Terry Straus

Indinawemaaganag gaye ayaawiyaan: Nora Moore Lloyd waabanda'iwe keyaa inawendiyang

Community and Identity: A Tapestry of Relationships in the Work of Nora Moore Lloyd

At home in Chicago, Nora Moore Lloyd (Lac Courte Oreilles Band of Lake Superior Ojibwe, born 1947) begins work on another birch bark piece for the exhibition *Woven Being: Art for Zhegagoynak/Chicago-land* at Northwestern University's Block Museum of Art. It is difficult, delicate, and time-consuming work. The bark must be cleaned, dried, and substantially flattened for preservation and display. Most birch bark is harvested from living trees, which offer up their bark late in summer. Nora's bark, however, comes from branches felled by age or wind. Nora has shared that "over the years I've collected branches that fell naturally—some so old that the inside wood had completely rotted, leaving a circle of bark with a hole."[1] The pieces are fragile, so every step is undertaken carefully to prepare them for painting. After washing the birch bark pieces in a laundry tub, Nora uses a blow-dryer to dry them, going "back and forth, back and forth, for several minutes."[2] Because they hold the cylindrical shape of the tree's trunk, she then weighs the pieces down with heavy books to encourage them to lie flat. The last step is to flatten the birch bark pieces even more with a heat press that her daughter, Melissa, loaned her.

Birch bark is the basis for several of Nora's works included in *Woven Being*. Nora's two-sided banner, *Birchbark/Wiigwaas* [figs. 3.3a, 3.3b], heralds the presence of Anishinaabe culture in Chicago, and a series of paintings on birch bark, "Remembering Ancestors," delves into the artist's ongoing connection with her Lac Courte Oreilles tribal history and culture [figs. 3.1, 3.2 and pl. 12].[3] Birch bark has a special significance to the artist. It has long been indispensable to Ojibwe people, providing the material for many essential items, including waterproof baskets, wigwams, canoes, and sacred texts.[4] "What makes working with these particular bark pieces special," Nora says, "is that they come from my home on the Lac Courte Oreilles reservation."[5] In 1745, as the Lac Courte Oreilles Band moved south from upper Wisconsin, their first settlement was along a path between big and little Courte Oreilles Lakes. Now called Thoroughfare Road, that path is where the artist's property is located. "I'm positive that my ancestors shared oxygen and space with those birch trees in addition to leaving their tracks on the land. The birch trees, I know, may have just been seedlings from generations of birch on that land, but I believe there is a thread of connection."[6] Birch bark thus ties Nora to her ancestors and tribal traditions. With the "Remembering Ancestors" series, she extends this connection by painting the names of those ancestors on the carefully prepared bark segments, using the Canadian Aboriginal Syllabics.[7]

Further connecting the artist to her ancestors and to tribal and reservation history are six letters written by her great-great-uncle

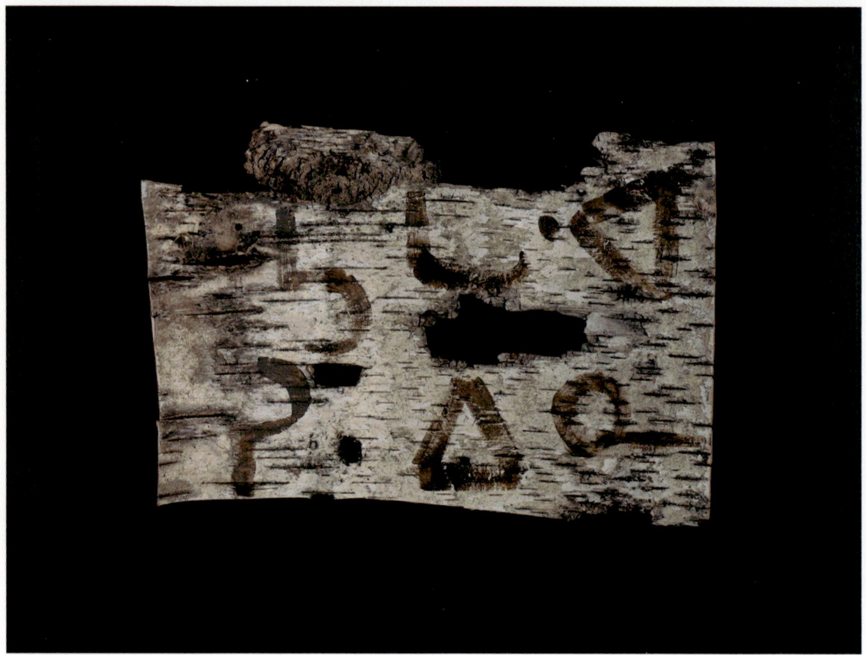

Fig. 3.1

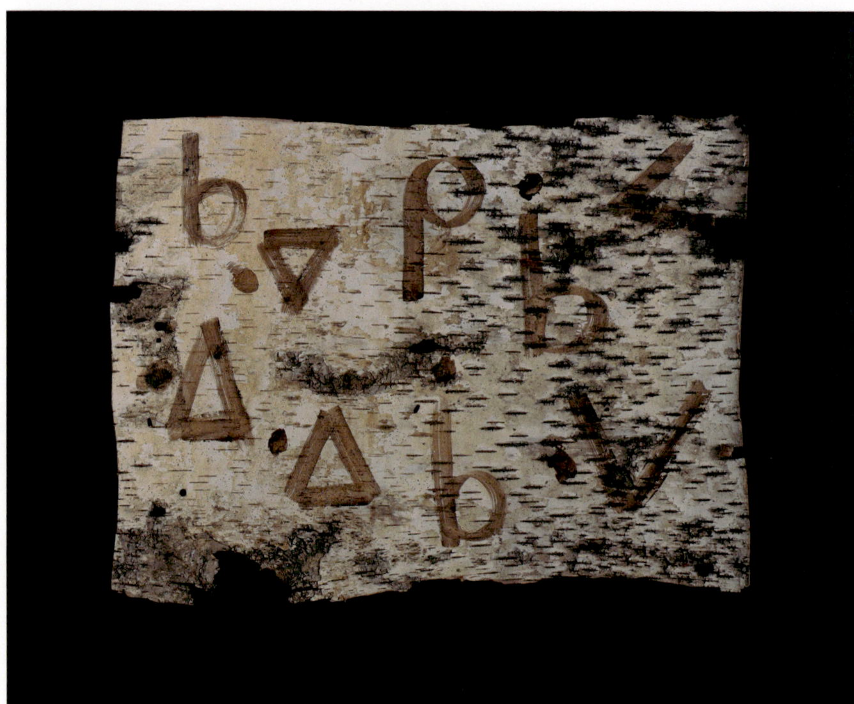

Fig. 3.2

Fig. 3.1 Nora Moore Lloyd (Lac Courte Oreilles Band of Lake Superior Ojibwe, born 1947), ᓴᑭᐱ·ᐊᐧ, *Zaasijiwan* (*Ripple on the Water*), also known as Frank Bluesky, from the series "Remembering Ancestors," 2023–24. Acrylic on birch bark, 13 × 17¼ inches framed. Collection of the artist. Photograph by Holly Trevan.

Fig. 3.2 Nora Moore Lloyd (Lac Courte Oreilles Band of Lake Superior Ojibwe, born 1947), ᑫᐧᑭᐸᐸᐃᐃᑫᐧ, *Gwekigaabowikwe* (*Lady Who Turns Around; Lady Who Turns Back*), from the series "Remembering Ancestors," 2023–24. Acrylic on birch bark, 16 × 20 inches framed. Collection of the artist. Photograph by Holly Trevan.

Frank Bluesky and passed down in the family. Nora enlisted Michael "Migizi" Sullivan, a Lac Courte Oreilles tribal member and respected Ojibwe linguist, to read, translate, and recite these letters in Anishinaabemowin, culminating in the work *Voices from Home*, which has both textual and aural components. She came by these letters through her grandmother Anna. When Anna was about two years old, her parents died, and she was taken in by her maternal grandparents, Chief Bluesky, called Ozaawashkogiijig, and his wife, Zaagigwanebi. Some years later, when the Presbyterian missionary women closed the mission boarding school Anna attended, they took custody of Anna and removed her from her grandparents, taking her to Warsaw, Indiana, without consultation or consent.[8] There, Anna met and married Arthur Moore, who was not Native. The couple left Indiana for Illinois to raise their children—Nora's father, DeWitt Moore, and his sister, her aunt Martha MacKenzie.

Frank Bluesky, Anna's uncle, wrote the letters to Anna between 1892 and 1900. They make clear the abiding connection the Bluesky family felt with Anna, who had been taken from her family and community. Frank Bluesky did not speak English and could not write Ojibwe. Sending letters to his niece meant locating and working through a translator and then finding a way to transport the letters from northern Wisconsin to southern Indiana—in other words, it was a labor of love. Reaching through time, Frank Bluesky's letters anticipate ongoing efforts by reservation-based family members to keep up relations with off-reservation family and friends over long distances and periods. *Voices from Home* includes reproductions of the letters, their translation from English into Anishinaabemowin, and their recitation in Anishinaabemowin, enacting a powerful reclamation of Bluesky's original words and of Anna's stolen heritage. The artwork's audio also expands the kaleidoscope of intention and connection motivating the artist: preservation of family, individual, and tribal history; acknowledgment of the depth of interaction and exchange between Chicago and the Lac Courte Oreilles reservation; and the relevance of tribal history to Chicago and Chicagoans.

In another work, *Treaty with the Chippewa, September 26, 1833*, Nora draws attention to the 1833 Treaty of Chicago by printing it on five plexiglass sheets backed by images of birch bark. The 1833 treaty, together with the earlier 1821 Treaty of Chicago,[9] dramatically changed the role and residence of tribal people in the Chicagoland region. By 1839, thousands of Native people were forced to move to reservations or to other Indian communities outside the land cession area, although numerous Native settlements persisted or were reestablished. Prior to this, early non-Indian residents in the growing city had depended on local Native people in many ways, including for trade routes and knowledge of local geography and ecology. These relations were often brokered by Native women who married non-Native men.[10]

As Chicago developed and new immigrants became increasingly present and powerful, less is known of the city's Native population. However, it is clear that throughout the nineteenth century, Native

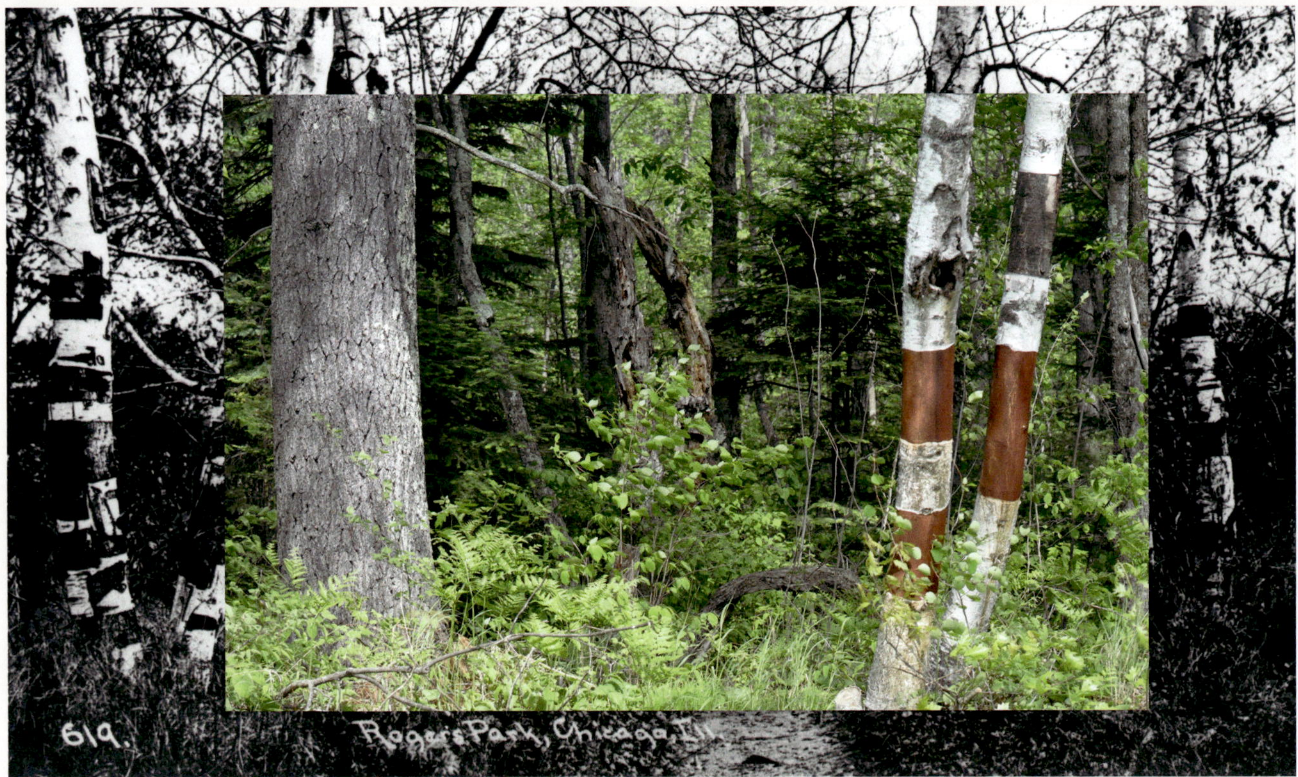

Fig. 3.3a

residents and visitors were present in the city. In the early twentieth century, Native Americans arrived from nearby reservations and communities, pulled in part by wartime employment and pushed by reservation poverty.[11] Reservation-to-city migration continued through the Second World War, such that there was already a substantial Native population in the city at the time of the passage of the federal Indian Relocation Act of 1956.[12] Supporting the 1950s federal policy of termination, the relocation program, which lasted from 1952 to 1973, promised temporary housing and employment for tribal members in seven major urban centers, including Chicago [fig. 5.4]. Impatient with the "Indian problem," the policy sought to terminate the special, constitutionally assured legal and political status of tribes and the attendant treaty rights of tribal members.[13] The process of relocation and resocialization in urban areas was intended to erase tribal identity, family bonds, and access to health, education, and other treaty rights of Natives enrolled in federally recognized tribes. Indians in Chicago did not behave according to these expectations.

In 1953, seeking to connect with other Natives and to help those newly arrived in the city, a consortium formed one of the first urban Native centers in the country, the American Indian Center of Chicago (AIC) [fig. 6.1].[14] While Natives who gathered at the AIC and elsewhere throughout the city came from different tribal nations, they shared experiences with reservation life, issues with the Bureau of Indian Affairs, and difficulties adjusting to urban lifeways. Gradually, an urban community with new traditions emerged, supplementing

Figs. 3.3a and 3.3b Nora Moore Lloyd (Lac Courte Oreilles Band of Lake Superior Ojibwe, born 1947), *Birchbark/Wiigwaas*, 2020. Textile banner printed on two sides, 50 × 84 inches. Collection of the artist.

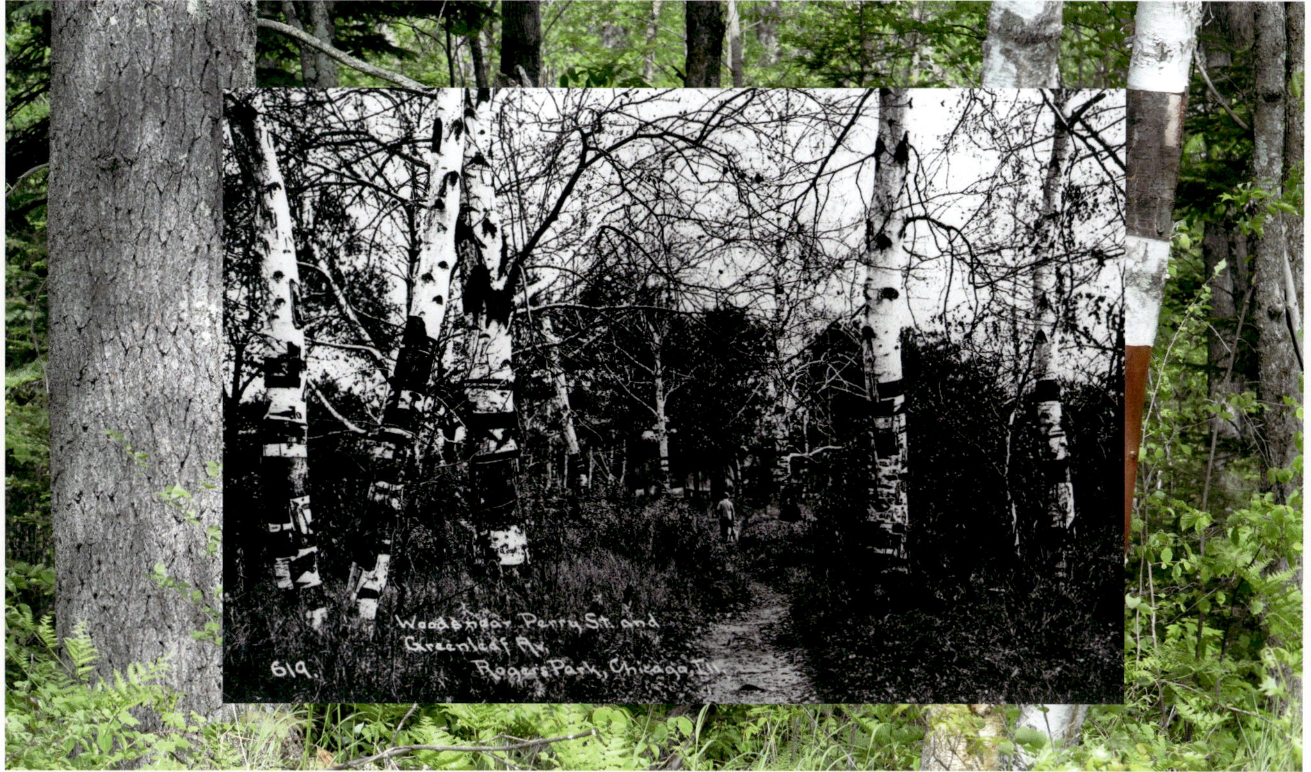

Fig. 3.3b

tribal identities. The AIC, which was initially supported by federal funds, became the organizational center of the new intertribal community.[15] Early leaders there became critical to the creation and cohesion of a Native community in the city. A locus of intertribal Indian identity, the center also nurtured tribal identity and supported the notion that treaty rights depended on tribal membership, not on reservation residence. Nora's experience clearly attests to this.

Nora grew up unaware of her Ojibwe heritage. She began to investigate her heritage and ancestry when her aunt Martha discovered Frank Bluesky's letters among Anna's possessions after her death and shared them with other family members. Supported by her husband, Bill, Nora first traveled the four hundred miles to the Lac Courte Oreilles (LCO) reservation in Wisconsin in 1983. Nora recalls:

On the first trip, everything fell into place—meeting the LCO college president, tribal judge, tribal chairman (and a Bluesky relative), LCO genealogist, and Pipe Mustache, the elder and LCO spiritual leader who became my mentor. That group, who welcomed me with open arms, recognized my family history was a blank canvas waiting to be filled in with Bluesky stories. The genealogist even had twenty pages of my ancestors' names that she began preparing in the sixties . . . a huge undertaking pre-computers, prompted by her curiosity about the disappearance of Chief Bluesky's granddaughter. The page with Anna ends with ". . . married Arthur Moore ???"[16]

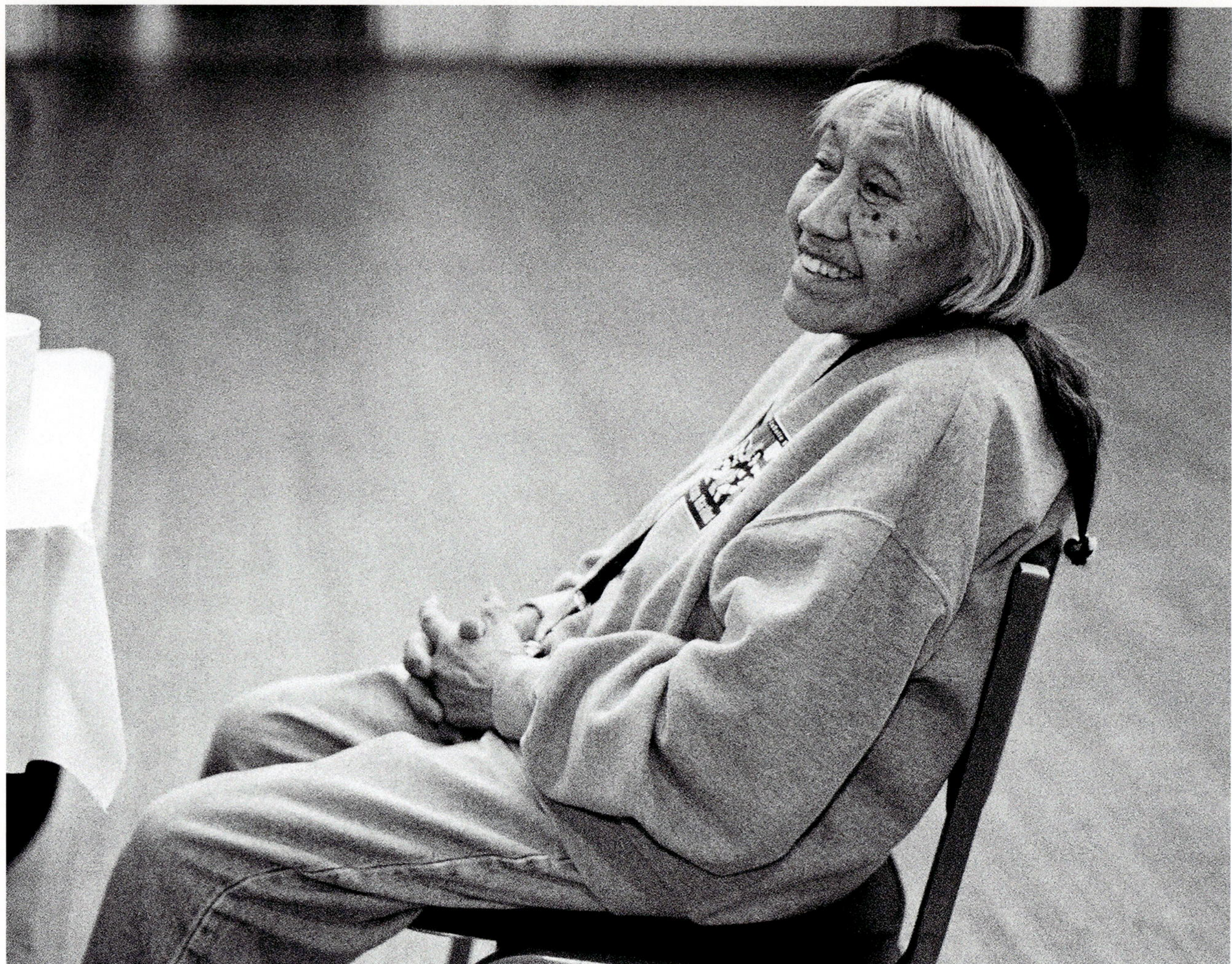

Fig. 3.4

Following her discovery of her Ojibwe heritage, Nora ventured to connect with the AIC, and "it was the elders again who took me under their collective wing, teaching me cultural protocol that children usually learn at a young age."[17] The importance of elders in Chicago's urban Native community recurs thematically in the artist's photographs. In *Woven Being*, Nora presents twelve photographs of elders taken between 1998 and 2024 [fig. 3.4 and pl. 10]. They are connected by twine, a metaphorical tying together of a new community that is also joined to diverse tribal communities across North America. Nora's connection to her Lac Courte Oreilles ancestors and identity has been nourished by her participation in Chicago's urban Native community. The AIC and other local Native organizations have similarly served and continue to serve many Native people in the city, supporting connection or reconnection with tribal identity.

Nora's recognition of the critical importance of elders to the Chicago Native community influenced the constellation of artists she identified for *Woven Being*: Sharon Skolnick (Fort Sill Apache/Lakota, born 1946), Joe Yazzie (Navajo, born 1942), and Mark LaRoque (White Earth Ojibwe, born 1948). These artists also

Fig. 3.4 Nora Moore Lloyd (Lac Courte Oreilles Band of Lake Superior Ojibwe, born 1947), *Angie Decorah (Ho-Chunk)*, from the series "Chicago's Native American Community: Our Elders Look Back," 1998–ongoing. Archival digital photograph from original 35 mm negative, 8 × 10 inches. Collection of the artist.

reflect dual tribal and urban experiences, foreground the role of art in the creation and expression of community, and represent a commitment to intergenerational mentorship. Sharon Okee-Chee Skolnick, like many of the artist-elders in Chicago, performed significant community service in addition to creating community-recognized and appreciated works of art. She spent her early childhood years in foster care and orphanages, distant from her tribal community.[18] In the 1960s, she was among the first students to attend the Institute of American Indian Arts, in Santa Fe.[19] Sharon's untitled painting evokes the culture of her Plains ancestry through the depiction of horses painted on buffalo hide, an art form that has been practiced by Plains artists over centuries [fig. 3.5 and pl. 11]. Here, horses romp within an unlikely border of prairie flowers beneath a purple-blue sky, elements that are atypical in traditional hide painting. In this work, Sharon merges tribal tradition, popular representation, and individual creativity. Her art is eclectic; in addition to painting (in acrylics; she has professed, "I don't have patience to work in oils"), her practice includes sewing, beading, doll making, dance, literature, and film.[20] She has a background as a community leader in arts organizations, having served on various boards and co-founded the Chicago Native Artists Guild through the AIC. She also established Okee-Chee's Wild Horse Gallery, the first gallery for Native American artists in the city, through which she introduced many in the broader Chicago arts community to local and national Native American artists [fig. 6.4].[21]

Joe Yazzie came to Chicago in 1964, leaving his tribal community in Pinedale, New Mexico, to pursue his interest in art. "I wanted to be an artist since I can remember. . . . It's taken me this long to get there, so that's all I do now," he shared in a 2012 article in the *Navajo Times*.[22] Joe is a Vietnam veteran, and his images often include warrior elements. He has called his work "art that looks like painting, but it's done on a computer." As described in the *Navajo Times* article, "Yazzie does sketches in pencil or ink, scans them into his computer and uses design software to add color and layers." This process distinguishes his work [fig. 3.6 and pl. 11]. He began making drawings using a computer in order to connect with younger generations, blending designs inspired by traditional themes and patterns with technology.[23] The works are then printed on canvas—or, in one series, on skateboard decks [fig. 3.7].

Mark LaRoque, the youngest of the artists in Nora's *Woven Being* constellation, has a diverse practice: he is a poet, painter, speaker, and, more recently, pipestone sculptor. (Mark LaRoque's poem "THE WOVEN BEING" has been published for the first time in this volume [pp. 78–79].) Like Sharon Skolnick and Joe Yazzie, he is committed to the Chicago Native community alongside his ties to his reservation home in White Earth, Minnesota. His painting titled *If* depicts snags on a dark ridge, evoking a psychological state through landscape [fig. 3.8 and pl. 11]. Light swirls above darkness, devastation, and death, in what can be read as an invitation to hope. Among the artist's paintings, this work is notable for the vision it represents. Much of Mark's work foregrounds the Chicago Native community, as does the work of his former mentor, the celebrated Ojibwe poet and playwright E. Donald "Eddie" Two-Rivers, who died in 2008.[24] Eddie Two-Rivers's creativity and persistence over many years fostered a turning point within Chicago's Indian arts community. From his first publication, *A Dozen Cold Ones by Two Rivers: Native American Poetry in an Urban Setting* (1992), to his establishment as a leading poet in the community, his message was always one of nurturing and mentoring others. In 1997, Eddie was the founding director of Red Path Theater Company, where he laid a foundation for fostering artistic expression in the community and for broader recognition of Native artists. His work, deeply rooted in his experience of Chicago, revealed and enhanced the role of the arts in the creation of urban Indian community identity.

The insight of another community artist provides an important addendum here. James Yellowbank (Ho-Chunk, 1948–ca. 2020s), a leading activist in the Chicago Indian community, established the Indian Treaty Rights Committee, which empowered local community members to act on behalf of tribal and Indian rights. After many years of political action, James determined that he could inform and inspire a broader vision of past problems and future possibilities through art and music, and he turned from demonstrating to singing and composing. With her constellation, Nora brings long-overdue attention to the critical role of elders like Eddie Two-Rivers and James Yellowbank, Sharon Skolnick, Joe Yazzie, and Nora herself, who move between the Chicago Indian community and their home reservation communities. Their relationships with each other, mentoring of younger artists like Mark LaRoque, and support of community youth are guiding tenets of Nora's vision in *Woven Being*.

Native people of many different tribes and backgrounds arrived in Chicago for various purposes. They often found each other in the neighborhoods where they were housed by the Bureau of Indian Affairs relocation office. However, there was no community center and, indeed, no community. The AIC was a means of building that community, providing an organizational hub around which disconnected and disparate Native people could come together. In early events sponsored by the center, members shared their diverse traditions, including forms of dress, dance, and music. Gradually, local traditions developed from shared experiences and intertribal commonalities, and an urban Indian culture emerged that was essential to community continuity. In this creative endeavor, Chicago Native elders in the arts occupied a central role.

Woven Being: Art for Zhegagoynak/Chicagoland aptly acknowledges the role of the arts in the creation and persistence of the Chicago Indian community, while recognizing the continuing connection of community members to their Native tribes and traditions. Reflecting on the exhibition process, Nora has noted, "I think preparing for an exhibition, revisiting thoughts that started the creative process and sharing with others, absolutely helps define self, because it reinforces memories and strengthens neuronal

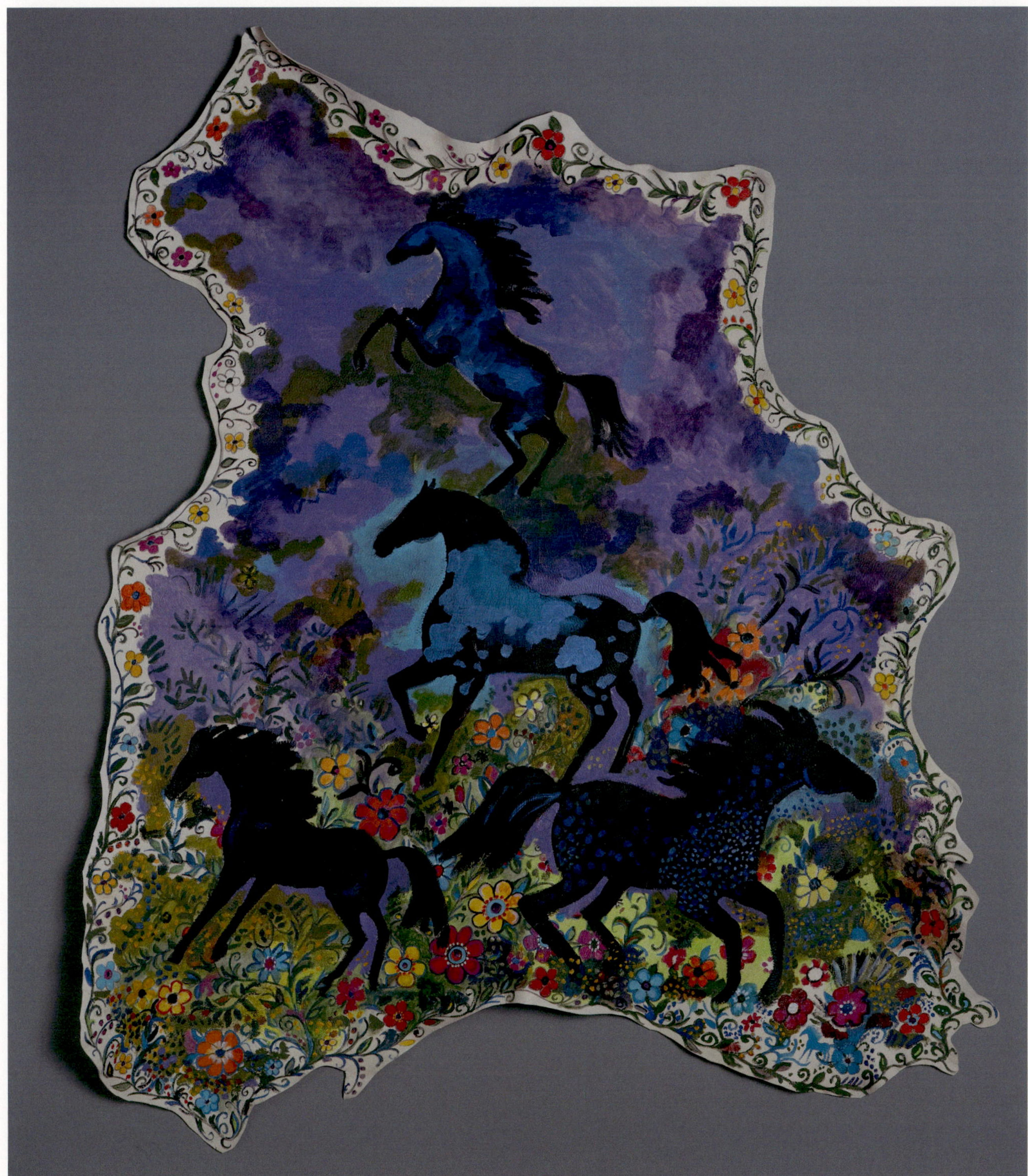

Fig. 3.5

Fig. 3.5 Sharon Skolnick (Fort Sill Apache/
Lakota, born 1946), *Courage Is Like a Wild
Horse*, 2002. Acrylic paint on deer hide,
46 × 43 inches. Private collection.
Photograph by Holly Trevan.

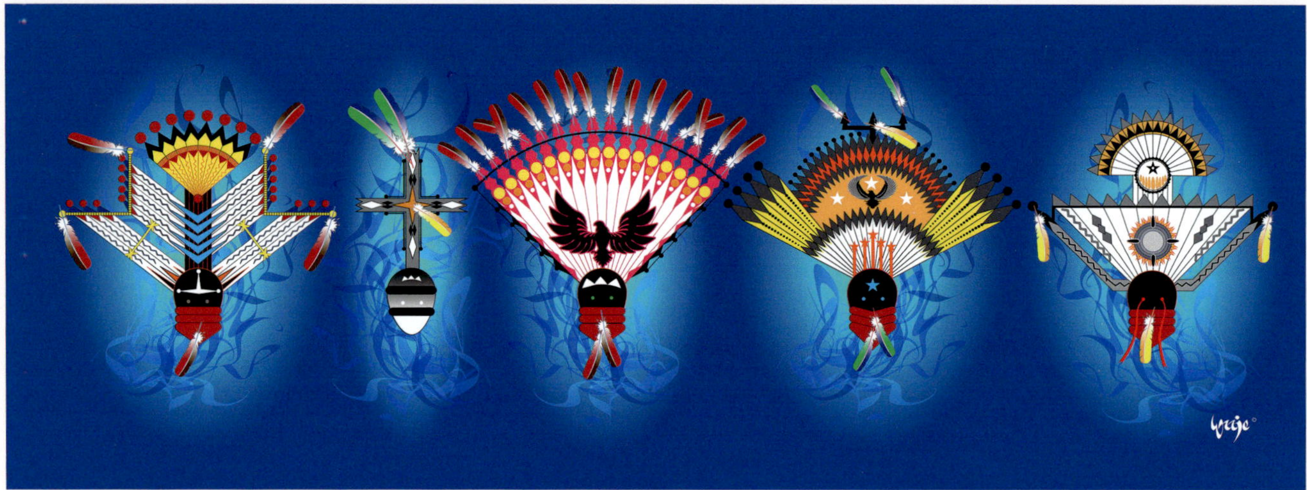

Fig. 3.6

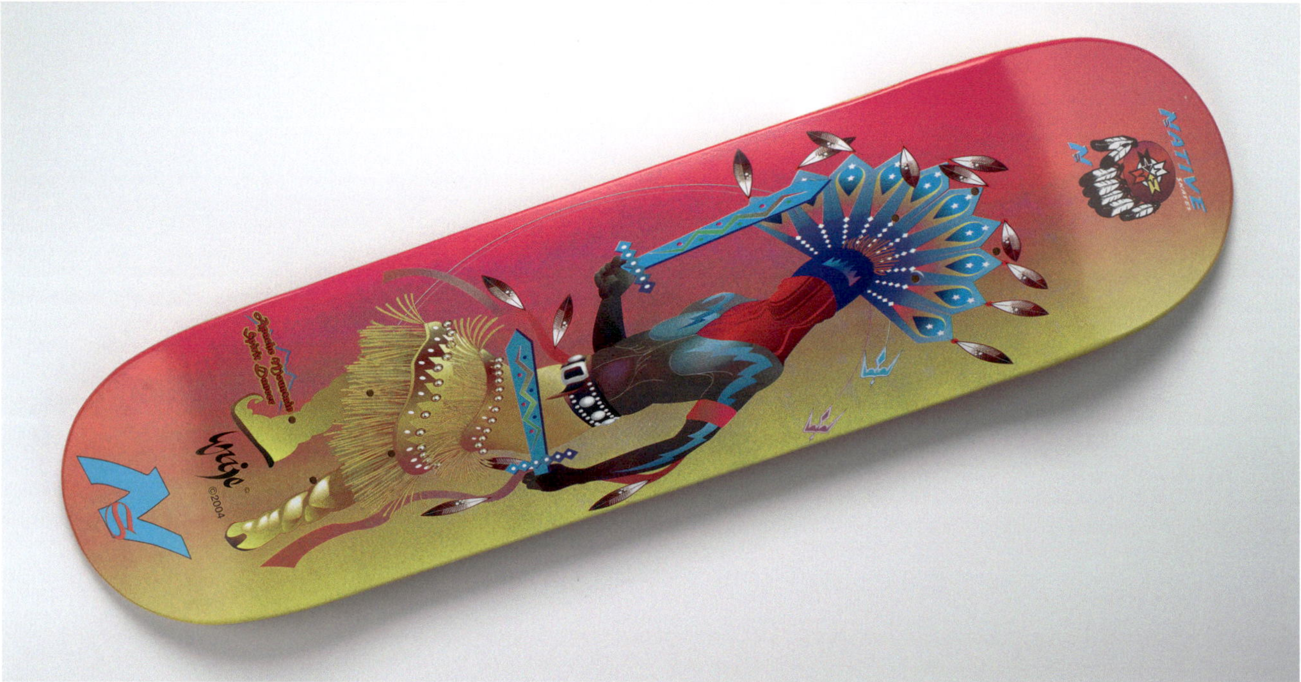

Fig. 3.7

pathways and connections."[25] A triangular creative tension is clear, with individual imagination, tribal traditions, and Chicago Indian community history at the vertices, connected by a curatorial practice that foregrounds the perspectives of Indigenous artists. It is a fresh and welcome approach to the exhibition of Native American arts in a museum.

Fig. 3.6 Joe Yazzie (Navajo, born 1942), *Apache Strong*, 2024. Giclée on canvas, 12 × 32 inches. Courtesy of the artist and Art Studio Prints.

Fig. 3.7 Joe Yazzie (Navajo, born 1942), *Apache Mountain Spirit Dancer*, 2008. Wooden skateboard deck, ink, paint, and glue, 8 × 31½ inches. National Museum of the American Indian, Smithsonian Institution, Washington, DC, 27/553. Photograph by NMAI Photo Services.

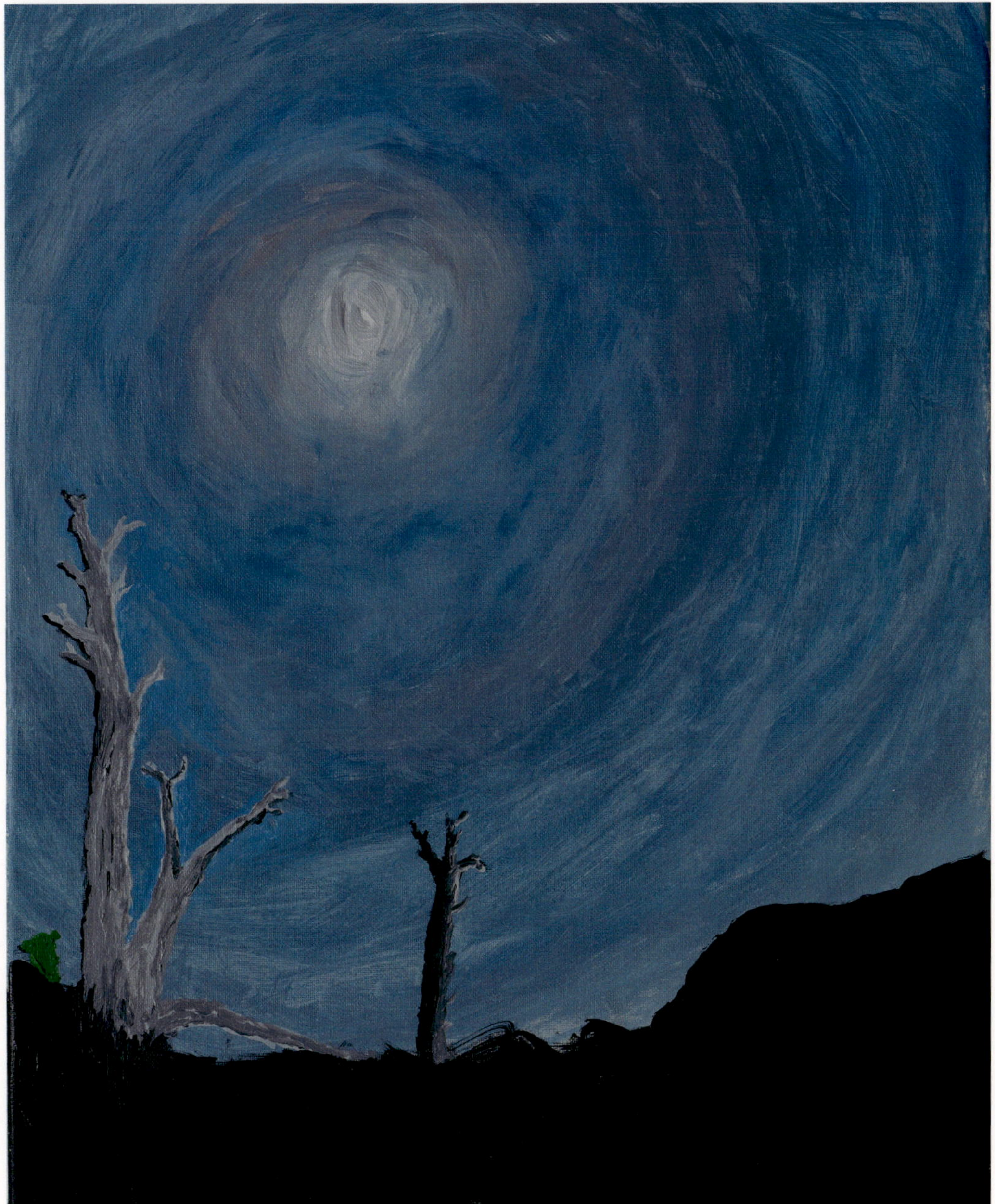

Fig. 3.8

Fig. 3.8 Mark LaRoque (White Earth Ojibwe, born 1948), *If*, 2022. Acrylic on canvas, 20 × 16 inches. Collection of the artist. Photograph by Holly Trevan.

The literal translation of *Indinawemaaganag gaye ayaawiyaan: Nora Moore Lloyd waabanda'iwe keyaa inawendiyang*, the Ojibwe title for this chapter, is "My Relatives and the Being Which I Am: Nora Moore Lloyd Presents the Way That We Are Related." Ojibwe translation provided by Forrest Bruce (Fond du Lac Ojibwe).

1   Nora Moore Lloyd, conversations with the author, January 2024.
2   Lloyd, conversations.
3   Lloyd created an iteration of *Birchbark/Wiigwaas* for the 2017 exhibition *Property* at the Roman Susan Art Foundation, Chicago.
4   In Anishinaabemowin, the Ojibwe language, the birch tree is called the "tree of life," and every part, from leaves to roots, provides something of value. "*Wiigwaazii: The Evolving Traditions of Birch* Exhibit," Madeline Island Museum, La Pointe, Wisconsin, 2019, web.
5   Lloyd, conversations.
6   Lloyd, conversations.
7   Nora has made the artistic choice to use Ojibwe syllabics here; however, the Ojibwe syllabary was never adopted by the Lac Courte Oreilles Tribe.
8   Before the implementation of the Indian Child Welfare Act (ICWA) of 1978, many Native children were removed from their families by social workers and missionaries and adopted out, mostly into white families. A concerted effort, aided by Chicagoans Sol Tax and Alderman Leon Despres, eventually led to the passage of the ICWA, which placed any removal of tribal children from their families entirely under the jurisdiction of the tribe. The ICWA was upheld by the US Supreme Court in 2023, following legal challenges that began in 2018.
9   The 1821 treaty between the United States, Ottawa, Chippewa, and Potawatomi included the cessation of almost four million acres of Native land. For a digital copy of the treaty, see the National Archives Catalog at catalog.archives.gov/id/100378017.
10 For an in-depth look at the agency and influence of Native women who married French men in the Great Lakes region before colonization, see Susan Sleeper-Smith, *Indian Women and French Men: Rethinking Cultural Encounter in the Western Great Lakes*, Native Americans of the Northeast (Amherst: University of Massachusetts Press, 2001).
11 For more on the early twentieth-century history of Natives in Chicago, see Rosalyn LaPier and David R. M. Beck, *City Indian: Native American Activism in Chicago, 1893–1934* (Lincoln: University of Nebraska Press, 2015).
12 In 1940, Chicago had the thirteenth-largest Native population among US cities; by 1960, it had risen to the third largest. Elaine M. Neils, *Reservation to City: Indian Migration and Federal Relocation* (Chicago: University of Chicago Department of Geography, 1971), 152, table 18. Neils also notes, as do others, that Natives were largely undercounted in urban areas. See Neils, *Reservation to City*, 15; and Donald L. Fixico, "The Federal Relocation Program of the 1950s and the Urbanization of Indian Identity," in *Removing Peoples: Forced Removal in the Modern World*, ed. Richard Bessel and Claudia B. Haake (Oxford: Oxford University Press, 2009), 107–29, web.
13 House Concurrent Resolution 108 of 1953, which announced the termination policy, imposed an immediate end to the federal relationship with a select group of tribes, expunging federal treaty obligations, despite the assurance in Article VI of the US Constitution that "treaties are the supreme law of the land." For an overview of this policy, see "Termination," Bureau of Indian Affairs Records, National Archives, web.
14 Jacqueline Lopez provides a brief overview of the American Indian Center's role supporting Indigenous art and artists in her chapter in this volume [pp. 121–23]. For more on the AIC, see aicchicago.org.
15 Initially supported by the federal government in what can be seen as a halfway measure to encourage assimilation and diminish access to treaty rights, the AIC instead became a community support for Indian identity and rights. Grant P. Arndt, "Relocation's Imagined Landscape and the Rise of Chicago's Native American Community," in *Native Chicago*, ed. Terry Straus and Grant P. Arndt (Chicago: McNaughton & Gunn, 1998), 114–27.
16 Lloyd, conversations.
17 Lloyd, conversations.
18 Sharon Skolnick (Okee-Chee) and Manny Skolnick, *Where Courage Is Like a Wild Horse: The World of an Indian Orphanage* (Lincoln, NE: Bison Books, 2001). In 1997, Skolnick headed the foster care and adoption program at Chicago's American Indian Health Service, the mission of which anticipated the goals of the 1978 Indian Child Welfare Act. Sharon Skolnick, "Interview with Sharon Skolnick, Artist and Coordinator of the Foster Care Program at the American Indian Health Service, Chicago, Illinois," by

ANNE TERRY STRAUS

Roberta Fiske-Rusciano and R. Hajnal, Chicago Ethnic Arts Project Collection, May 19, 1977, audio, 00:15, web.

19 Skolnick, "Interview with Sharon Skolnick," 12:00.

20 Skolnick, "Interview with Sharon Skolnick," 07:22; *This Is Indian Land: Okee-Chee's Vision*, directed by Sharon Okee-Chee Skolnick (Chicago: Shadow Bechtol Studio, 2017).

21 For more on the Wild Horse Gallery, see Jacqueline Lopez's chapter in this volume [p. 125].

22 Alysa Landry, "Diné Artist Appeals to All Ages*," Navajo Times*, December 6, 2012, web. All quotes by Joe Yazzie are drawn from this interview.

23 Landry, "Diné Artist Appeals to All Ages."

24 An excerpt from Eddie Two-Rivers's poem "Indian Land Dancing" appears as an epigraph in this volume [p. 128].

25 Lloyd, conversations.

Jeanne LaTraille
(Oneida, 1922–2008)

"Memory of an Elk (Elkskin Dress)"

Originally published in *Native Chicago*, ed. Terry Straus and Grant P. Arndt (Chicago: McNaughton & Gunn, 1998).

He was proud and stately

This elk of majestic manner

He roamed the land

He wore his freedom as a rightful banner

He was awesome

A king in his domain

With wisdom and dignity he did reign

He was proud and stately

A vision to behold

His head held high in summer

and in the winter's cold

His time has passed but he lives on

For his spirit still dwells there but

It also dwells within the Elkskin

dress I wear

He hears the beat of the drum

Yes, his spirit dances with me

His spirit dances proud and free

I'm honored to wear the Elkskin dress

As proud as I can be

As I dance his Spirit dances with me

As I don the dress I feel a change

A change you cannot see

In a different role I'm cast

No longer in the present

But in the distant past

I'm all the Indian Women

Who used to be

For I have the Elk-Spirit dancing

with me.

MIGWETCH, ELK SPIRIT!

Mark LaRoque
(White Earth Ojibwe, born 1948)

"THE WOVEN BEING"

Written in 2024, on the
occasion of the exhibition
*Woven Being: Art for
Zhegagoynak/Chicagoland.*

TEARS

The fabric of life becomes dark with tears

   Caused by war   or is it

by the birth of another weaver

HANDS

Memories   yet to become a part of the woven being

Created by hands of our own making

Making beauty and destruction

With the same breath

DARK and LIGHT

Dark turns to light

   With the drying of tears

      On the fabric of the woven being

Turned by the light of a new day

CHANGE

It is time to change the direction of the woven being

Turn away from walking into darkness

FREE WILL

With the free will the creator gave us

Weave again the will to change

This being called humanity

This   woven being.

John Low
(Pokagon Band of Potawatomi)

Ė zhë nénmëk Andrea Carlson ė wzhetot

Thoughts on Andrea Carlson and Her Art

I have known Andrea Carlson (Grand Portage Ojibwe/European descent, born 1979) since 2021, when we were selected as co-curators for a redesign of the lobby of the MacArthur Foundation's headquarters in the Marquette Building in downtown Chicago. At the time, Andrea was living in Chicago. We were given the opportunity to "indigenize" the lobby through an on-site exhibition that would provide a counternarrative to the building's original mosaic mural, commissioned from Tiffany & Company, and bronze bas-relief panels and figures.[1] These artworks celebrate stereotypes of the so-called discoverers of Chicago, European explorers Jacques Marquette and Louis Joliet, and of Native leaders mostly from the early nineteenth century. What I learned about Andrea early on is that she has a keen sense of history, design, and activism. In this essay, I share what I know about Andrea and her art, writing from the perspective of a Pokagon Potawatomi elder and scholar. In doing so, I have been inspired by the work of Leanne Betasamosake Simpson (Anishinaabe/Ojibwe, born 1971) concerning *Biskaabiiyang*, meaning "a new emergence":

Within Nishnaabeg theoretical foundations, Biskaabiiyang . . . encompasses a visioning process where we create new and just realities in which our ways of being can flourish. Nonetheless, it is not just a visioning process. We must act to create those spaces— be they cognitive or spatial, temporal or spiritual.[2]

Fig. 4.1 George Morrison (Grand Portage Ojibwe, 1919–2000), *Untitled*, 1972. Pen and black ink on blue paper, sheet: 9 × 12 inches. Minneapolis Institute of Art, gift of Jean Elleard Stewart, 2000.188. Photograph by Minneapolis Institute of Art, © George Morrison Estate. Courtesy of Bockley Gallery, Minneapolis.

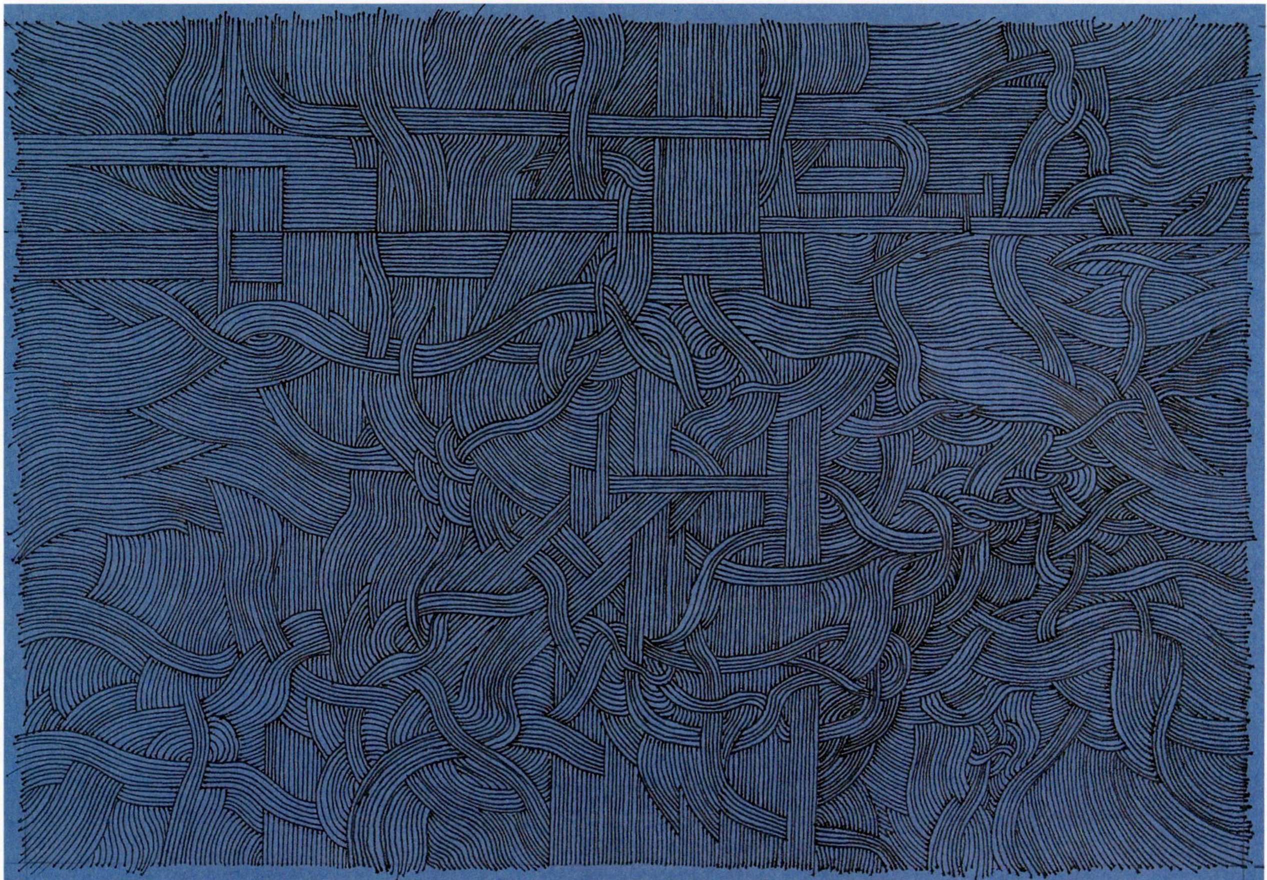

Fig. 4.1

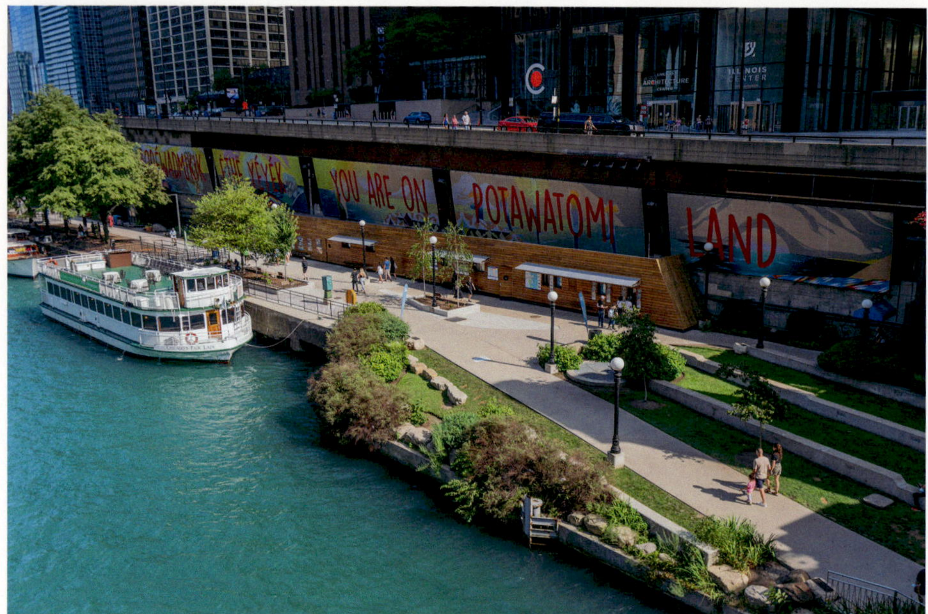

Fig. 4.2

Andrea is of Anishinaabe/Ojibwe and European descent. She resides in Minnesota on land ceded under the 1854 Treaty of La Pointe and belongs to Gichi-Onigaming (Grand Portage Ojibwe) through her father's side of the family. Her clan is Mikinaak (Snapping Turtle). She says you can see Lake Superior from her home, with all its myriad emotions, from calm and peaceful to furious and dangerous. In many Algonquian tribes, including the Ojibwe and Potawatomi, women are the caretakers of water, and I imagine her fulfilling that traditional role where she now lives. She intends to transfer ownership of the land back to her tribe after her family is gone. She knows the importance of land to Indigenous peoples and communities. Land is sacred to us. She tells me that her studio is only about a mile from the grave of internationally acclaimed artist George Morrison (Grand Portage Ojibwe, 1919–2000) [fig. 4.1]. This is not name-dropping. It simply reflects the reverence she has for this elder who has walked on, but not before clearing paths for other Indigenous artists.

Andrea lived for a while in Chicago, and she may return someday. I hope so. I miss her presence in the city and in the American Indian community here.[3] She supports other Indians (not all do); she is an activist, and she uses her art to resist the metanarratives of colonization and self-colonization. She frequently grapples with the vastness of decolonization in her artwork and writing; additionally, she is currently analyzing land narratives, assimilation metaphors, and Indigenous futurisms.[4]

I consider Andrea a friend, a colleague, and an ally in struggles against oppression, and I admire and respect her for all her talents and heart. In the interest of full transparency, I am not an artist or art critic. I am a historian and an elder of my tribe, the Pokagon Band of Potawatomi. Like many of you, I love some art and am indifferent to

Fig. 4.2 Andrea Carlson's mural *Bodéwadmikik ëthë yéyék / You Are on Potawatomi Land* adorned the Chicago Riverwalk (Wacker Drive east of the Michigan Avenue Bridge) from 2021 to 2023. Photograph by Patrick L. Pyszka, City of Chicago.

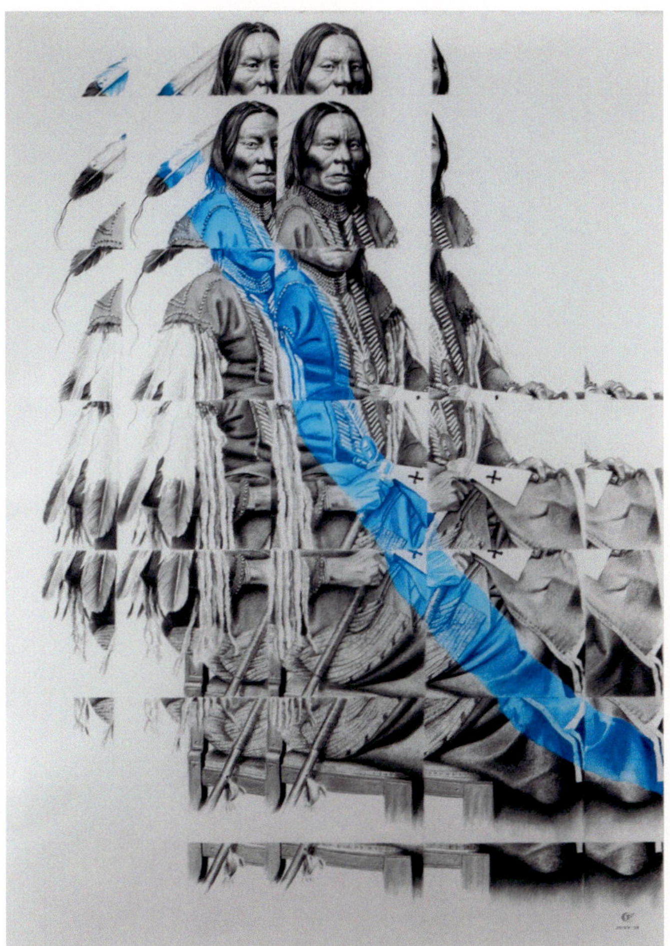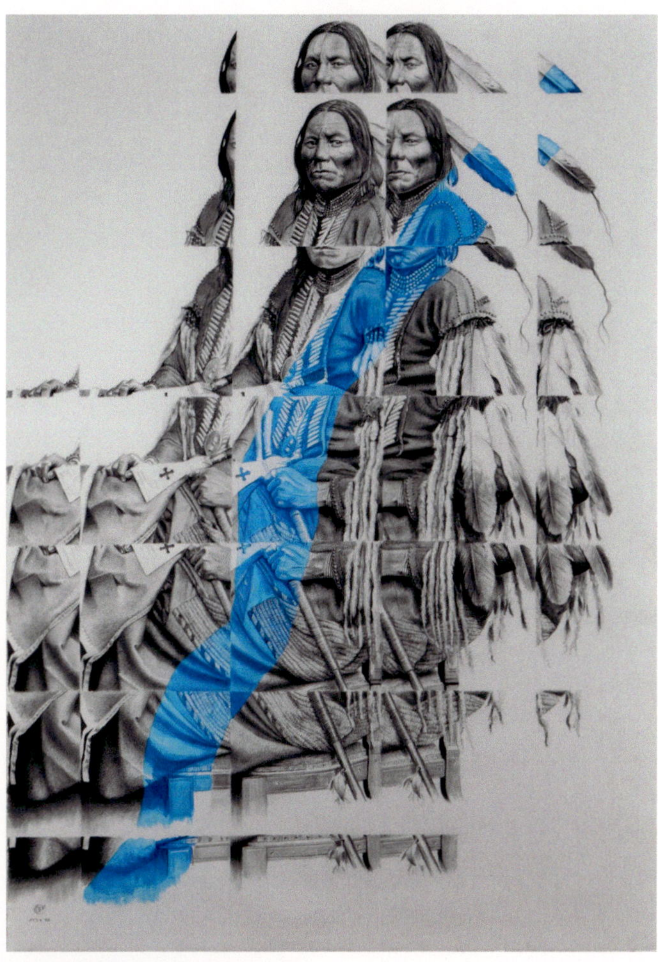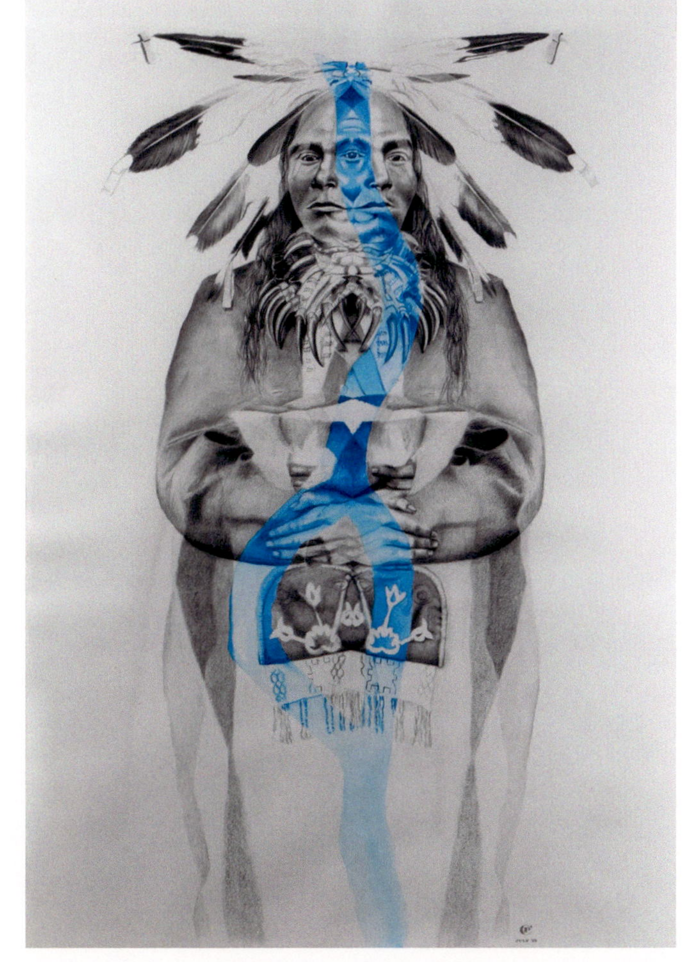

Fig. 4.3 Chris Pappan (Kaw [Kanza]/Osage/Lakota, born 1971), *Howageji Nizhuje Akipé (Where the Rivers Meet)*, 2023. Graphite and gouache on Rives BFK paper, three drawings: 44 × 30 inches each. Blue Rain Gallery, Santa Fe.

Fig. 4.3

or unimpressed by other art. Andrea's art affects me in a good way, and it may change how you, too, see the world around you. Andrea has honored me by asking me to write an essay for this book, and I say *migwétth* (thank you) to her for the opportunity.

Andrea has a bachelor of arts in American Indian studies and art from the University of Minnesota Twin Cities and a master of fine arts from the Minneapolis College of Art and Design. The subject of numerous exhibitions and recipient of many awards and residencies, she is also a co-founder and board member of the Center for Native Futures (CfNF), the only all-Native artist-led visual arts nonprofit currently operational in Chicago. Her art reflects her deep bonds as an Ojibwe person to land, community, and history.

My tribe, the Pokagon Potawatomi, sued for the return of the Chicago lakefront, including the land that Northwestern University's Chicago and Evanston campuses sit on, in 1914 and appealed its land claim all the way to the United States Supreme Court, where it was rejected.[5] It was a wonderful and inspiring early effort at Land Back.[6] Andrea has said, "The location of Zhegagoynak (Chicago) is in the very heart of Potawatomi's traditional territory. Although Ojibwe and Potawatomi people are ethnically related and we hold each other close, I don't want to prioritize my sense of belonging. I don't want to participate in the prolonged displacement of Potawatomi people."[7]

In 2021, Andrea responded to questions about the Potawatomi and connections to Chicago with a large site-specific installation along the Chicago Riverwalk.[8] It brightly declares, "Bodéwadmikik ėthë yéyék / You Are on Potawatomi Land" [fig. 4.2]. She told me:

Of course, I know the Potawatomi, Ojibwe, and Odawa are the People of the Three Fires. But that doesn't mean what is yours is mine. We were allies, relatives, friends, intermarried, all of it. But we are distinct peoples with our separate sovereignties. I would not appreciate a Potawatomi person coming to my home in Grand Portage and claiming it as their homeland, and I don't think the Ojibwe people should be coming to Chicago and telling the Potawatomi and everyone else that this land is their land too. It's not right.[9]

To break from colonial structures of expertise and authority that are inherent in museums, The Block has organized the *Woven Being* exhibition into "constellations," clusters of related works selected by the four collaborating artists. Each constellation comprises works by artists with connections to Chicago and the Great Lakes region, either through history or through residency. Andrea describes the works in her constellation as "held together with gravitational pulls," each selected for their ability to "persuade or dissuade, intrigue, and inspire."[10]

For her constellation, Andrea selected the Chicago-based artists Chris Pappan (Kaw [Kanza]/Osage/Lakota, born 1971) and Debra Yepa-Pappan (Jemez Pueblo/Korean, born 1971), who are also CfNF co-founders, along with fellow Ojibwe artists Frank Big Bear (White

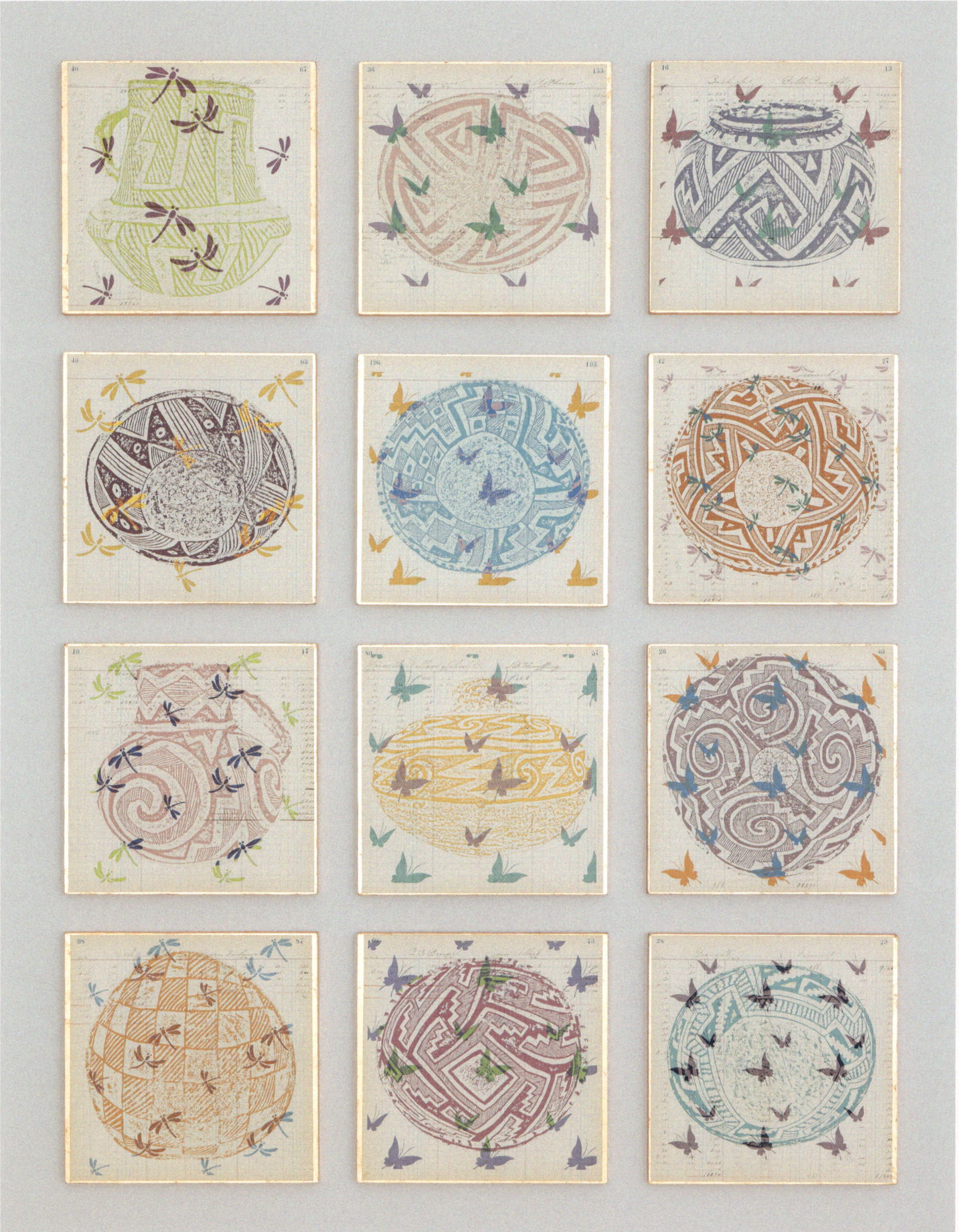

Fig. 4.4

Fig. 4.4 Debra Yepa-Pappan (Jemez Pueblo/Korean, born 1971), *Ancestors Speak (a visual repatriation)*, 2023. Digital images printed on antique ledger paper, copper leaf, and birch panels, twelve panels: 12 × 12 inches each. Collection of the artist. Photograph by Claire Britt.

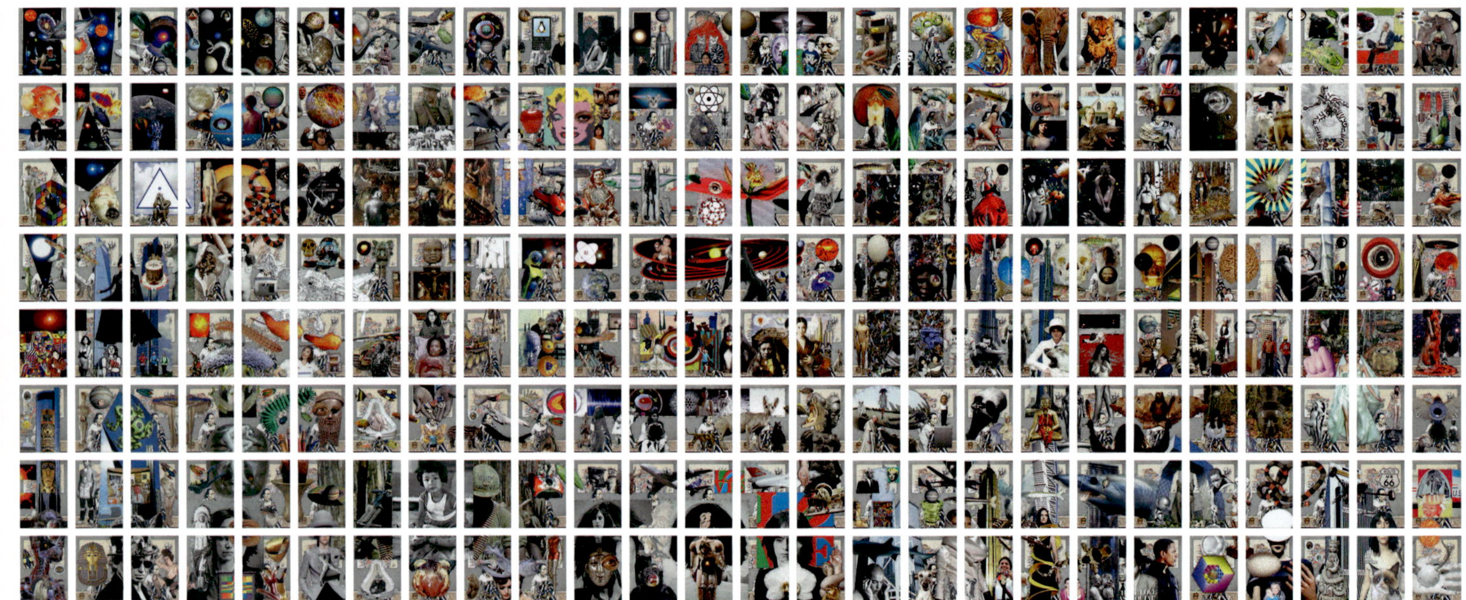

Fig. 4.5a

Fig. 4.5a Frank Big Bear (White Earth
Ojibwe, born 1953), *The Walker Collage,
Multiverse #10*, 2016. Mixed media on
invitation cards for an exhibition by
the artist's son, Star Wallowing Bull,
432 cards: 8½ × 6 inches each, overall:
78 × 378 inches. Commissioned by
Walker Art Center, Minneapolis, T.B.
Walker Acquisition Fund, 2018.30.1-432.
Courtesy of the artist and Bockley Gallery,
Minneapolis.

JOHN LOW

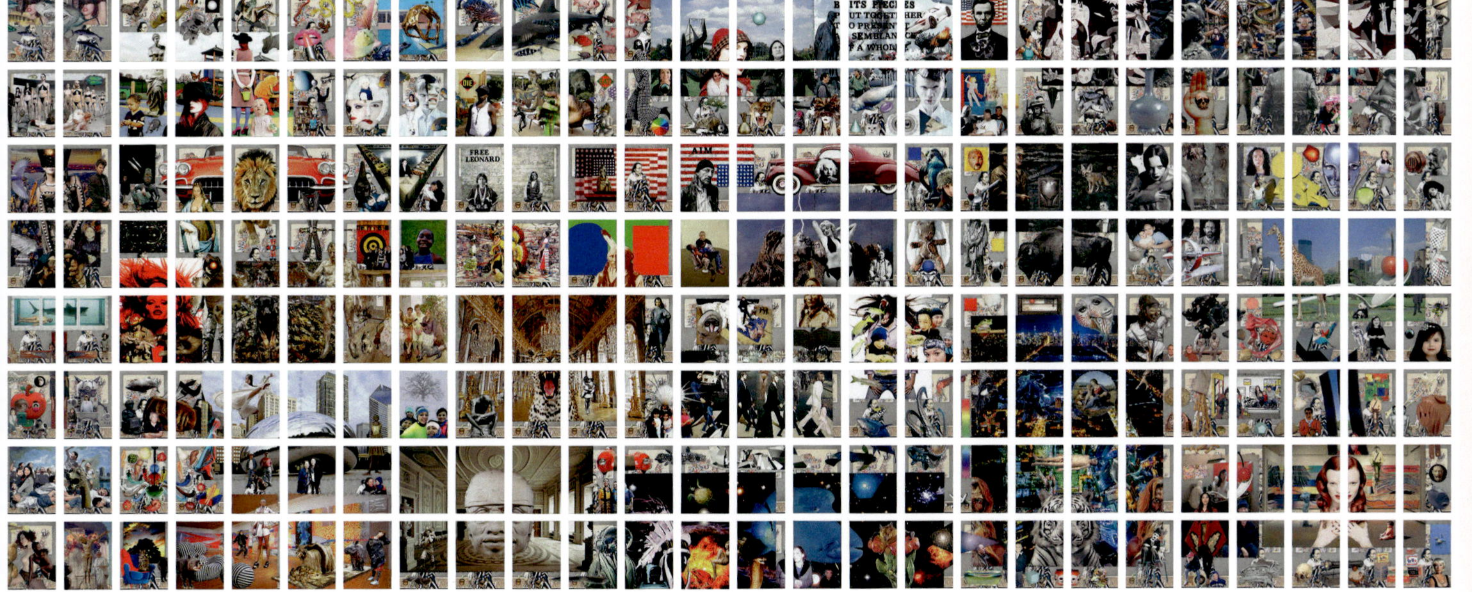

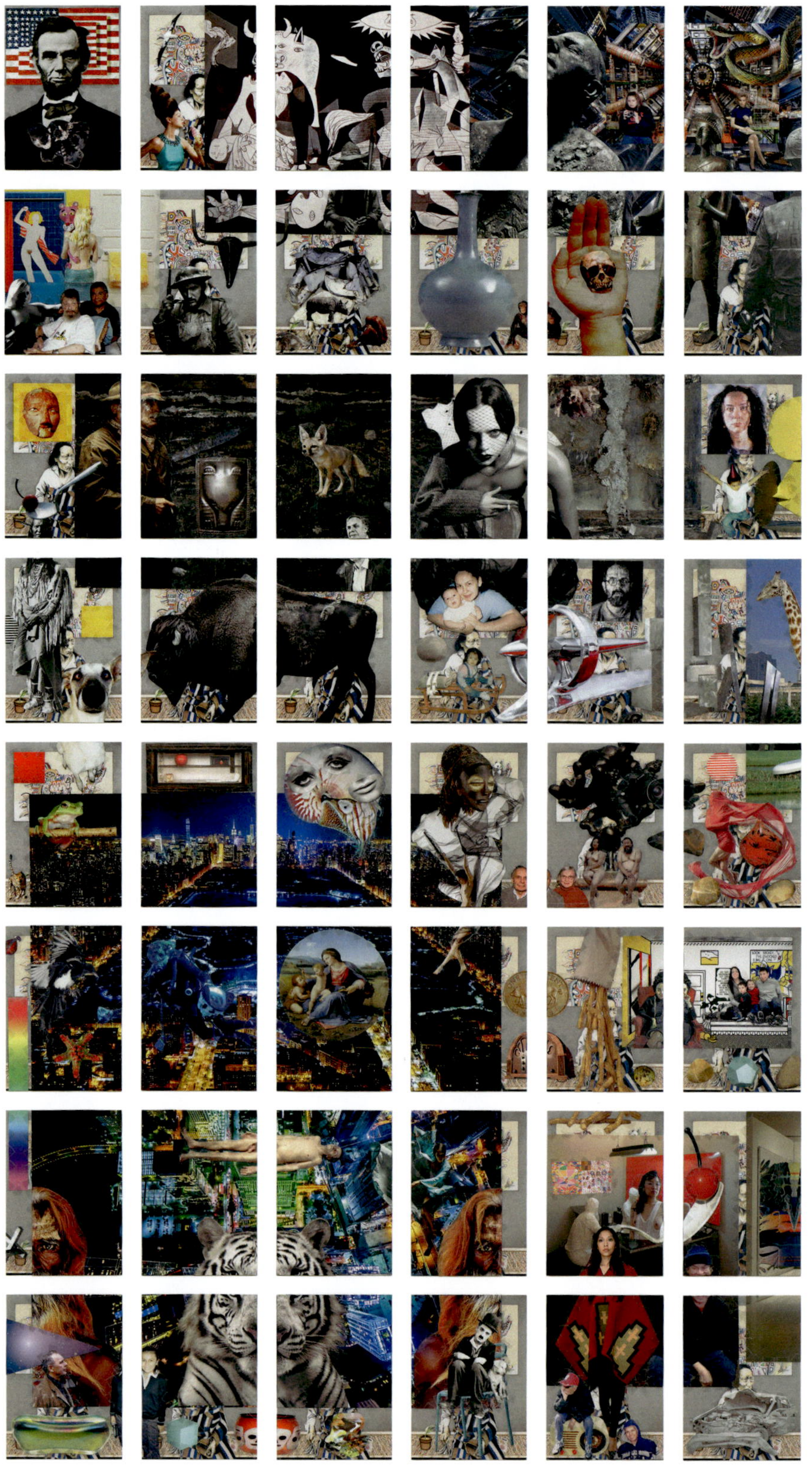

Fig. 4.5b

Fig. 4.5b Frank Big
Bear (White Earth
Ojibwe, born 1953),
*The Walker Collage,
Multiverse #10*
(detail), 2016

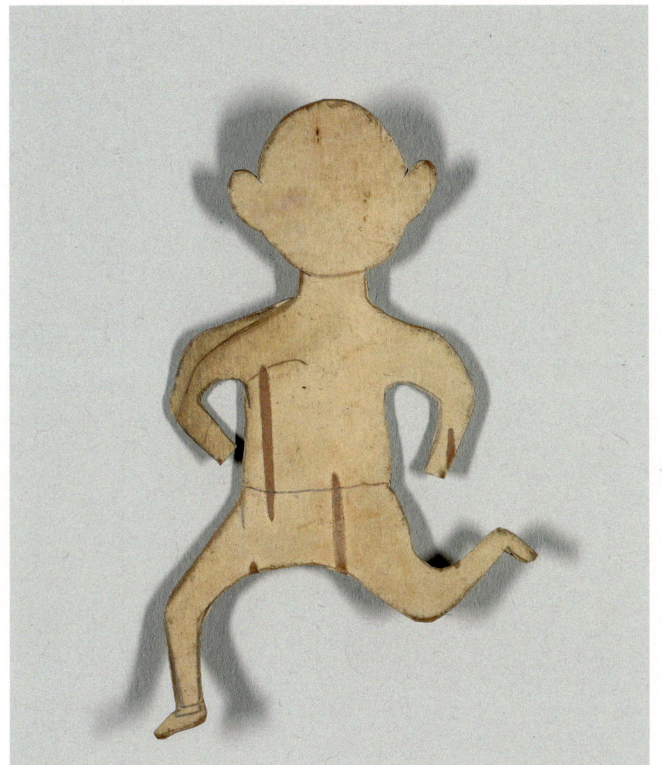

Fig. 4.6

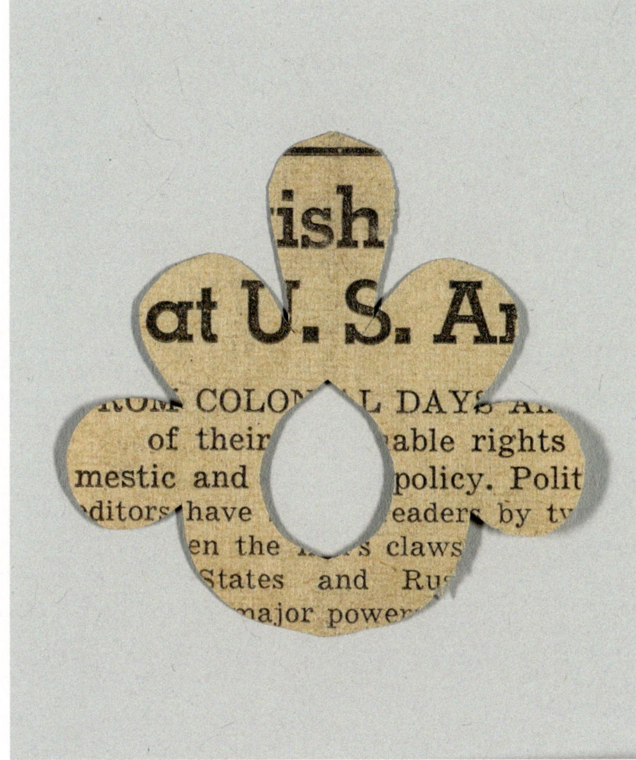

Fig. 4.7

Fig. 4.6 Nancy Fisher Cyrette (Grand Portage Ojibwe, 1900–1985), *Birch Bark Human Figure*, before 1958. Birch bark, 2⁹⁄₁₆ × 1⁹⁄₁₆ inches. Minneapolis Institute of Art, bequest from the Karen Daniels Petersen American Indian Collection, 2008.99.23.

Fig. 4.7 Nancy Fisher Cyrette (Grand Portage Ojibwe, 1900–1985), *Paper Pattern in Floral Motif*, before 1958. Newsprint, 1¹⁵⁄₁₆ × 1¹⁵⁄₁₆ inches. Minneapolis Institute of Art, bequest from the Karen Daniels Petersen American Indian Collection, 2008.99.42.

Earth Ojibwe, born 1953), Nancy Fisher Cyrette (Grand Portage Ojibwe, 1900–1985), Jim Denomie (Lac Courte Oreilles Band of Ojibwe, 1955–2022), and George Morrison [see figs. 1.7, 2.3, 4.1, 4.3–4.7 and pl. 9]. According to Andrea, these artists reflect, in varying ways and degrees, features that intrigue her and inform her own art, including "replications of images, breaking down of images, [and] breaking down structures of time and space."[11]

From her own work, Andrea selected only *The Indifference of Fire* for inclusion in her constellation [fig. 4.8; see also fig. 1.3 and pl. 9]. She made the painting on twenty-four pieces of paper, arranged in a grid to create a unified image. In the center, she depicts a dream catcher based on one made by her great-uncle, Raymond Duhaime (Grand Portage Ojibwe, 1909–1986).[12] This is flanked by depictions of black ash baskets by the artist Kelly Church (Match-E-Be-Nash-She-Wish Band of Pottawatomi/Ottawa, born 1967) [fig. 4.9], and of white-throated sparrows, who have four chromosomal genders.[13] The painting reflects her "interest in fragmentation and replication of imagery as an approach."[14] Andrea sometimes draws or paints imagery in multiples to add movement and break the idea of a static image or singular version of a figure, a technique that can also be read as representing a duration of time. Paper is an important medium for Andrea, for whom it resonates in part because of its links to colonial bureaucracies. She observes, "Paper took our land from us—treaties, deeds, laws, regulations—and paper can return our land to us."[15] Paper, thus, is closely tied to her interest in "how information moves across landscapes, from exchanges to cultural

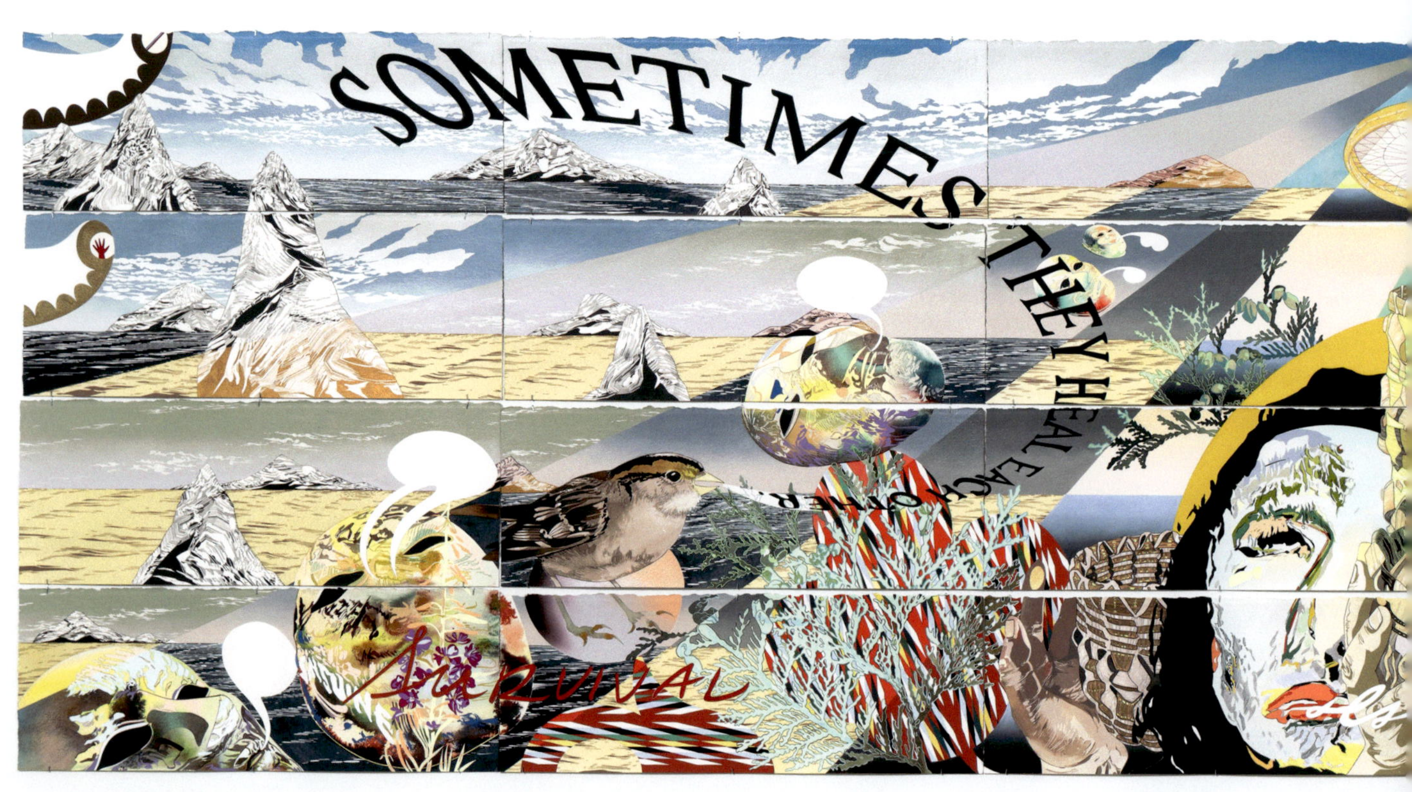

Fig. 4.8

JOHN LOW

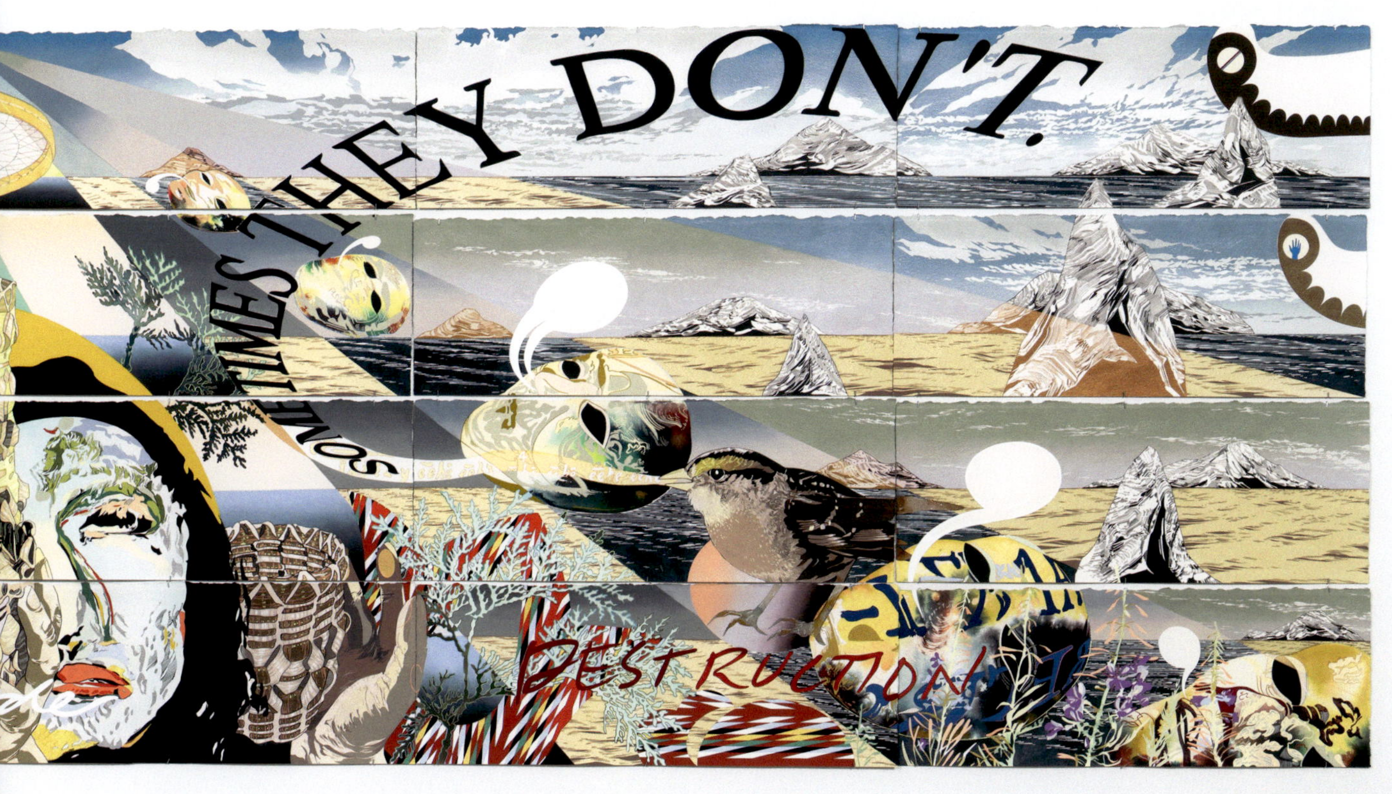

Fig. 4.8 Andrea Carlson (Grand Portage Ojibwe/European descent, born 1979), *The Indifference of Fire*, 2023. Oil, acrylic, gouache, ink, colored pencil, and graphite on paper, twenty-four panels: 11½ × 30 inches each, overall: 46 × 182 inches. Gochman Family Collection, New York.

diplomacy, while contrasting [with] and critical to violent conversions and assimilation."[16]

In her work, Andrea is calling out and talking back to colonization and neocolonization:

[I think about the] history of objects [and their associated] narratives. I get upset and that motivates me [to think about] how art can thumb its nose at colonization and organizations that continue to hurt Indian peoples. [They are] places of violence. The stage of a museum allows me to speak directly to it. Some might think it hypocritical, but I need to use these stages to make change. That's not a bad place to do it from. An artist can do things a curator cannot, as an outsider.[17]

Claiming of land, possession and dispossession of land, commodification of land, and destruction of and extraction from the land constitute the lived American Indian experience. Observing American Indians repeating the lessons of the colonizers by making claims on the lands of other Natives pains Andrea. *The Indifference of Fire* is a thoughtful and provocative continuation of conversations she began when she was in Chicago. Capturing a fragmented landscape of land, sea, and sky, it confronts tensions relating to Indigenous identity and survival and settler colonial projects of taking. Andrea says:

Landscape painting is fraught with colonial histories, with triumphal views of land possession and control. In my work, I subvert and complicate the legacy of landscape painting with multidimensional, prismatic landscapes. Indigenous movements like Land Back and efforts to peel back colonial intrusions on Indigenous land are becoming [part of] the conversation about my work, too. I've begun using profits from the sale of landscapes to purchase land to be held in tribal trust. This is a strategy that many Native artists are starting to employ, including Natalie Ball and Nicholas Galanin.[18]

Andrea's art has both narrative texts and subtexts embedded within its imagery, and *The Indifference of Fire* tells a story in its own right. Describing the work and its place in the *Woven Being* exhibition, the artist uses a series of evocative phrases that weave together the threads of land, Chicago's history, the impacts of colonialism, and hope for the future:

Chicago as landscape—Indigenous landscapes as connection. Responsibility rather than possession and control. Fractured space as a denial of land. Land, art, art as collection/possession. [This] exhibit is seen as a gift to Chicago. Space and time as fractured. Landscape art knowledge as fractured. [The colonial project as] divide and conquer? Internalized colonization—woven beings in tatters. Stories on a fractionalized landscape. [The] influence of artists breaking down static images with prismatic

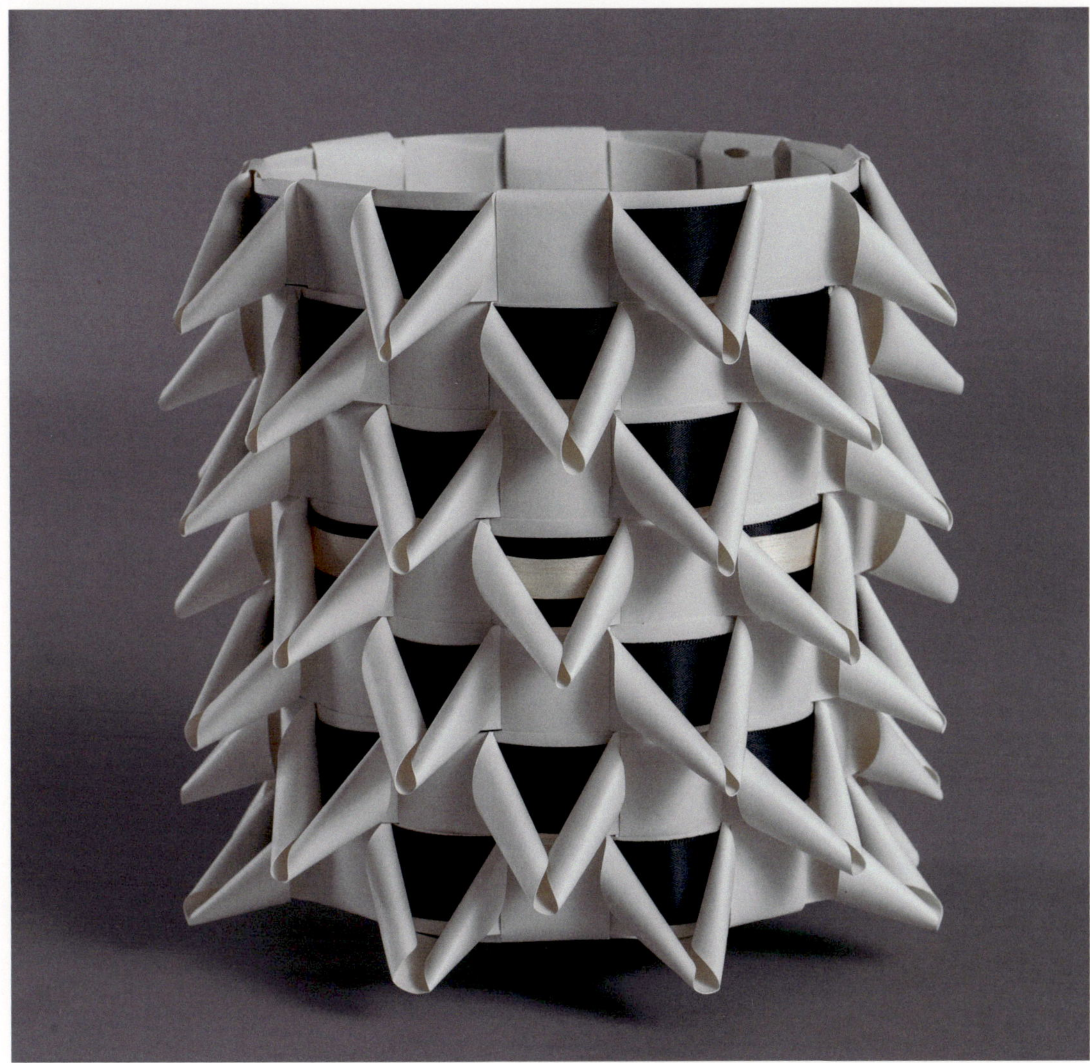

Fig. 4.9

Fig. 4.9 Kelly Church (Match-E-Be-Nash-She-Wish Band of Pottawatomi/Ottawa, born 1967), *Seventh Generation Black Ash Basket—Sustaining Traditions*, 2024. Vinyl window blind, black ash, and ribbon, 8 × 6 inches. Collection of the artist. Photograph by Holly Trevan.

images . . . pulling out of a singularity into a multiplicity. Woven beings, stitched together, stronger together, but still independent and unique. Talking back to Triumphalism, success and power of colonization, [a flipping of "old master" paintings such as] Dutch landscapes, and [a critique of the] European pride of taking.[19]

Centrally located in *The Indifference of Fire* is the mirrored image of a Native face overlaid with the word *ishkoday* (sacred fire). This image implies duality; we are the land, and the land is us. It also reminds us that fire is a gift from the Creator that makes life possible for us two-legged folk. Beyond warming us and allowing us to cook our food, fire is an essential element in rituals including sweat lodge and longhouse ceremonies. It guides us on our four-day journey after our life on this earth is over. Fire can destroy, reducing almost anything to ashes and carbon. Fire, unlike humans, never acts with intent or agenda. The consequences of its burning can be perceived as either positive, as in the flames of a sacred fire, or negative, as

when a building, forest, or city is reduced to ash. Chicago has a
long history with fire—for instance, the burning of Fort Dearborn
by the Potawatomi during the Battle of Fort Dearborn in 1812, the
Great Chicago Fire of 1871, and the forging of steel for skyscrapers.
Today, some Native and non-Native people claim that Chicago was
the homeland of the Ojibwe, Odawa, and Potawatomi, known as the
Council of Three Fires, and this erases the historical reality that Chicago was the sole territory of the Potawatomi before our removal.[20]
Fire has no responsibilities. It is the energy of life and death. As the
artist has pointed out, "Fire can be used for good purposes and bad.
It can heal and aggrieve. The Three Fires Confederacy is real; the
Potawatomi, Ojibwe, and Odawa are related by blood, intermarriage,
and history. But we have differences, too, and we are distinct. That
deserves respect."[21]

Andrea hopes for a different kind of interaction between Native
peoples in and around Chicago. It is this desire, in part, that led to
the creation of the Chicago-based CfNF.[22] Andrea describes this
initiative as a way to grab hold of the "popularity of the Land Back
movement and parlay it into sustainable agency and control," while
also noting the irony of "Native artists always having to ask for space
when it was space taken from us."[23]

The title of this exhibition and book, *Woven Being: Art for Zhe-
gagoynak/Chicagoland*, captures Andrea's hopes for Chicago. The
Block—indeed, all of Chicagoland—is situated on Potawatomi land—
Zhegagoynak. As Indigenous people, we are woven together, and our
art reflects aspects of those connections. We must care for those
interwoven relationships, or they will tatter and fray. That is a powerful message! The works in Andrea's constellation pull and push on
each other and, by doing so, contribute to themes and conversations
and engage with one another. As Leanne Betasamosake Simpson,
referenced earlier, might say, Andrea is creating new perspectives
and understandings about Indigenous peoples of Chicago with this
installation: a new emergence, a *Biskaabiiyang. Migwétth* (thank you).

The literal translation of *Ė zhë nénmëk Andrea Carlson ė wzhetot*, the Potawatomi title for this chapter, is "My Thoughts on Andrea Carlson and What She Makes." Potawatomi translations throughout this chapter have been provided by Bmejwen Kyle Malott (Pokagon Band of Potawatomi).

1   The exhibition *Nwi Yathmomen: We Will Tell Our Story* opened in October 2024.
2   Leanne Betasamosake Simpson, *Dancing on Our Turtle's Back: Stories of Nishnaabeg Re-creation, Resurgence and a New Emergence* (Winnipeg: Arbeiter Ring, 2011), 73, 75.
3   I use the terms "American Indian" and "Native American" interchangeably and, when possible, refer to the specific appropriate tribe/tribal nation.
4   Andrea Carlson, Zoom interview by the author, December 18, 2023.
5   I have written about the Pokagon Band claims in chapter 3 of my book *Imprints: The Pokagon Band of Potawatomi Indians and the City of Chicago* (East Lansing: University of Michigan Press, 2016), 67–94. For a more detailed articulation of this argument, see my article "Chicago Is on the Lands of the Potawatomi: Why Land Acknowledgments for Chicago Should Acknowledge This Historical Fact," *Chicago History Magazine* 46, no. 2 (2023): 16–27.
6   Land Back, also referred to as #LandBack, is a movement of Indigenous peoples around the world that emerged beginning in 2010 to strengthen their sovereignty and community well-being by reclaiming ancestral lands. See, for example, Harmeet Kaur, "Indigenous People across the US Want Their Land Back—and the Movement Is Gaining Momentum," CNN, November 26, 2020, web.
7   Monica Whitepigeon, "Native in the Arts Spotlight: Visual Artist Andrea Carlson Talks about Her Chicago *You Are on Potawatomi Land* Mural," *Native News Online*, July 15, 2021, web.
8   The installation was on view in 2021–23. The installation site is adjacent to the site of the first settler colonial structure in Zhegagoynak (Chicagoland), Fort Dearborn, built in 1803.
9   Carlson, Zoom interview.
10 Carlson, Zoom interview.
11 Carlson, Zoom interview.
12 Raymond Duhaime's dream catcher is in the collection of the Grand Portage National Monument Heritage Center, Minnesota.
13 Andrea Carlson, email to author, November 19, 2023.
14 Carlson, email to author.
15 Carlson, email to author. Andrea also uses tools and materials that hold connections to Western colonial powers, such as Dutch masters' paintbrushes and Arches imperial-size paper (22 × 30 inches), which includes an insignia and watermark that reads "1492," the year of the company's founding. For more on the history of Arches Papers, see arches-papers.com/who-is-arches/history-arches.
16 Carlson, email to author.
17 Carlson, email to author.
18 Carlson, Zoom interview.
19 Carlson, Zoom interview.
20 Low, "Chicago Is on the Lands of the Potawatomi," 20–24.
21 Carlson, Zoom interview.
22 For more on the Center for Native Futures, see centerfornativefutures.org/about-us.
23 Carlson, Zoom interview.

Mark Turcotte
(Turtle Mountain Band of Ojibwe,
born 1958)

"Woman Calls Water"
for S. K. Power

Originally published in *Prairie
Schooner* 74, no. 3 (2000): 74–76.

In a dream of mixed
blood memory I fall
toward the tear
that rests upon the cheek
of my Dakota Grandmother.

I fall toward the tear that holds
the reflection
of my face,
where I see, past
my ear over my shoulder,
a landscape that unfurls before
the rolling winds.

Freight trains burrow slowly
along the distant rails,
seeming to heatwave, melt
into the sky.

The great grasses ripple amber
to gold, dissolve into the curve
of Earth, forever turning,
    forever scarred, healing
wound upon wound.

        * * *

*There were no ruts
before they brought the wheel*, she says.
*Only the cut of a hoof, the scratch
of the point of a stick
drawing circles within human circles,
hoops spinning, untangling to the Sun.*

*There were no ruts
before they brought the wheel*, she says.
*The river bank and shoulder
were strong before they brought
the wagons, before
the teams of oxen carried off away
the humming, hissing skins
of all our brother buffalo.*

I dive toward the tear
that falls along the cheek
of my Dakota Grandmother.

I dive deep into the tear
that holds the river
of her remembering,
the river of our rage,
where a highway receding has cut
the heart, the circles of the land
into maps and lines of longitude.

I swim within the tear
that crashes to the dust, followed
by another and another,
swelling to flood the plain,
to wipe away the dirt, then
bury all the bones again.

        * * *

Heid E. Erdrich
(Turtle Mountain Band of Ojibwe, born 1963)

"Incantation on a Frank Big Bear Collage"

Originally published in *Cream City Review* 38, no. 1 (2014): 40.

Bar the windows, the Red Owl looming into view,
cut by bars, stripes from the American flag.
Bar the eyes, but not the breasts,
cut from marble pale nudes out of Art History books.
Bar the luscious behind of Marilyn Monroe.
Cut the cut body builder, the honey-baked ham, the recombinant Christ.
Bar the windows, the Red Owl looming into view,
cut by bars, stripes from the American flag.
Bar the warriors on the Wallowing Bull work.
Cut the Bog man so he sits right on Custer's face.
Bar emblems and icons and emblem-ography.
Cut the Blue Period into the blues guitar.
Bar the windows, the Red Owl looming into view,
cut by bars, stripes from the American flag.
Bar the door to your studio—photographers still get in.
Cut happy Anne Frank into newsreel out of Guernica.
Bar the Gertrude Stein and her little dog, too.
Cut the death stars from cosmic maps and eclipse them.
Bar the windows, the Red Owl looming into view,
cut by bars, stripes from the American flag.
Bar the Sepia-toned Warrior and the horse he rode in on.
Cut the lines, curves, tones that say *It's full of stars*.
Bar the windows, the Red Owl looming into view,
cut by bars, stripes from the American flag.
Bar the fringe on the two-hide dress.
Cut the sneak-up dancer into action.
Bar the wheel spokes and the battle scene.
Cut the curve of the rubber glove, the dial-up lovely child.
Bar the windows, the Red Owl looming into view,
cut by bars, stripes from the American flag.
Bar the lines in my poem, the lines of my smile.
Cut clean with keen comment, slashed and clashed colors.
Bar the windows, the Red Owl looming into view,
cut by bars, stripes from the American flag.

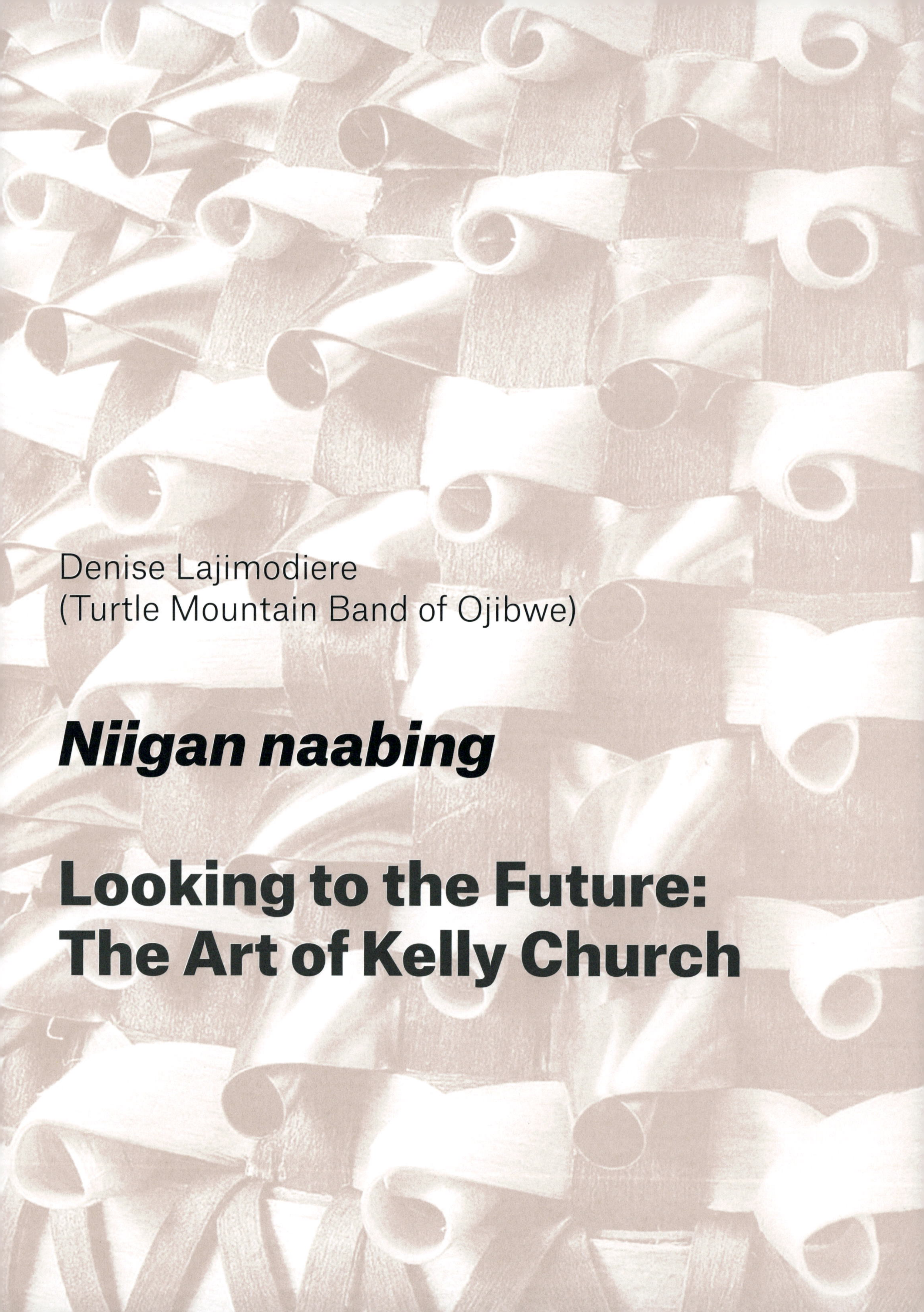

Denise Lajimodiere
(Turtle Mountain Band of Ojibwe)

Niigan naabing

Looking to the Future:
The Art of Kelly Church

Zhegagoynak, known today as Chicago, was once the homeland of Anishinaabe: Pottawatomi, Ojibwe, and Ottawa. The Anishinaabe of the Great Lakes migrated according to the seasons and subsisted on what they were able to hunt, fish, and harvest. Within less than one hundred years, between 1778 and 1871, federal laws and treaties were enacted throughout the United States resulting in loss of land.[1] The Indian Removal Act of 1830 also displaced and separated entire communities from their traditional homelands.[2]

During this time, the implementation of the American Indian boarding school system imposed upon Native children a Eurocentric educational model based on an assimilationist approach.[3] Between 1819 and 1969, the US Department of the Interior operated 408 Indian boarding schools. As part of a program of cultural genocide and assimilation, Native children were forced to attend these schools, which replaced their languages and cultures with English, Western agriculture, and Christianity. Native children were taken from their families, physically and psychologically abused, molested and sexually assaulted, and even killed. Captain Richard Pratt started the first off-reservation boarding school, in Carlisle, Pennsylvania. His motto was "Kill the Indian in him, and save the man."[4] Children as young as four years old were taken from their families and sent to year-round boarding schools, often far from home. Their hair was cut, and they were made to dress in uniforms and taught domestic skills. They were punished for speaking their tribal languages. By 1926, nearly 83 percent of Indian school-age children in the United States were attending boarding schools.[5] Many never returned home. It is said that Native children did not graduate from these boarding schools, they survived them.

Despite the efforts of forced assimilation, Native people are still here. As artist Kelly Church (Match-E-Be-Nash-She-Wish Band of Pottawatomi/Ottawa, born 1967) says, "We are survivors and we are thriving."[6] We are learning and practicing our languages. We continue to hunt and fish. We harvest and process the trees of our forests, relying on the teachings passed down through generations of oral traditions that convey knowledge of sustainable practices and look ahead to the generations that come after. The strength and resilience to keep the language, teachings, and culture alive to continue indefinitely is not only a testament to the spirit of our people—it is who we are as Native people. It is who we are as Anishinaabe.

The creations of Kelly Church begin with teachings that have been practiced by the Anishinaabe since before this country existed. She takes the traditional teachings of the past to create woven vessels that share her concerns and hopes for the life of today and for the generations of tomorrow. The words "healing," "strength," "resilience," and "sustainability" apply to these weavings, which are created with intentionality and thought [see pl. 5]. Each of Kelly's baskets tells a story, sharing her voice as a Native woman, mother, artist, activist, and culture sharer. Kelly says, "Being able to create with the same teachings and materials as my ancestors gives me a connection to my relatives and weaves together our experiences and our voices of

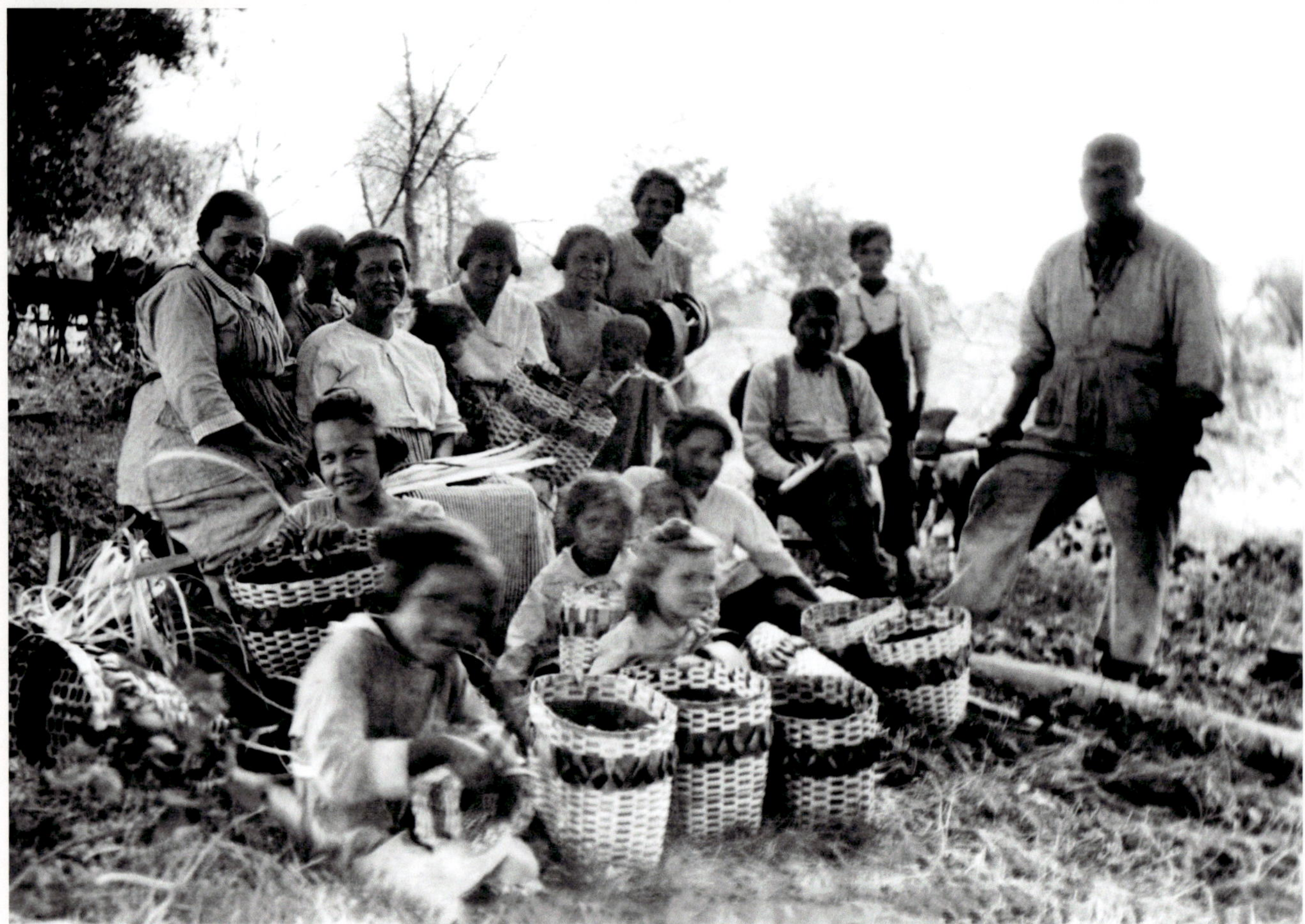

Fig. 5.1

the past and present. We still scout for trees, give thanks, and harvest the same way we always have. We process the materials with time-tested instructions passed on to each generation of the next teachers. It is a responsibility and honor that leads me on a path to ensure the sustainability and continuity for future generations" [fig. 5.1].[7]

For *Woven Being: Art for Zhegagoynak/Chicagoland*, Kelly has assembled a constellation of works by artists Cherish Parrish (Match-E-Be-Nash-She-Wish Band of Pottawatomi/Ottawa, born 1989), Avis Charley (Spirit Lake Dakota/Diné, born 1976), Roy Boney (Cherokee Nation, born 1978), Teri Greeves (Kiowa, born 1970), Lisa Telford (Haida, born 1957), Courtney M. Leonard (Shinnecock, born 1980), Virgil Ortiz (Cochiti Pueblo, born 1969), Jason Quigno (Saginaw Chippewa, born 1975), and Monica Rickert-Bolter (Prairie Band Potawatomi/Black, born 1986). For Kelly, what draws these artists together is the way they express, through their art, who they are today and where they see Native people in the future. Their answer to that last question: everywhere and anywhere. Native communities in Chicago have diverse languages and traditions, but they share the experience of federal policies that have negatively impacted Native people. Each of these artists creates a vision of belonging for future

Fig. 5.1 Photographer once known, *Medawis Family of Basket Makers, Salem Township, Michigan*, 1919. Collection of Richard Church (Odawa/Pottawatomi).

generations using their language, their traditions, and the stories that have been sustained through time.

Kelly and her daughter, Cherish Parrish, weave baskets using strips made from the growth rings of black ash trees. They use the backside of an old axe to pound on the harvested wood; it makes a beautiful resounding echo that Kelly calls "the heartbeat of the black ash tree."[8] The pounding separates the fibers between the growth rings. Each ring is then scored with a knife and split in half from end to end, revealing a beautiful, silky-smooth material inside. The outer layer is shaved smooth, and each strip is cut into desired lengths, depending on the form of the creation to be woven. Once moistened with water, the strips become flexible, allowing the weaver to manipulate them into vessels of seemingly endless variety. Among various forms, Kelly uses the strips she harvests and processes to create egg-shaped baskets, which she calls "fibergé eggs" [fig. 5.2; see also fig. 1.4].[9] Each basket represents the beginning and the continuation of traditional teachings; inside, she places a story to be carried forth for future generations. These stories might take the form of a vial containing a black ash seed and the casing of an emerald ash borer (EAB), to bring awareness to the destruction of ash trees by the invasive beetle; or water from Lake Michigan, encapsulated to show it as it is today, should the Line 5 pipeline ever be compromised; or teachings about trees and weaving saved on a flash drive to pass on to future Anishinaabe generations.

Cherish Parrish uses exceptionally thin strips of black ash to weave the female form. Her baskets take the shape of our jingle dress dancers, who bring healing, or of pregnant women, representing carriers of culture both biologically and as teachers, passing on traditions to the next generation [fig. 5.3]. Her mastery and understanding of black ash as a material is the key to her creation of innovative baskets that are unique in shape and form, in a style that is wholly recognizable as hers. She carefully chooses her strips by feeling the thickness, then cuts them to her preferred width and weaves lifelike figurative forms imbued with the grace and importance of women.

Both Kelly Church and Cherish Parrish use blades of sweetgrass to weave the bottoms of their baskets or as a fragrant rim, giving each piece a beautiful finish. When soaked in water, sweetgrass becomes strong and can hold the wood splint bottoms together. When braided, it becomes even stronger. Braided blades of sweetgrass also serve as the medium for a large-scale installation, *Honoring Our Children: Never Forgotten*, which Kelly made for the *Woven Being* exhibition [pl. 6]. It consists of an outer circle of sweetgrass braids, each about eight feet long, that are suspended and hang to the floor. Entering the circle, visitors encounter a transparent pedestal with shorter sweetgrass braids confined inside and a digital memory book resting on top. The shorter braids represent the Native children who were taken from their parents at formative ages and sent to boarding schools, where their braids were cut off upon arrival. The uncut braids represent the children as they were, as themselves. The sweetgrass braids

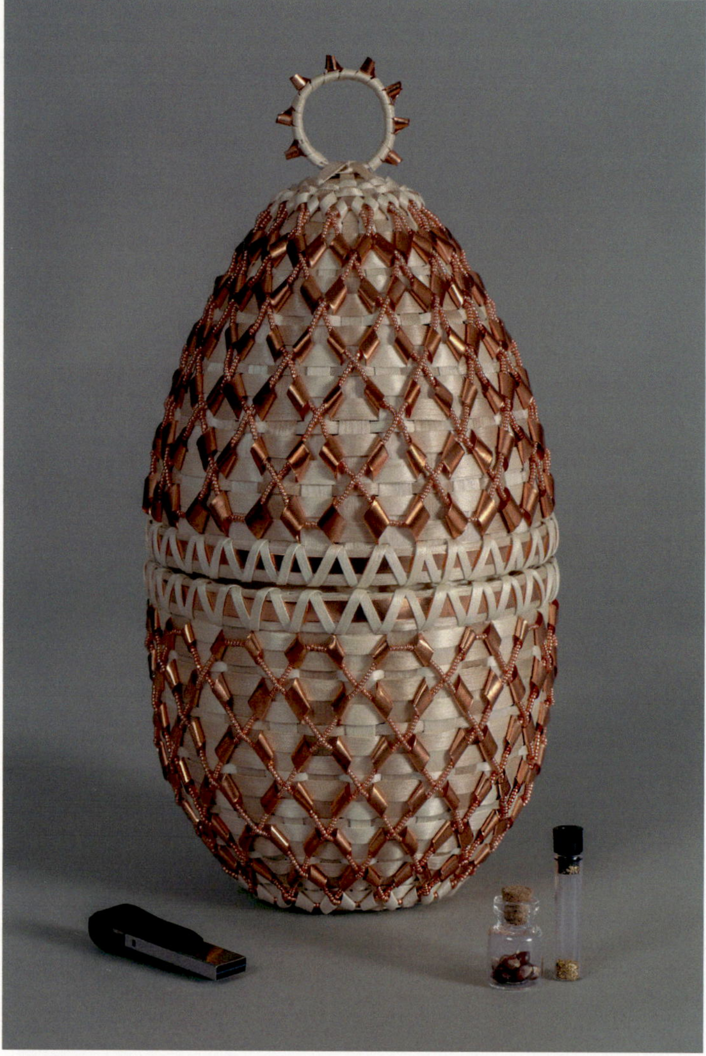

Fig. 5.2

have copper beads woven into them, representing the healing that needs to take place, not just for those who were forced to attend boarding schools but also for their descendants.

The book of memories within the sweetgrass circle opens to the recorded stories of survivors who have shared their experiences and photographs from the boarding school era. The installation is meant to educate us on a part of Native history that is only beginning to be told. It seeks to bring awareness to those children who suffered or never returned home from these schools.[10]

The Urban Indian Relocation Program, initiated in 1952, encouraged and sometimes forced Natives from tribes around the United States to move to cities such as Chicago, Denver, and Los Angeles for jobs and other opportunities.[11] The program increased the Native population in these cities, and the term "urban Indian" was coined. The promises of jobs and support did not always pan out, leading to further displacement. The Bureau of Indian Affairs Chicago Field Office distributed brochures and posters to encourage the move

Fig. 5.2 Kelly Church (Match-E-Be-Nash-She-Wish Band of Pottawatomi/Ottawa, born 1967), *Looking to the Future—What Would You Choose?*, 2024. Black ash, copper strips, size 15 beads, sinew, vial with corn seeds, vial with gold flakes, and flash drive with video, 9¼ × 4¾ inches. Collection of the artist. Photograph by Holly Trevan.

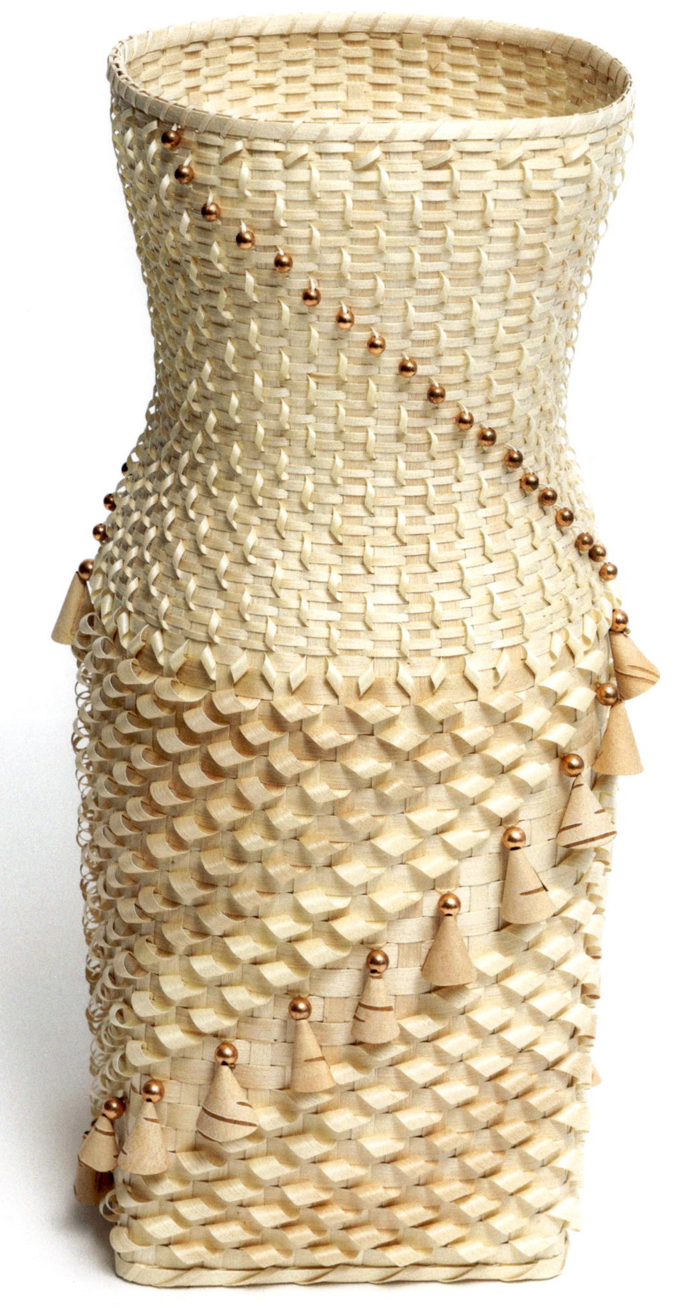

Fig. 5.3 Cherish Parrish (Match-E-Be-Nash-She-Wish Band of Pottawatomi/Ottawa, born 1989), *Jingle Dress Dancer 1: Nenookasi (Hummingbird) and the Great Fire*, 2024. Birch bark, black ash, sweetgrass, and copper beads, 15 × 6 × 6½ inches. Collection of the artist. Photograph by Holly Trevan.

Fig. 5.3

to Chicago by promoting what were portrayed as exciting new opportunities [fig. 5.4]. Avis Charley makes ledger art and figurative paintings that bring attention to the urban Native experience. Her painting for *Woven Being* borrows from the visual language of relocation brochures and posters but responds to who we are today from a Native perspective and addresses healing for inclusion and acceptance [fig. 5.5].

The Natives who answered calls to relocate brought to Chicago elements of their home cultures, including familiar foods and cooking, forms of dress, and art forms. They also brought their languages, as demonstrated by the *Cherokee Speaker* newsletter, which included contributions printed in a new typeface created in Chicago for the Cherokee Syllabary [figs. 5.8a, 5.8b].[12] Artist Roy Boney alerted Kelly to these examples of Cherokee cultural production that were generated in Chicago. Roy's work *ᏒᎢᏬ ᎢᎣᎠ (Come to Chicago)*, featuring a portrait of his great-aunt Myrtle, who moved to the city in the 1950s due to relocation, is also included in Kelly's *Woven Being* constellation [fig. 5.9].

Today, Natives in Chicago continue to network as an intertribal community, sharing and connecting.[13] Kelly selected Teri Greeves's *My Family's Tennis Shoes*, which comprises two pairs of elaborately beaded Converse shoes, one for an adult and one for a baby, and Lisa Telford's *Going Places*, a pair of high-heeled shoes woven from cedar bark, for her *Woven Being* constellation for the way they evoke the movement of Native people and the teachings they brought from their old homes to their new homes, maintaining their sense of identity in unfamiliar places [figs. 5.6, 5.7 and pl. 12].

Kelly collaborated with Courtney M. Leonard on *Convergence and Continuity*, a work representative of the waters that flow through and connect our Indigenous nations and Indigenous communities in cities [pl. 3]. As a Shinnecock person of North America's Eastern Seaboard, Courtney makes work that explores her close personal ties to the ocean and its many life forms.[14] Kelly has likewise created works that reference her strong sense of connection and obligation to the lakes and rivers of the Midwest, which help sustain life, including the black ash trees used in basket weaving. For nations located near waterways, seas and fresh waters have provided routes for travel and trade, sustenance, and, perhaps most importantly, connections with other communities.

Birch bark is a versatile material that is sustained by and associated with water. As Simon Pokagon (Pokagon Band of Potawatomi, 1830–1899) wrote in his 1893 booklet, *The Red Man's Rebuke*, this "most remarkable tree with manifold bark [was] used by us instead of paper, being of greater value to us as it could not be injured by sun or water" [see pp. 56–61 in this volume].[15] In the past, the bark of the birch tree was used to create twenty-foot canoes that could easily hold over one thousand pounds and traverse the waters around Chicago and across the Great Lakes. Today, Anishinaabe people are still building birchbark canoes, using knowledge passed down through generations or, in some instances, recovered through close

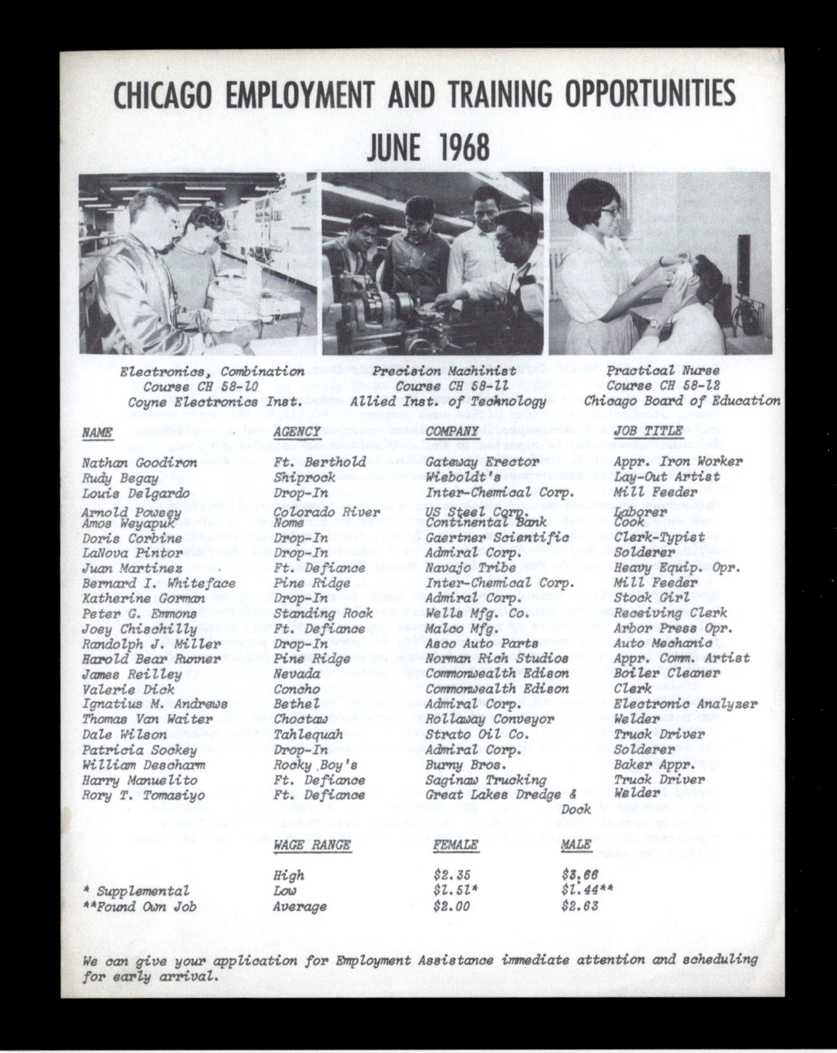

CHICAGO EMPLOYMENT AND TRAINING OPPORTUNITIES
JUNE 1968

Electronics, Combination Course CH 58-10 Coyne Electronics Inst.	Precision Machinist Course CH 58-11 Allied Inst. of Technology	Practical Nurse Course CH 58-12 Chicago Board of Education

NAME	AGENCY	COMPANY	JOB TITLE
Nathan Goodiron	Ft. Berthold	Gateway Erector	Appr. Iron Worker
Rudy Begay	Shiprock	Wieboldt's	Lay-Out Artist
Louis Delgardo	Drop-In	Inter-Chemical Corp.	Mill Feeder
Arnold Powsey	Colorado River	US Steel Corp.	Laborer
Amos Weyapuk	Nome	Continental Bank	Cook
Doris Corbine	Drop-In	Gaertner Scientific	Clerk-Typist
LaNova Pintor	Drop-In	Admiral Corp.	Solderer
Juan Martinez	Ft. Defiance	Navajo Tribe	Heavy Equip. Opr.
Bernard I. Whiteface	Pine Ridge	Inter-Chemical Corp.	Mill Feeder
Katherine Gorman	Drop-In	Admiral Corp.	Stock Girl
Peter G. Emmons	Standing Rock	Wells Mfg. Co.	Receiving Clerk
Joey Chischilly	Ft. Defiance	Malco Mfg.	Arbor Press Opr.
Randolph J. Miller	Drop-In	Asco Auto Parts	Auto Mechanic
Harold Bear Runner	Pine Ridge	Norman Rich Studios	Appr. Comm. Artist
James Reilley	Nevada	Commonwealth Edison	Boiler Cleaner
Valerie Dick	Concho	Commonwealth Edison	Clerk
Ignatius M. Andrews	Bethel	Admiral Corp.	Electronic Analyzer
Thomas Van Waiter	Choctaw	Rollaway Conveyor	Welder
Dale Wilson	Tahlequah	Strato Oil Co.	Truck Driver
Patricia Sockey	Drop-In	Admiral Corp.	Solderer
William Descharm	Rocky Boy's	Burny Bros.	Baker Appr.
Harry Manuelito	Ft. Defiance	Saginaw Trucking	Truck Driver
Rory T. Tomasiyo	Ft. Defiance	Great Lakes Dredge & Dock	Welder

	WAGE RANGE	FEMALE	MALE
	High	$2.35	$3.66
* Supplemental	Low	$1.51*	$1.44**
**Found Own Job	Average	$2.00	$2.63

We can give your application for Employment Assistance immediate attention and scheduling for early arrival.

Fig. 5.4

study of surviving canoes and trial and error [see fig. 1.5].[16] In addition to canoes, technologies for using birch bark to construct lodges for shelter, vessels for holding maple sugar or cooking, and beautiful utilitarian containers and quilled boxes [see fig. 2.8] have been passed on among Anishinaabe communities.

Kelly Church is among the artists who continue the tradition of using birch bark to make *mazinibakajige*, meaning "pictures upon the bark." The bark is harvested in the spring, when sap is flowing. Tobacco and prayers are offered. The tree is not harmed. Layers are peeled onion-skin thin. The process is painstaking and must be done slowly and carefully. Designs are created by folding the thinly peeled layers of summer birch bark and then biting them with the eyeteeth into shapes such as flowers, turtles, dragonflies, and butterflies [see, for example, the front and back inside covers]. No two bitings will ever look exactly the same, nor will the same designs by different practitioners. Birch bark biting teaches patience, respect, kindness, and creativity, and calls on the imagination. The passing

Fig. 5.4 Chicago Field Office, Bureau of Indian Affairs, *Chicago Employment and Training Opportunities*, June 1968. The Newberry Library, Chicago.

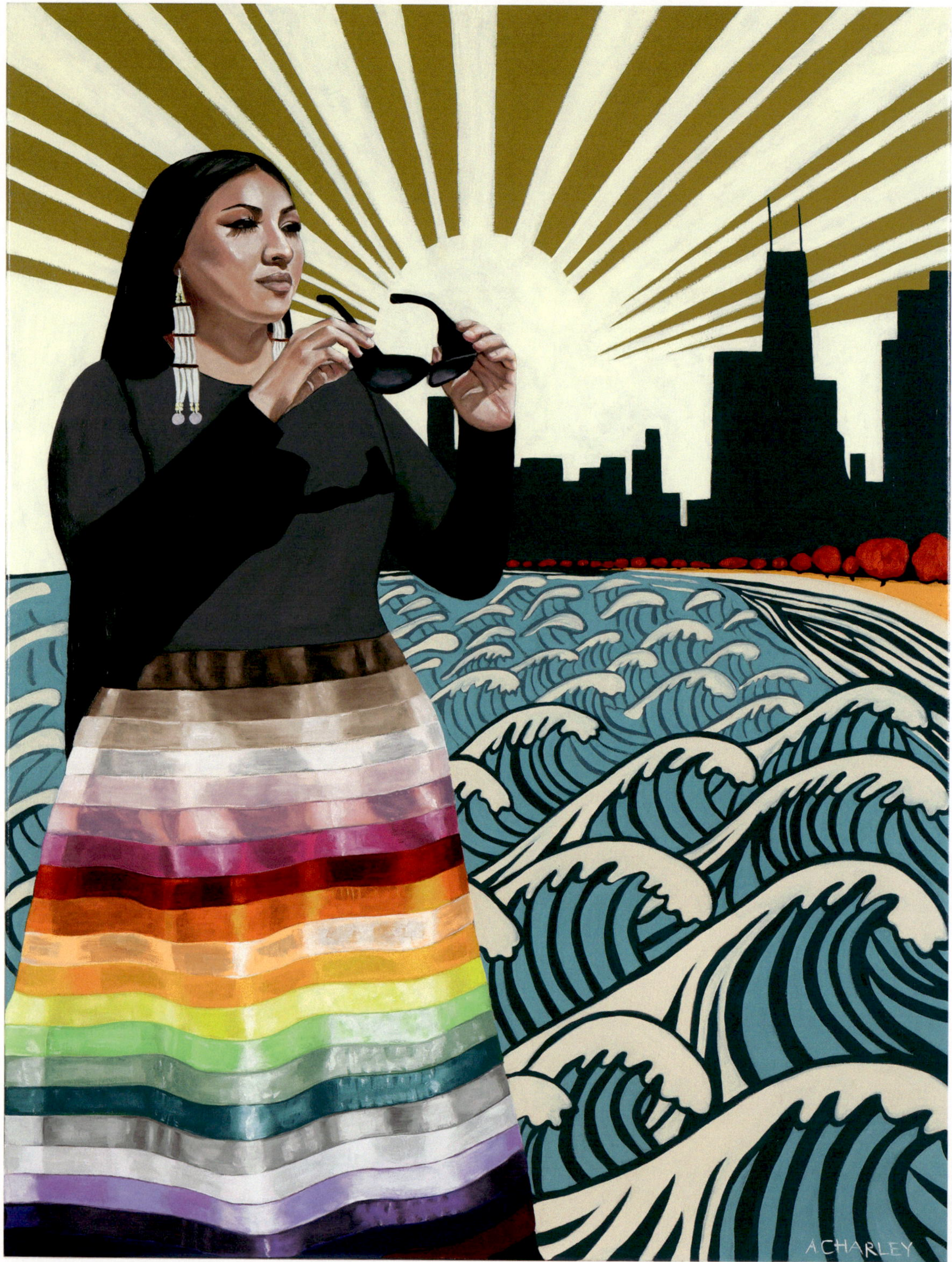

Fig. 5.5

Fig. 5.5 Avis Charley (Spirit Lake Dakota/ Diné, born 1976), *She Brings the Light*, 2024. Oil on canvas, 40 × 30 inches. Collection of the artist.

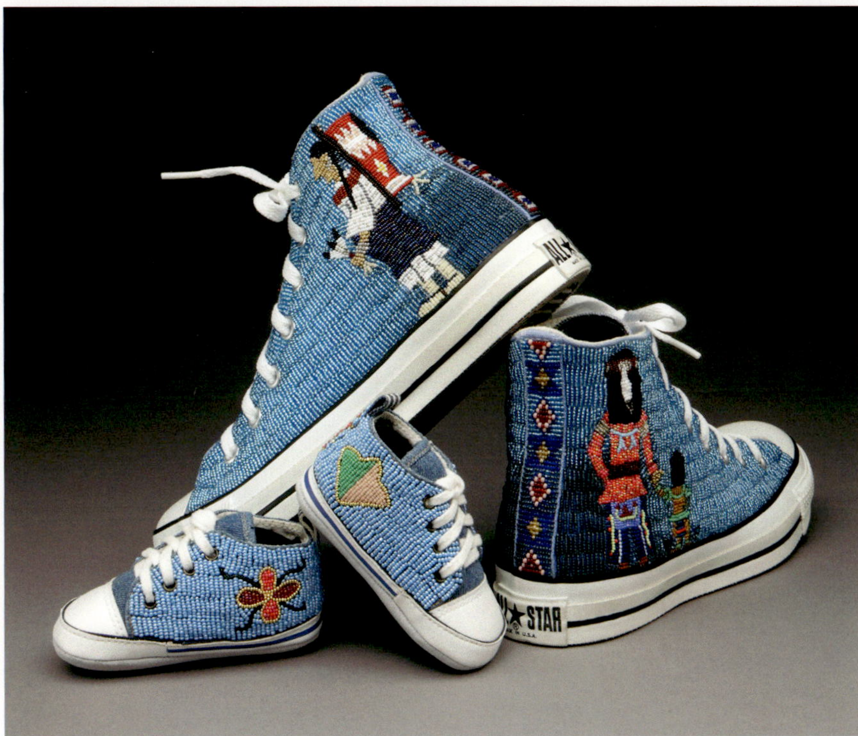

Fig. 5.6

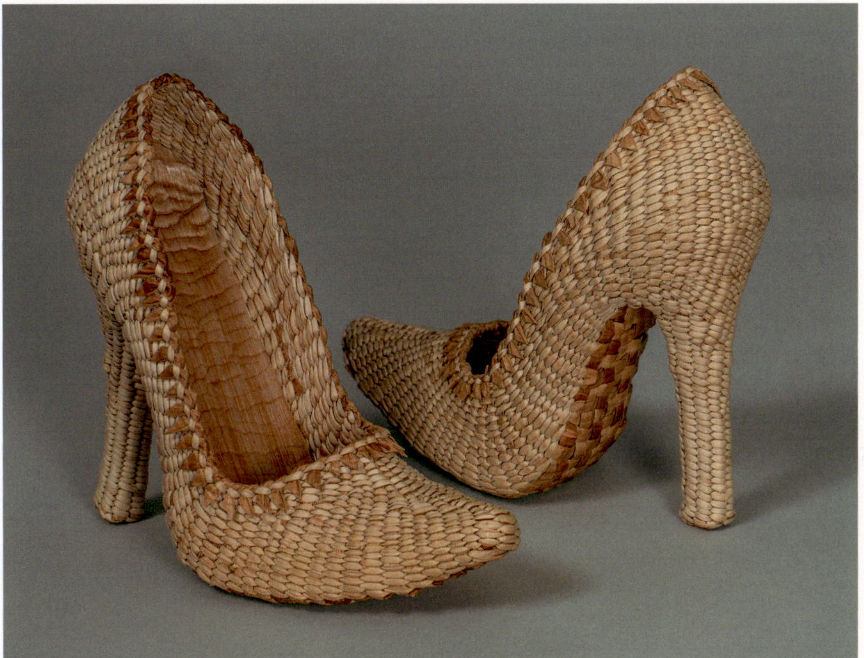

Fig. 5.7

Fig. 5.6 Teri Greeves (Kiowa, born 1970), *My Family's Tennis Shoes*, 2003. Cotton, rubber, glass beads, metal, thread, and ink, women's shoes: 6 × 3½ × 10½ inches each; baby's shoes: 2¾ × 2 × 4¾ inches each. School for Advanced Research, Santa Fe, NM, gift of the artist, 2003, SAR.2003-16-1A-D. Photograph by Addison Doty.

Fig. 5.7 Lisa Telford (Haida, born 1957), *Going Places*, 2024. Red and yellow cedar bark, 5 × 3¼ × 8 inches. Collection of Kelly Church. Photograph by Holly Trevan.

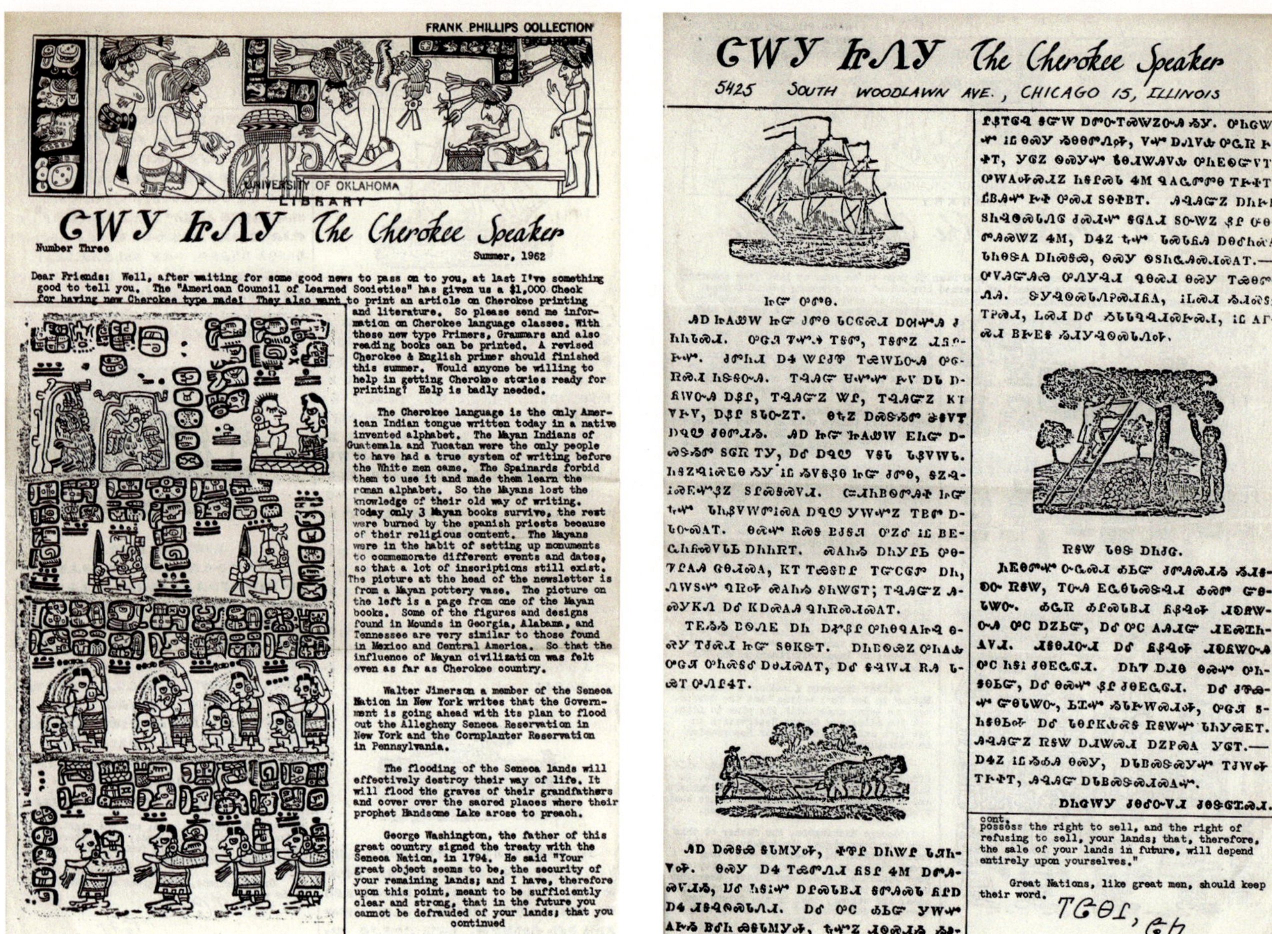

Fig. 5.8a

Fig. 5.8b

on of this and many other traditions continues to grow and sustain this knowledge for future generations. Large-scale reproductions of *mazinibakajige* by Kelly Church, Wanesia Misquadace (Minnesota Lake Superior Chippewa Tribe, Fond du Lac Band), and me adorned the windows of The Block for the run of the *Woven Being* exhibition, allowing for easier appreciation of these intricate details [pl. 1]. These examples, created by three different artists, show the individuality of each artist's work and the beautiful designs that can be created by "drawing with your teeth." I learned the art of birch bark biting from Kelly after buying a piece of her work while at the Eiteljorg Museum of American Indians and Western Art, in Indianapolis. Fascinated, I contacted Kelly, and she generously sent me copies of her bitings and instructions on how to peel and bite the birch bark. I have been fortunate to have the eyeteeth needed to practice this art.[17]

Kelly's work titled *Emergence* represents the many tribal cultures that call Chicago home [pls. 13–15]. It comprises fibers of basswood, black ash, and red willow harvested from Michigan woods and forests, intertwined to suggest a large cocoon from which emerges a half-female, half-male butterfly rendered in quillwork. Hanging above

Figs. 5.8a and 5.8b *Cherokee Speaker* (Chicago) no. 3 (Summer 1962). Sequoyah National Research Center, University of Arkansas at Little Rock.

and resting beneath the cocoon are fourteen butterflies, each created by an artist from a different tribal nation. Kelly says, "My intention with this piece is to help viewers . . . understand that Chicago was Anishinaabe land originally. Natives were removed and, ironically, relocated back to Chicago. While the original inhabitants were Anishinaabe, there are over 540 tribal nations in the US and over 30,000 Natives in Chicago today, and not just Anishinaabe."[18] She chose to include works by the artists Roy Boney, Virgil Ortiz, Jason Quigno, and Monica Rickert-Bolter in her constellation for the way they "share our voices, our hopes, and what we envision our futures to be. Their works help us to imagine these futures and see our place in many spaces, continuing to give voice to who we are as Native people, of Chicago and of the US."[19]

Roy Boney, a teacher of the Cherokee language, uses his artistic skills to create futuristic paintings and drawings of animals behaving as humans. Kelly follows his work drawing Native heroes for the covers of Marvel comics.[20] She is interested in how he connects our communities with spaces not commonly occupied, showing today's youth and future generations that we belong wherever we can see ourselves [see fig. 5.9].

Virgil Ortiz makes ceramic sculptures depicting figures that represent the nineteen Pueblo peoples in New Mexico, bearing witness to the Pueblo Revolt of 1680 and its aftermath.[21] Through his art, he uses ancestral memories to share his view of the world and his experiences, imagining a future place and space for the Pueblo people to have and hold [figs. 5.11, 5.12]. Kelly sees similarities between her practice and Virgil's harvesting of clay for his creations using traditional methods passed on by his ancestors, as well as the way he shares his voice and his hopes for future generations.[22] "His work starts us in the future, helping us see places and people we have yet to experience or meet. His work opens our minds to what the future might hold."[23] Kelly likewise relates to the work of Jason Quigno, whose stone sculptures bring to life stories of his Anishinaabe heritage and of his own experiences as a contemporary Native artist. In Kelly's words, Jason "takes the materials of the past to tell his story today."

Monica Rickert-Bolter uses computer graphics technologies to convey her experiences and thoughts as an urban Native residing in Chicago [fig. 5.10 and pl. 3].[24] Her work in *Woven Being* continues her "Hair Stories" series, in which she explores connections between hairstyles, personal expression, and significant life events for women who are Indigenous, Black, and/or people of color. She says, "These pieces get into the complexities of mixed-identity hair, challenging societal norms, and how we all have our own stories to tell."[25] Monica is also a co-director, with Debra Yepa-Pappan (Jemez Pueblo/Korean), of the Center for Native Futures (CfNF), which empowers Native artists who live in and around Chicago and beyond by giving them a space and place of their own. The organization's vision is to bring together "Native artists to imagine ourselves richly, where art

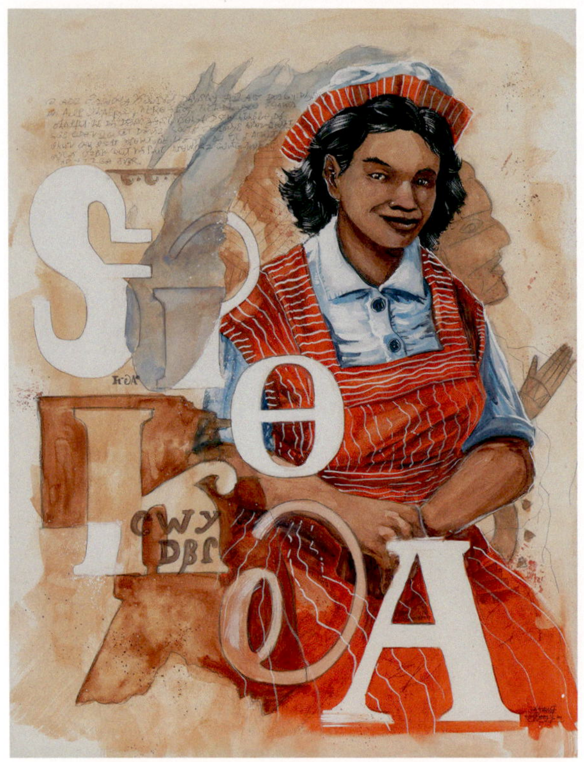

Fig. 5.9

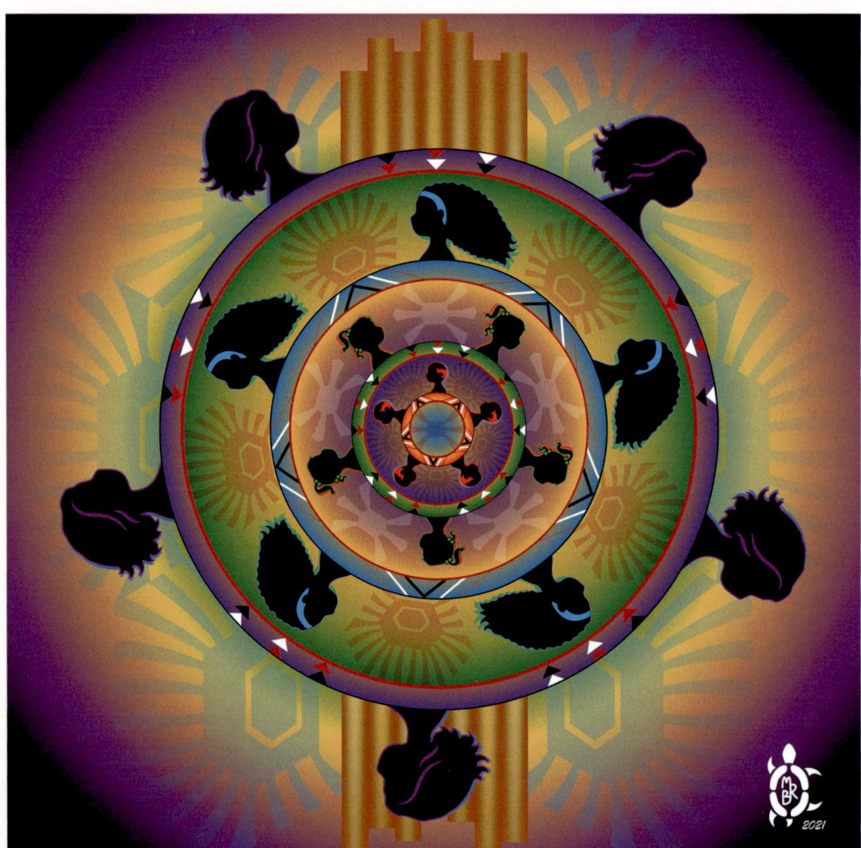

Fig. 5.10

Fig. 5.9 Roy Boney (Cherokee Nation, born 1978), *ᏍᎤᎥᎾ ᏓᏐᎠ (Come to Chicago)*, 2024. Acrylic on illustration board, 30 × 24 inches. Collection of the artist.

Fig. 5.10 Monica Rickert-Bolter (Prairie Band Potawatomi/Black, born 1986), *Mshike Kwe*, from the series "Hair Stories," 2021–24. Digital painting on aluminum, four panels: 30 × 30 inches each. Collection of the artist.

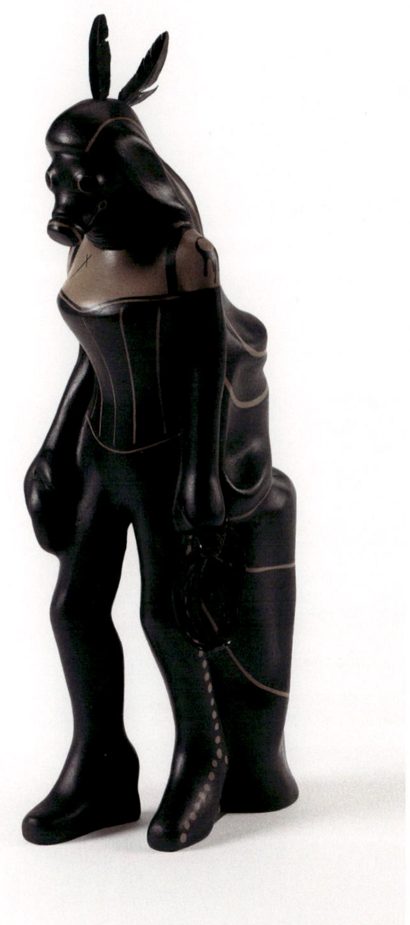

Fig. 5.11

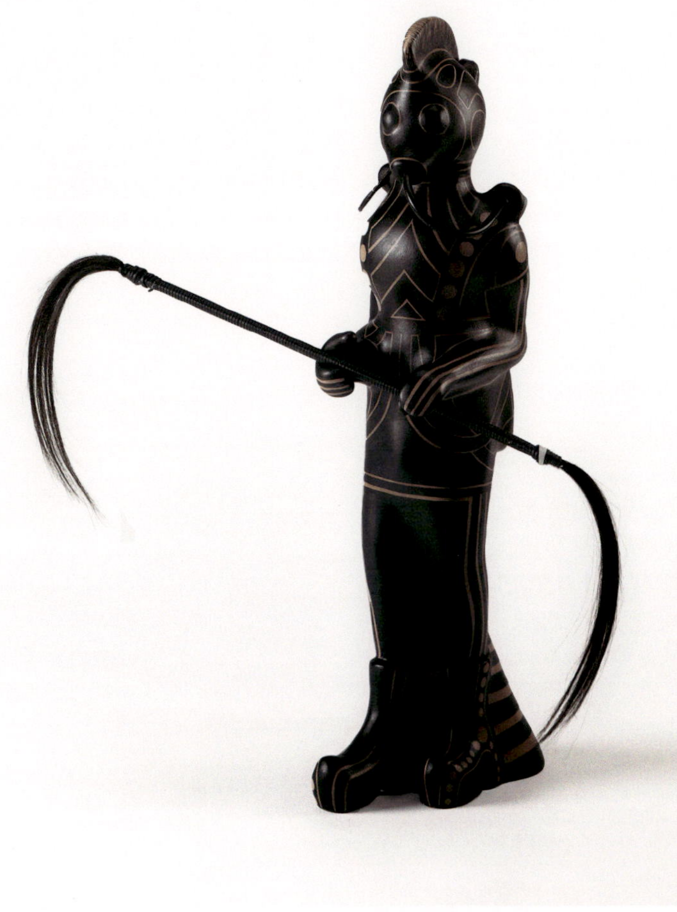

Fig. 5.12

Fig. 5.11 Virgil Ortiz (Cochiti Pueblo, born 1969), *Tracker | Mapoowana*, 2012. Clay and slip, 15½ × 8½ × 5 inches. Denver Art Museum, gift of Vicki and Kent Logan, 2016.119a-c. Photograph © Denver Art Museum © Virgil Ortiz.

Fig. 5.12 Virgil Ortiz (Cochiti Pueblo, born 1969), *Tracker*, 2012. Clay and slip, 22 × 15 × 9 inches. Denver Art Museum, gift of Vicki and Kent Logan, 2016.117a-d. Photograph © Denver Art Museum © Virgil Ortiz.

can provide a lens to learn from the past, nurture our present, and realize a thriving future."[26] CfNF makes it possible for Native artists to be heard and seen, but most importantly, it adds value to what Chicago is and offers.

Kelly's work *Seventh Generation Black Ash Basket—Sustaining Traditions* is a fitting summation of the vision she expresses through her constellation for *Woven Being.* The work, a basket made of vinyl strips from window blinds with a single strip of black ash woven through it [fig. 4.9], speaks to the loss of ash trees due to the invasive emerald ash borer (EAB). The EAB was identified near Detroit in 2002 by researchers at Michigan State University, and the US Department of Agriculture considers it the most destructive forest pest ever seen in North America.[27] For Kelly, the very real eventuality that we could lose the black ash tree altogether tells us that we need to work harder to look out for our future generations. Through her art and through lectures around the United States, she actively educates the public about this potential loss and ways to sustain black ash basket making. Her *Seventh Generation Black Ash Basket* reflects the reality that, while it is possible to pass on weaving methods with manmade materials, we will lose the knowledge of the harvest and processing of the black ash tree if we do not collect seeds and make the teachings available while we are still able. This basket both shows continuity and makes tangible a permanent loss, one that we may avoid if we act now. These powerful themes of loss and rebuilding, adversity and resilience, run throughout Kelly's *Woven Being: Art for Zhegagoynak/Chicagoland* constellation, which "speaks to who Natives are today and where they see our future generations; how they are sustaining traditions of the past while sharing their voices today and into the future."[28]

The Ottawa translation of this chapter's title has been provided by Isadore Toulouse (Wiikwemkoong First Nation).

1   The National Archives provides a list of treaties between the United States and Indigenous nations, available at archives.gov/research/native-americans/treaties.
2   Much has been written about the Indian Removal Act, which was signed by President Andrew Jackson in 1830. The Library of Congress has created a guide to primary documents, available at guides.loc.gov/indian-removal-act.
3   I have written about boarding schools in the United States in *Stringing Rosaries: The History, the Unforgivable, and the Healing of Northern Plains American Indian Boarding School Survivors* (Fargo: North Dakota State University Press, 2019).
4   The complete text of Pratt's 1892 speech in which he used this phrase is available at carlisleindian.dickinson.edu/teach/kill-indian-him-and-save-man-r-h-pratt-education-native-americans.
5   David W. Adams, *Education for Extinction: American Indians and the Boarding School Experience, 1875–1928* (Lawrence: University of Kansas Press, 1995), 27.
6   Kelly Church, written communication to author, April 2024.
7   Kelly Church, written communication to author, February 2024.
8   Church, written communication, February 2024.
9   This is a pun on "Fabergé eggs," decorative egg-shaped containers made by the jewelry firm House of Fabergé in Saint Petersburg, Russia, between 1885 and 1916. See faberge.com/the-world-of-faberge/the-imperial-eggs.

10   Healing from boarding school trauma is a focus of my book *Stringing Rosaries* (see note 3 above). It is also the work of the National Native American Boarding School Healing Coalition: boardingschoolhealing.org.

11   See, for instance, James B. LaGrand, *Indian Metropolis: Native Americans in Chicago, 1945–1975* (Champaign: University of Illinois Press, 2002); and Elaine M. Neils, *Reservation to City: Indian Migration and Federal Relocation* (Chicago: University of Chicago Department of Geography, 1971).

12   While in Chicago, the educator, historian, and cultural preservationist John K. White (Shawnee/Cherokee/Scots descent) raised money and oversaw the creation of a new font for printing the Cherokee language, working with Torvald Faegre, a student at Chicago's Roosevelt University. The font was used in White's English and Cherokee language newsletter, the *Cherokee Speaker*, issues of which were published in 1961 and 1962. John K. White, "On the Revival of Printing in the Cherokee Language," *Current Anthropology* 3, no. 5 (December 1962): 511–14. The Newberry Library, in Chicago, is the repository of White's papers, and biographic information about White can be found in its collection database at archives.newberry .org/repositories/2/resources/1008.

13   These connections are supported by organizations such as the American Indian Center, founded in 1953, and the Chicago American Indian Community Collaborative, founded in 2012.

14   Courtney M. Leonard also has a connection to the Great Lakes, as she currently makes her home in Minnesota and is assistant professor of art at St. Olaf College.

15   Simon Pokagon, *The Red Man's Rebuke* (n.p.: C. H. Engle, 1893), web. Quoted in Bmejwen Kyle Malott and Blaire Morseau, introduction to *As Sacred to Us: Simon Pokagon's Birch Bark Stories in Their Contexts*, ed. Blaire Morseau (East Lansing: Michigan State University Press, 2023), 1.

16   For instance, in 2021, Ojibwe master canoe builder Wayne Valliere was an artist in residence at Northwestern University's Center for Native American and Indigenous Research, where he worked with community members to build a birchbark canoe [see fig. 1.5]. Made from birch bark and other organic materials, the canoe is viewed as a relative; it is currently housed in Northwestern's Evanston campus Visitors Center. See Center for Native American and Indigenous Research, Northwestern University, "These Canoes Carry Culture," web.

17   My poem "Birch Bark Biting" appears in this volume [pp. 118–19].

18   Church, written communication, April 2024. According to the Bureau of Indian Affairs, there are 574 federally recognized tribes in the United States. "Indian Entities Recognized by and Eligible to Receive Services from the United States Bureau of Indian Affairs," *Federal Register* 89, no. 5 (2024): 944–48. As of the 2020 US Census, 34,543 Native Americans lived in Chicago. Elvia Malagón, "As Chicago's Native American Population Grows, More Efforts Are Underway to Build Community," *Chicago Sun-Times*, April 8, 2022, web.

19   Church, written communication, April 2024.

20   Lindsey Bark, "Boney Creates Variant Cover for Marvel Voices: Heritage," *Cherokee Phoenix*, November 6, 2021, web.

21   Vincent Schilling, "Watching over the Past: Virgil Ortiz's Futuristic Creations Are Perpetuating Cochiti Pueblo Pottery-Making Traditions," *American Indian* 23, no. 2 (2022), web.

22   Virgil Ortiz, "Art Rooted in the Earth," interview by Barron B. Bass, May 4, 2022, in *Frame of Mind*, podcast, produced by the Metropolitan Museum of Art and Goat Rodeo.

23   Church, written communication, April 2024.

24   National Museum of the American Indian, "Ancestors Know Who We Are: Monica Rickert-Bolter," web.

25   Monica Rickert-Bolter, email to Janet Dees, June 24, 2024.

26   Center for Native Futures, "About Us: Our Vision," web.

27   Cameron Rudolph, "MSU Researcher Shows Emerald Ash Borer Threatening Tree Species Vital to Indigenous Cultures," AgBioResearch, Michigan State University, September 19, 2023, web; "Emerald Ash Borer," USDA National Invasive Species Information Center, web.

28   Church, written communication, April 2024.

"Aged Indian Remembered Chicago as Little Village"

Reprinted from the *Kalamazoo Gazette*, October 26, 1912. Library of Michigan, Lansing.

AGED INDIAN REMEMBERED
CHICAGO AS LITTLE VILLAGE

Traverse City, Mich., Oct. 23.—Joe Manitou, the most picturesque and best known Indian in northern Michigan, was buried at Gills' Pier, Leelanau county, today. Joe had made his home at Cedar for the last 15 years and was known to every tourist who visited that section during that time. His father was a full blooded Pottawatomie chief and was a power in Indian circles around Chicago in the early days.

It was one of Joe's favorite pastimes to relate to tourists his experiences in the vicinity of Chicago when he was a boy. He remembered when the present site of the Windy city held only 10 Indian tepees in one of which his father's family resided. He had a wonderful memory and could recall many incidents that occurred in the Indian wars in the north central state dating back to the first years of the nineteenth century. It is not known just how old Joe was, but it is claimed he was between 115 and 120 years of age at the time of his death. One son living at Cedar survives him.

Denise Lajimodiere
(Turtle Mountain Band of Ojibwe, born 1951)

"Birch Bark Biting"

Originally published in Denise Lajimodiere, *Thunderbird* (Fargo: North Dakota State University Press, 2017).

I study the spring peeled
bark, gathered when leaves
unfolded.
Thunderbirds, wings spread
wide, gaze back at me.
I peel the amber bark
into thin layers, careful
not to tear claw marks,
place the folded bark in my
mouth, biting down with eye
teeth, closed eyes see designs,
unfold a flower, turtle,
or dragonfly, hold
it to the light, feathery bite
marks glow through
transparent wings.

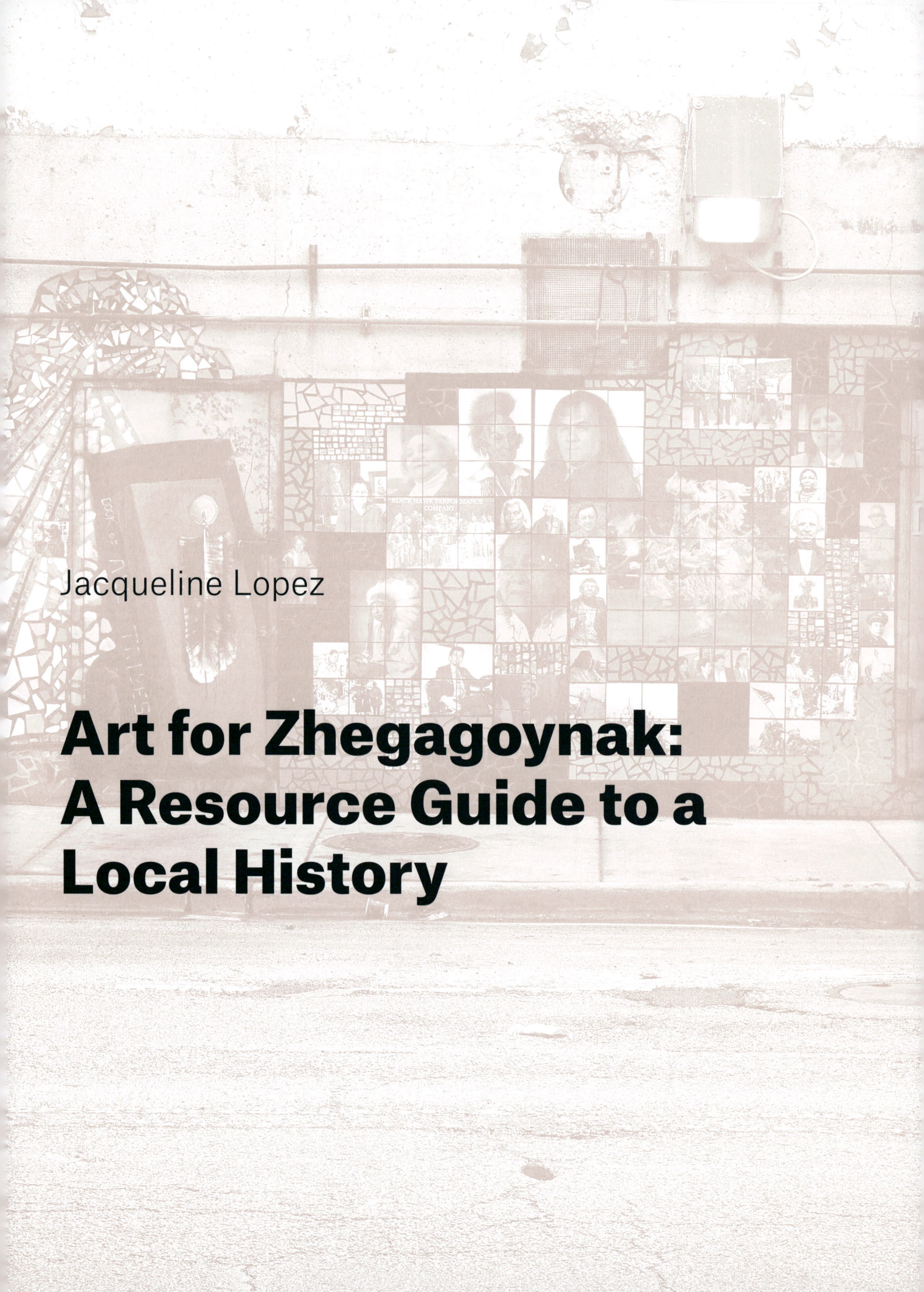
Jacqueline Lopez

Art for Zhegagoynak:
A Resource Guide to a
Local History

Since long before white settlers came to this region, art has been integral to Native identity in Zhegagoynak (Chicagoland). In this space, diverse Indigenous peoples have created, collected, and displayed art—though written records of these works and collections may not exist. Since the mid-twentieth century, Indigenous-led, community-based art initiatives have continued to be essential hubs for mentorship, culture keeping, social networking, community care, activism, and economic power. According to Pamala Silas (Menominee Tribe of Wisconsin/descendant of the Oneida Nation), a longtime member of Chicago's Native community and the current associate director of community outreach and engagement at Northwestern University's Center for Native American and Indigenous Research, "Art and culture are considered as luxuries in mainstream society, not as critical mechanisms for the health and prosperity of a community."[1] Through art, Indigenous Chicagoans have created spaces of belonging, asserted their own notions of Native identity, and worked to ensure more opportunities for future generations. With gratitude to the many members of the Chicago Native community who shared their insights and memories, this chapter endeavors to tell some of that story.

These pages are intended as a resource for future researchers, scholars, and artists, who will continue to expand upon this history. While several organizations, galleries, and initiatives are highlighted here, this chapter captures only a small part of the tapestry of the city's intergenerational and interconnected Indigenous art history, with a focus on the mid-twentieth century to the present. Since time immemorial, Indigenous artists have moved through this region, creating art in communion with the landscape, telling the story of their connection to Zhegagoynak across time and space. In conducting this research, a common thread emerged, tracing the ways in which Indigenous artists in Chicago have utilized their art to deepen their connections to their pasts while remaining focused on the future and the world they hoped to create for the many generations that follow. While this guide is bound to what exists in the written record, it aims to highlight these connections between the past, present, and future of Native art in Zhegagoynak. In terms of structure, it begins with a narrative timeline of key organizations and initiatives, starting with the opening of the American Indian Center in Chicago in 1953 and ending with the establishment of the Center for Native Futures in 2023. This is followed by a chronology of various Native-led exhibitions, many of which have not previously been part of the published record, and additional sources to guide further reading.

TIMELINE OF KEY ORGANIZATIONS AND INITIATIVES, 1953–2023

American Indian Center (Established 1953)
The American Indian Center of Chicago (AIC) was founded in 1953, during the height of the federal government's relocation and termination programs, which brought thousands of Native Americans into

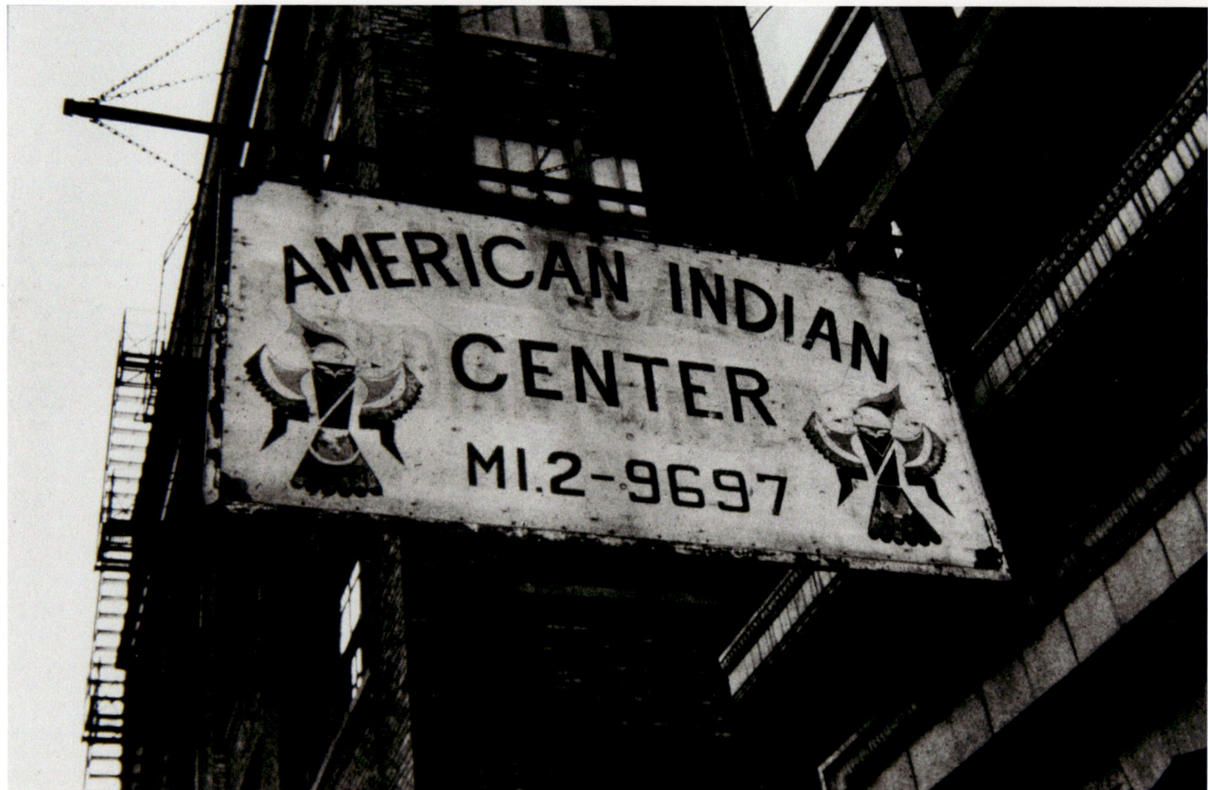

Fig. 6.1

Chicago from reservations all over the country [fig. 6.1].² Organized by Native activists in Chicago in cooperation with local social clubs and organizations, the AIC began as a space to help newly arrived Native families navigate life in the city and find community with one another.³ Since it opened, the AIC has served as a hub of Native art, life, and culture in Chicago, filling gaps in state-run social programs and providing a space for community members to deepen their connections to their roots while establishing themselves in the city. It was one of the first urban Native centers to be established in the United States, and it remains central to the Chicago Native community. In the decades before a formal gallery existed, the AIC served as a space for Native artists to host art shows and sales; groups like the Chicago Indian Artists Guild and individual artists like Robert Wapahi (Dakota Santee Nation) presented pop-up exhibitions there.⁴ In the 1990s, the AIC shifted to more structured arts programming, focused on re-centering Native creators as artists and connecting the younger generations to their tribal identities. According to the AIC's interim executive director, Dave Spencer (Choctaw/Diné), "The goal was to rebalance powwow with fine arts. Powwow is intertribal, which is important to identity as an urban Native, where focusing on arts, and specifically first-voice representation in arts, is a way to connect to tribal-specific identities and traditions."⁵ Among its art-focused programming, the AIC presents exhibitions in its gallery and offers a variety of programs that feature artists and artmaking. In 2003, the AIC celebrated its fiftieth anniversary with a gallery exhibition

Fig. 6.1 Leroy Wesaw (Pokagon Band of Potawatomi, 1952–2022), *American Indian Center Sign when the Center Was Located on LaSalle Street*, date unknown. Exhibition records for *Seeing Indian in Chicago*, 1958–84. The Newberry Library, Chicago.

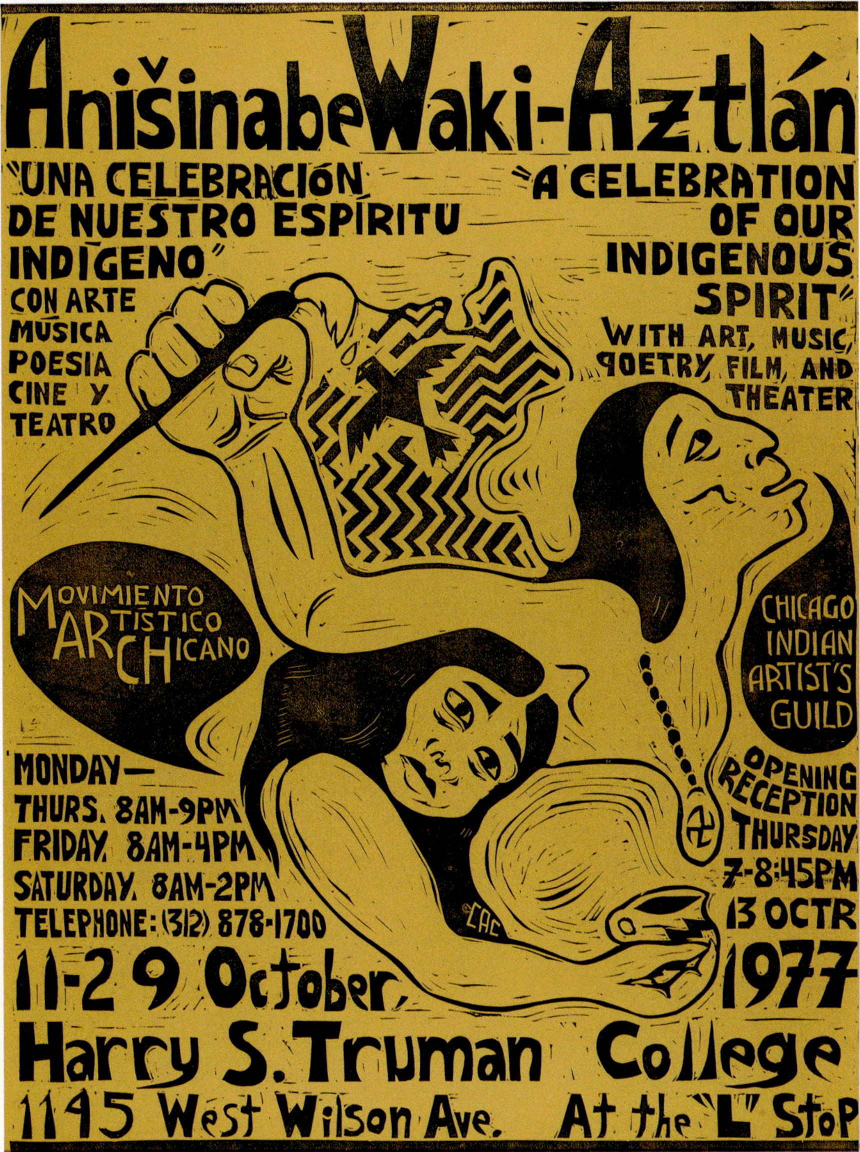

Fig. 6.2

Fig. 6.2 Carlos A. Cortéz (American, 1923–2005), *Anisinabe Waki-Aztlan*, 1977. Linoleum cut on paper, sheet and image: 24 × 18⅛ inches. Smithsonian American Art Museum, Washington, DC, gift of Tomás Ybarra-Frausto, 1995.50.4. © 2024 Carlos A. Cortéz Archive.

titled *50 Years of Powwow*, which highlighted the arts and culture of the Chicago Native community. The exhibition went on to travel internationally, celebrating the rich history of Chicago's Indigenous community.

Chicago Indian Artists Guild (Active 1970s)

The Chicago Indian Artists Guild (CIAG) was formed in 1972 by a group of Native artists in Chicago. In a 1977 interview, artist Loniel Poco (Quahada Comanche), then director of the AIC and a founding member of the guild, said most of the founders had arrived in the city during relocation and got the idea to form the group during an art festival at Hull House.[6] Though unsuccessful at securing state funds to support its work, the CIAG presented exhibitions at the AIC, calling its pop-up galleries "the Thunderbird," and continued

Artists in Exhibition

Christine Sabbia (Menominee)
Johnny Chevez (Navajo/Chippewa)
Ron Perrone (Blackfoot Sioux)
Debbie Whitebear (Seminole)
Patricia Xerikos (Chippewa)
Robert Wapahi (Lakota)
Francis Yellow (Lakota)
Valjean Hessing (Choctaw)
Micky Welsh (Mohave)
Michael Harris (Pokagon/Ottawa/Chippewa)
Eugene Pine (Chippewa/Winnebago)

The Cultural Center Planning Committee, made up of Native people from the American Indian community and other friends, has a dream of a cultural center where both visual and performance artists' skills can be showcased. Operating as a cultural center without walls, the committee plans cultural events that will benefit the American Indian community. The First Annual Art Exhibit and Sale is such an event. It is the first time that the committee planned and carried out an art show. A lot of effort was involved in the preparations; people volunteered long hours and contributed much needed skills and knowledge. A special "thank you" goes out to all the visual and performance artists that are participating in this show, making it an impressive success.

The most important factor involved is your attendance at this event. Without you, there would be no show. You can continue to support the work of the Native American Cultural Center Planning Committee by donating your time, talent and/or money. Please make checks payable to AIEDA/Cultural Center.

If you would like to be on our mailing list, please do so by signing our guest book. You will receive copies of Urban Visions, our newsletter, plus other news important and relevant to Native issues. In the spirit of friendship we thank you for participating in the First Annual Art Exhibit and Sale.

Don't forget the Second Annual Film and Video Festival scheduled for November 20 and 21, 1993 at Facets Multi-Media, 1517 W. Fullerton Avenue, Chicago, Illinois. Call Beverly Moeser at (312) 907-6447 or Ed Two-Rivers at (312) 784-0808 for further information.

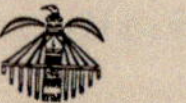 ## Program 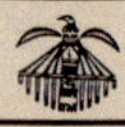

Sunday, October 10, 1993
Mitchell Indian Museum, Kendall College, Evanston, Illinois
Room 02

12:00 p.m.   **Azilicea (Cedaring) Ceremony**

12:30 p.m.   **Jeanne LaTraille (Onieda): Poet**
Allen Turner (Lakota): Storyteller

1:30 p.m.   **Bob Jackson (Cherokee): Traditional Flute Player**
Lenora Enoah (Navajo): Poet

2:30 p.m.   **Julia Hattory (Chippewa): Poet**
Marty Yellowbank (Winnebago): Poet
Sisters in Spirit: Musical Group

3:30 p.m.   **Deboraha Vitello (Cherokee): Poet**
Mark LaRoque (Chippewa): Poet
Robert Wapahi (Lakota): Storyteller

Native American Drumming & Dancing
in the Cafeteria
(on the hour)
Hosted by Leonard Malatare
& Chi-Town Drum

Event Coordinator: E. Donald Two-Rivers
Event Stage Manager: Bernard Catches
Event Host: Tim Hays

Fig. 6.3

to foster contemporary and traditional art education, often centered around challenging stereotyped conceptions of what constituted Native art [fig. 6.2].[7] Also in 1977, Sharon Okee-Chee Skolnick (Fort Sill Apache/Lakota), another of the guild's founding members, said, "People want a traditional-looking thing—they think an Indian artist should paint traditional-looking things . . . but I just paint as I feel" [see fig. 3.5].[8] Similarly, Poco spoke of young Native artists emulating art styles that mainstream audiences expected, even if they were not rooted in any real Native community's tradition.[9] The CIAG strove to push against these pressures by providing a space for open creativity that was not bound to non-Native perceptions. Guild members, like Skolnick and Poco, hoped to inspire and train younger generations of Native artists to make a space for themselves in both the art world and the city. Poco said, "I would like to see a renaissance of Indian art, a rebirth if you will, of some of the Indian artists of today. I would encourage them to draw for all Indians' sake. . . . There are not that many Indian artists as far as the rest of the population. I think Indian artists will be kind of like a boon in later years. Indian artists work[ing] now aren't going to have the recognition due [to] them in, say, thirty to forty years from now. Their work hasn't been

Fig. 6.3 Brochure for the First Annual Art Exhibit and Sale of the American Indian Economic Development Association, 1993. Native American Educational Services, American Indian Economic Development Association Records, box 6, folder 7. Hanna Holborn Gray Special Collections Research Center, University of Chicago Library.

that well known."[10] The guild hoped to rectify this situation, aiming to ultimately open a permanent Native-owned gallery through which to share all styles of Native art in Chicago (see Wild Horse Gallery below).[11]

Wild Horse Gallery (1980s–1990s)

Today's Indian Artists Are Creating Tomorrow
—Wild Horse Gallery business card[12]

Sharon Okee-Chee Skolnick realized her dream from her days in the Chicago Indian Artists Guild when she opened Wild Horse Gallery in the mid-1980s [fig. 6.4]. The gallery served as a platform for Indigenous art and artists in Chicago and continued the CIAG's work as a site for mentorship, culture keeping, and social networking. Through Wild Horse Gallery, Skolnick supported the next generation of Native artists by providing a gateway to the city. Skolnick was known for letting artists new to Chicago stay in the gallery if they had no place to live when they first arrived in the city. She also provided portfolio advice, bought artwork from young artists so they could pay rent, and advised them on obtaining representation. Skolnick and Wild Horse further acted as a hub for connecting artists with Indigenous art opportunities, as the city would often contact her first with any prospective programming.

American Indian Economic Development Association (1985–2001)

The American Indian Economic Development Association (AIEDA) was formed in 1985 with a mission to promote economic development within the Chicago Native community. This Native-run organization focused on advocacy and programming for Chicago's urban Native population. By 1990, the AIEDA determined that Native Americans were underrepresented in museums and galleries and saw the economic benefit of creating more opportunities in arts and cultural institutions. To that end, it formed a subcommittee focused on creating a Native American cultural center in Chicago, seeking to "establish a Chicago-based institution which would serve as a

Fig. 6.4 Wild Horse Gallery business card. Collection of Nora Moore Lloyd. Photograph by Holly Trevan.

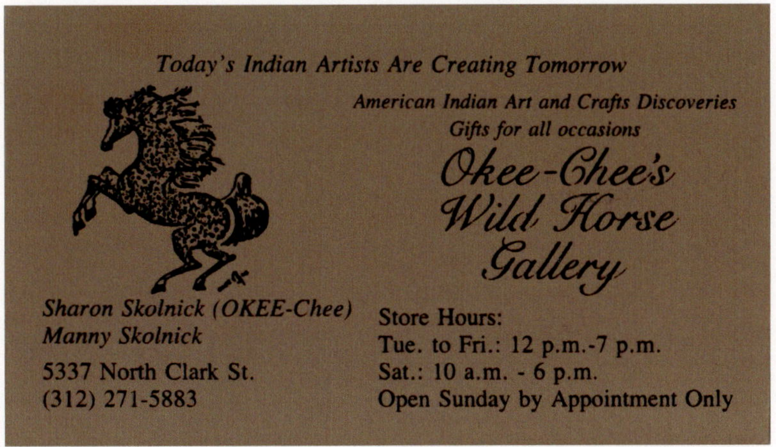

Fig. 6.4

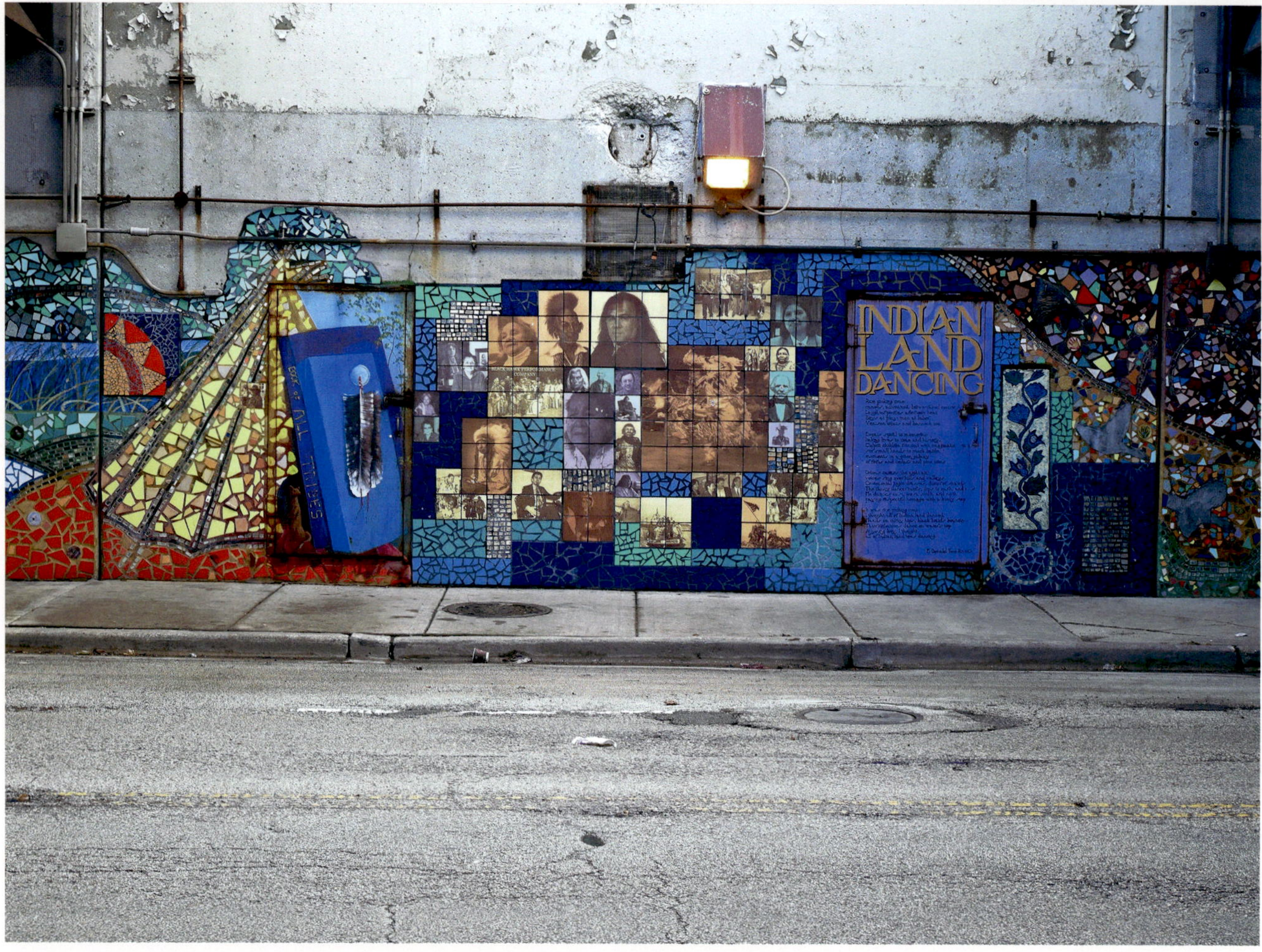

Fig. 6.5

living museum, preserving and interpreting aspects of Native American Indian (NAI) cultures, while exploring new income-producing opportunities for Native Americans. This facility will organize, promote and preserve Native American arts and crafts through the support of NAI artists, the expansion of public awareness and the definition and development of markets."[13] Through its cultural center, the AIEDA created a Native artist registry and offered a hub for finding Native artists, performers, and teachers citywide. It established an art residency at Chicago's River Park, where participants could learn arts such as sweetgrass basket weaving, writing, painting, singing, and sewing. It worked with other Native organizations to sponsor events, like the First Nations Film and Video Festival of Chicago, which continues to promote original works by Indigenous film and video creators.[14] The AIEDA arranged internships for Native artists in Chicago museums and Native-focused art galleries, including the Field Museum, Jan Cicero Gallery, the Mexican Fine Arts Center Museum (now the National Museum of Mexican Art), and the Mitchell Museum of the American Indian (now the Gichigamiin Indigenous Nations Museum). It co-sponsored events with museums, cultural institutions, and Native-led arts organizations to give Native artists

Fig. 6.5 *Indian Land Dancing* (wide section), Foster Avenue underpass, date unknown. Chicago Public Art Group Photo Archives.

JACQUELINE LOPEZ

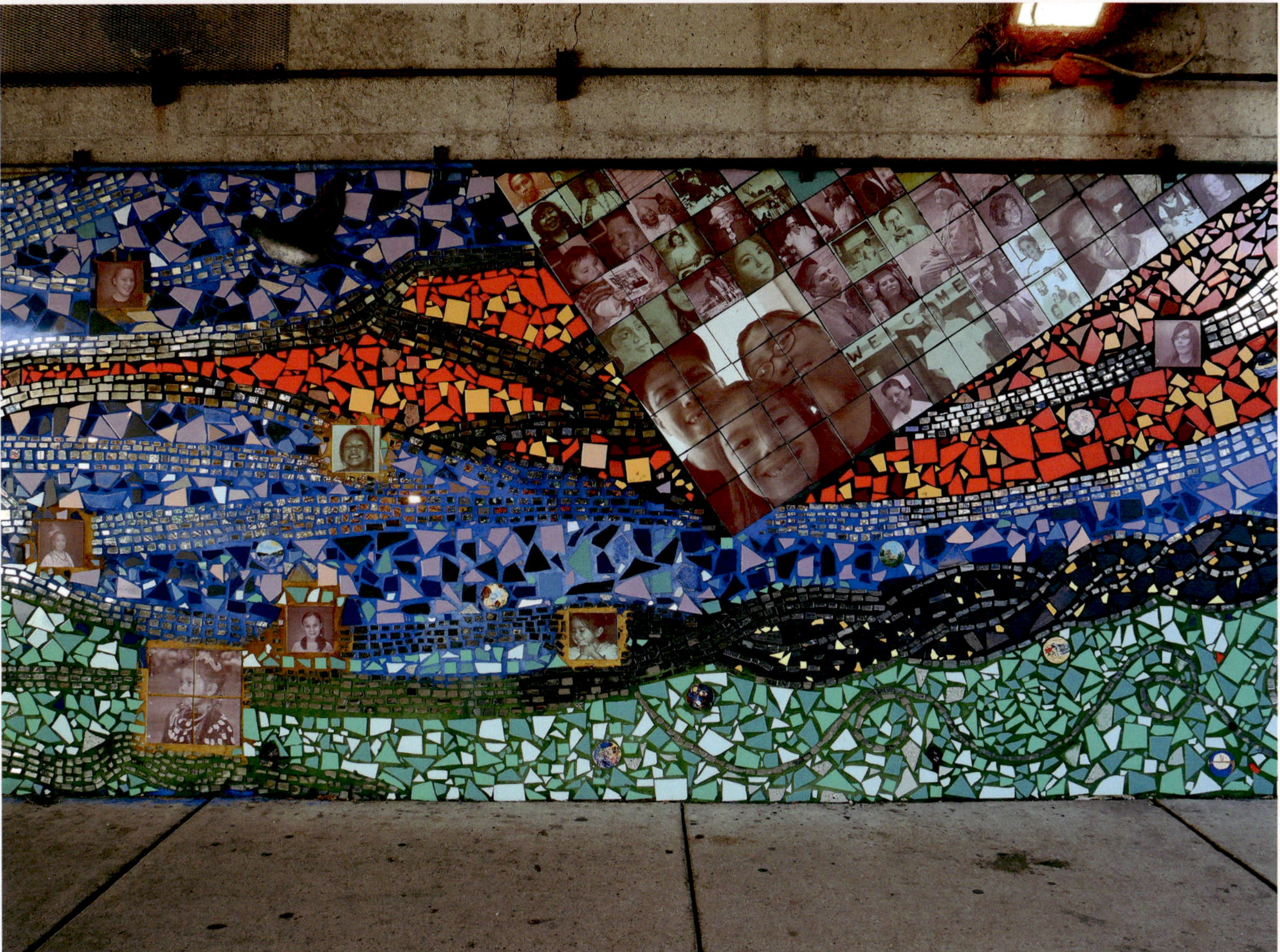

Fig. 6.6

Fig. 6.6 *Indian Land Dancing* (portraits),
Foster Avenue underpass, date unknown.
Chicago Public Art Group Photo Archives.

experience in portfolio creation, contract literacy, and arts administration, as well as training in event planning, marketing, and audience
building [fig. 6.3]. Through the arts, the AIEDA advocated for the
economic potential of Native Americans in Chicago and ensured their
representation in industries from which they had historically been
excluded. By displaying contemporary Native art, these spaces gave
young Native artists a way to contend with their identities in the city.
Speaking in 1995, Chicago artist Jeff Abbey Maldonado (Alabama
Coushatta/Mexican) said, "I believe that when Native Americans
view Native American artwork that is different from the preconceived
notion, they view it as a living culture that's always growing, keeping the same values and beliefs, bringing the past and the present
together and focusing on the future."[15]

Trickster Gallery and Cultural Center (Established 2005)
Established initially to support and expand the reach of the Arts
Department of the AIC, the Trickster Gallery and Cultural Center
opened its doors in Schaumburg, Illinois, in 2005. It aims to promote
multicultural education to the surrounding community, through programming including artist residencies, presentations, talks, school

tours, and film screenings.[16] It also serves as a place for Native artists to express their creativity and find fellowship while connecting their art to their cultures and histories. Among other priorities, Trickster works to increase the visibility of Native veterans and their contributions to the US military. For example, its *Wall of Honor* features a mixture of artwork and framed photographs of Native veterans in uniform, spanning from the Indian Wars beginning in the seventeenth century to modern conflicts in Iraq and Afghanistan.[17] Speaking about the *Wall of Honor* in 2009, Vietnam veteran Joe Yazzie (Navajo), a Trickster artist in residence at the time, said, "We're just trying to honor some of the people who served this country. We have every right to be remembered."[18] Through art, the Trickster Gallery and Cultural Center not only educates the general public about the role of Indigenous Americans in Chicago but also provides a space for recognition, commemoration, and community healing.

Indian Land Dancing Mural (2009)[19]

Events spiral to memories,
linking lives to time and history.
Culprit children frenzied with imagination
stir small hands to mock battle,
moments in a green galaxy
of ferns and cedars and green pine trees.
—E. Donald "Eddie" Two-Rivers (Ojibwe), "Indian Land Dancing"[20]

Developed in partnership with Chicago's Native community and the Chicago Public Art Group, *Indian Land Dancing* is a vibrant bricolage mural on Foster Avenue in the city's Edgewater neighborhood [figs. 6.5, 6.6]. The public artwork encapsulates Chicago's relationship with Indigenous peoples—serving as a bridge between Native cultures of the past and present within Zhegagoynak. When interviewed about the work in 2009, artist Chris Pappan (Kaw [Kanza]/Osage/Lakota), who served on the mural's research committee, said, "We are contemporary, but we also have a foot in the past."[21] The American Indian Center, located near the mural, supported the project because of its focus on community involvement, as well as the location's significance for Chicago's Native history. According to historian Frances Hagemann, vice president of the AIC board when the mural was created, "The location is far more relevant than most people realize. Angle streets like Rodgers Avenue and Broadway are all former Indian trails that ran right through the Foster Avenue underpass."[22] Native artists, scholars, students, and elders came out to take part in the mural's creation, adding photographs, regalia, maps, and more. Nora Moore Lloyd (Lac Courte Oreilles Band of Lake Superior Ojibwe), whose work is featured in *Woven Being: Art for Zhegagoynak/Chicagoland*, was among the artists who participated. She recalls traveling early in the morning to transport elders to the site, to ensure they were able to add a piece of their stories to the mural.[23]

Center for Native Futures (Established 2023)
During the global COVID-19 pandemic in 2020, a small community
of Native artists developed the idea for a new nonprofit gallery space
in Chicago that would center the promotion of Native art and artists.
In 2023, the Center for Native Futures (CfNF) opened its doors in
the Loop's historic Marquette Building. Whereas early initiatives like
the Chicago Indian Artists Guild had been unable to secure outside
financial support, the Center for Native Futures received seed money
from organizations such as the Terra Foundation for American Art
and the MacArthur Foundation. Debra Yepa-Pappan (Jemez Pueblo/
Korean), a co-founder of CfNF and its director of exhibitions and programs, said, "These foundations, I think they're in that moment now
where they realize how they haven't supported Native art and they're
all here now willing to support us because of what we're doing."[24]
Building on the work of the earlier initiatives, CfNF continues to challenge assumptions about what constitutes "Native arts," and provides
space for new and established Indigenous artists to showcase their
contemporary works as part of a growing community focused on the
future of Native art in Chicago. "This initiative has been a long time
coming and the outpour of support is a clear indication that the city
wants more contemporary Native art," said Monica Rickert-Bolter
(Prairie Band Potawatomi/Black), CfNF co-founder and director of
operations. "CfNF is an investment in the community and a reaffirma-
tion of the need for Indigenous artists for future generations."[25]

TIMELINE OF SELECT EXHIBITIONS, INSTALLATIONS, AND EVENTS, 1977–2023

Author's note: This timeline highlights exhibitions, installations, and events for which I have been able to find documentation. When possible, artists' names and tribal affiliations are included as they appear in archival materials to retain the identification used at the time.

Harry S. Truman College, Chicago
Anišinabe Waki-Aztlán: Una Celebracion de Nuestro Espiritu Indigeno, October 11–29, 1977
Organized by Movimiento Artístico Chicano and the Chicago Indian Artists Guild

Newberry Library, Chicago
Seeing Indian in Chicago, July 22–September 21, 1985
Photographers: Dan Battise, Ben Bearskin, Orlando Cabanban, Joe Kazumura, F. Peter Weil, Leroy Wesaw "of the Chicago American Indian Community"

Mexican Fine Arts Center Museum, Chicago
Tehuanas in Mexican Art, December 18, 1992–March 7, 1993

Mitchell Indian Museum at Kendall College, Evanston, IL
First Annual Art Exhibit and Sale, October 9–10, 1993
Organized by the American Indian Economic Development Association and the Native American Cultural Center of Chicago

Newberry Library, Chicago
Winter: A Time of Telling, January 14, 1995
Organized by the Native American Cultural Center Planning Committee of the American Indian Economic Development Association
Storytellers: James Yellowbank, Nick Hockings, John White, Joell Orona, Ester Orona; artistic directors: Julia Brownwolf, James Yellowbank

Harry S. Truman College, Chicago
Chicago Portraits, May 26–June 28, 1995
Organized in cooperation with the American Indian Economic Development Association

Newberry Library, Chicago
Winter: A Time of Telling, February 3, 1996
Organized by the Native American Cultural Center Planning Committee of the American Indian Economic Development Association
Storytellers: Dovie Thomason, Julia Brownwolf, Ed Edmo, Florence Dunham

American Indian Center, Chicago
50 Years of Powwow, grand opening January 1, 2003

JACQUELINE LOPEZ

Traveled to:
Chicago Historical Society, grand opening February 8, 2003
Spurlock Museum, Urbana, IL, January 27–June 26, 2004
State of Illinois Museum Gallery, Springfield, October 25, 2004–
February 13, 2005
Castle Gallery, New Rochelle, NY, September 10–November 22, 2006
Mashantucket Pequot Museum, Mashantucket, CT, June 17–
September 9, 2007
Comanche National Museum, Lawton, OK, September 14, 2007–
January 3, 2008
Mayborn Museum, Waco, TX, 2009
Museo Nacional de Etnografía y Folklore, La Paz, Bolivia, August 2011
Museo Nacional de Arqueología y Etnología de Guatemala, Guate-
mala City, 2011

State of Illinois Museum Gallery, Springfield
Elders Speak, October 25, 2004–February 13, 2005
Exhibited with *50 Years of Powwow*

Trickster Gallery, Schaumburg, IL
Native Women's Visions: Honoring Community through Art,
September 23–December 30, 2005
Presented by the Native American Women's Artist Guild

Trickster Gallery, Schaumburg, IL
Tribalistic Symphony, August 2006
Artists: Jessica Pamonicutt, Joe Yazzie, Ken Newton, Mike Marin, Joey
Yazzie, Robert Wapahi

Elgin Community College, Elgin, IL
Native Women Artists: Creating Contemporary Life Journals,
March 2–15, 2007
Artists: LeAnn Hascon (Navajo), Sharon Okee-Chee Skolnick
(Apache/Sioux), Nora Moore Lloyd (Ojibwe), Julia Brown Wolf
(Lakota), Frances Hagemann (Ojibwa/Metis)
Coordinated in partnership with the American Indian Center, Trick-
ster Gallery, and Jessica Pamonicutt (Menominee Indian Tribe of
Wisconsin) and Marcelyn M. Kropp (Osage/Kaw)

Cahokia Mounds Museum Society, Collinsville, IL
American Indian Photography Contest/Gallery Show, 2009

Foster Avenue underpass at Lake Shore Drive, Chicago
Indian Land Dancing, completed July 2009
Mural developed in partnership with Chicago's Native community
and the Chicago Public Art Group

Trickster Gallery, Schaumburg, IL
Out of Context, Two Women Exhibition, August 1–October 31, 2009

Artists: Sharon Okee-Chee Skolnick (Fort Sill Apache), Nora Moore Lloyd (Lac Courte Oreilles Ojibwe)

Trickster Gallery, Schaumburg, IL
Wall of Honor, November 2009–ongoing
Coordinated by Joe Yazzie, artist in residence, and Monica Boutwell

American Indian Center, Chicago
Spring Art Expo: *Collective Energy: Diverse Visions*, May 7–8, 2010
Artists: Frances Hagemann, John Dall, Spirited Daughters Group, Norma Robertson, Joe Yazzie, Sharon Okee-Chee Skolnick, Warren Perlstein, Erin Dall, Nora Moore Lloyd, Eli Suzukovich, Angie DeCorah, Chris Drew, Terry Gate Chair, Amelia Ortiz, Darlene Ortiz, Barbara St. Germaine, Robert Wapahi

Trickster Gallery, Schaumburg, IL
5th Anniversary Benefit for the Arts, March 6, 2011

Newberry Library, Chicago
Indians of the Midwest: An Archive of Endurance, November 2– December 31, 2011
Also presented as the digital exhibition *An Archive of Endurance*, digital.newberry.org/scalar/archive-endurance/introduction

Cliff Dwellers Social Club, Chicago
Prelude to Powwow, November 4, 2011
Performers: Robert Wapahi (Lakota), Ansel Deon (Lakota/Diné), Norma Robertson (Lakota), John Coon (Lakota/Menominee), Christine RedCloud (Ojibwe), Winfield WoundedEye (Ojibwe/Northern Cheyenne); MC: Gerry Lang (Meherren); blessing: G. B. Starr-Bresette (Lake Superior Chippewa); flute: William Bucholtz (Split Feather Clan); organizers: Nora Moore Lloyd, Joe Podlasek, Cyndee Fox-Starr
Presented by the Cliff Dwellers and the American Indian Center

OpenWall, Chicago
Contemporary American Indian Artists Continue a Traditional Story, 2012

American Indian Center, Chicago
Voices from Our Community: A Hopeful Future Built on Strong Traditions, 2012
Presented as part of Chicago Artist Month 2012: Art Block by Block

Trickster Gallery, Schaumburg, IL
Warriors in Our Midst, 2016

Illinois State Museum Chicago Gallery
Voices from Our Community: A Hopeful Future Built on Strong Traditions, November 2016

Artists: Frances Hagemann (Ojibwe/Metis), Nora Moore Lloyd (Ojibwe), Norma Robertson (Dakota), Josee Starr (Arikara/Omaha/Odawa), Robert Wapahi (Dakota)
Presented as part of Native American Heritage Month 2016, in partnership with the Chicago American Indian Community

The Art Center Highland Park, IL
Contemporary Native American Art, 2018

American Indian Center, Chicago
Urban Sovereignty at the Center: American Indian Center Retrospective Part One, 2018

American Indian Center, Chicago
[The] Native Art Seen, April 27, 2018

4000N (formerly the Northwest Portage Park Walking Museum), Chicago
Established August 2018
Artist: Santiago X (Coushatta Tribe of Louisiana [Koasati] and Indigenous CHamoru from the Island of Guam [Hacha'Maori])
Created in partnership between the Chicago Public Art Group, American Indian Center, and Portage Park Neighborhood Association

American Indian Center, Chicago
Roots of Resilience: Native Youth Art Exhibit, August 31–October 12, 2018

American Indian Center, Chicago
Standing Rock: Photographs of an Indigenous Movement, October 17–November 9, 2018

American Indian Center, Chicago
Modern TRADITIONS, March 8–June 28, 2019
Artists: Melissa Melero-Moose (Northern Paiute), Andrea Carlson (Ojibwe), Silvester Hustito (Zuni), Thomas "Breeze" Marcus (Tohono O'odham and Akimel O'odham, Ponca, Otoe)

American Indian Center, Chicago
Reclaim: Indigenizing Colonized Spaces, July 17–September 23, 2019

American Indian Center, Chicago
Visions of Home: Celebrating the Art of Leonard Peltier, November 15, 2019–January 30, 2020

Center for Native Futures, Chicago
Grand opening exhibition, September 17, 2023

"American Indian Urban Relocation." National Archives and Records Administration. Last reviewed October 4, 2024. Web.

Anthony Rayson Zine Collection. DePaul Special Collections and Archives, Chicago.

An Archive of Endurance. Newberry Library, Chicago. Digital exhibition.

Bureau of Indian Affairs Relocation Materials. Edward E. Ayer Collection. Newberry Library, Chicago.

Chicago American Indian Oral History Pilot Project. *Native Voices in the City, 1982–1985*. Edward E. Ayer Collection. Newberry Library, Chicago.

Chicago Field Office Photographs. Edward E. Ayer Collection. Newberry Library, Chicago.

Penney, David W., and Gerald McMaster. *Before and After the Horizon: Anishinaabe Artists of the Great Lakes*. Washington, DC: Smithsonian Books, 2013.

Ramirez, Reyna K. *Native Hubs: Culture, Community, and Belonging in Silicon Valley and Beyond*. Durham, NC: Duke University Press, 2007.

Lloyd, Nora, Warren Perlstein, Joseph Podlasek, and David Spencer. *Chicago's 50 Years of Powwows*. In collaboration with Jane Stevens. Charleston, SC: Arcadia, 2004.

Townsend, Richard F., Robert V. Sharp, and Alan Bailey Garrick. *Hero, Hawk, and Open Hand: American Indian Art of the Ancient Midwest and South*. New Haven, CT: Yale University Press, 2004.

Two-Rivers, E. Donald. *Powwows, Fat Cats, and Other Indian Tales*. Lawrence, KS: Mammoth Publications, 2003.

Virgil Vogel Papers. Edward E. Ayer Collection. Newberry Library, Chicago.

1   Terry Straus and Grant P. Arndt, eds., *Native Chicago*, 2nd ed. (Chicago: Albatross Press, 2002), 370. Pam Silas was known as Pam Alfonso in this period.

2   For a detailed account of the federal government's relocation and termination programs, see Donald Lee Fixico, *Termination and Relocation: Federal Indian Policy, 1945–1960* (Albuquerque: University of New Mexico Press, 1992).

3   For a detailed discussion on the founding of the AIC, see Grant Arndt, "'Contrary to Our Way of Thinking': The Struggle for an American Indian Center in Chicago, 1946–1953," *American Indian Culture and Research Journal* 22, no. 4 (January 1, 1998): 117–34, web.

4   Dave Spencer, interview by the author, April 26, 2024.

5   Spencer, interview.

6   Loniel Poco, "Interview with Loniel Poco, Director of the Chicago Indian Artists Guild, Chicago, Illinois," by Roberta Fiske-Rusciano and R. Hajnal, Chicago Ethnic Arts Project Collection, Library of Congress, May 19, 1977, audio, web.

7   Poco, "Interview with Loniel Poco."

8   Sharon Skolnick, "Interview with Sharon Skolnick, Artist and Coordinator of the Foster Care Program at the American Indian Health Service, Chicago, Illinois," by Roberta Fiske-Rusciano and R. Hajnal, Chicago Ethnic Arts Project Collection, Library of Congress, May 19, 1977, audio, web.

9   Poco, "Interview with Loniel Poco."

10 Poco, "Interview with Loniel Poco."

11 Skolnick, "Interview with Sharon Skolnick." While this goal was never achieved by the guild as a group, Sharon Skolnick went on to open Wild Horse Gallery in the 1980s, and it served as a gallery for Native artists in Chicago for a decade.

12 Private collection of Nora Moore Lloyd.

13 "Executive Summary: Why This Center Should Be Established," 1990–96, Native American Educational Services, American Indian Economic Development Association Records, box 6, folder 1, Special Collections Research Center, University of Chicago Library.

14 "Annual First Nations Native American Film/Video Festival of Chicago," flyers, 1992–94, Native American Educational Services, American Indian Economic Development Association Records, box 6, folders 3–5, Special Collections Research Center, University of Chicago Library. See also the film festival's website, fnfvf.org.

15 Connie Lauerman, "'What Do They Have to Prove?' Native American Artists Grapple with Questions of Culture, Identity and Seeing beyond Stereotypes," *Chicago Tribune*, December 24, 1995.

16 Kara Silva, "Gallery Celebrates 5th Anniversary," *Chicago Tribune*, March 11, 2010.

17 Dan Simmons, "Remembering Name, Tribe, Serial Number: Veterans Wall Honors American Indians' Military Service," *Chicago Tribune*, November 29, 2009.

18 Simmons, "Remembering Name, Tribe, Serial Number."

19 Lead artists: Todd Osborne, Tracy Van Duinen, Cynthia Weiss; assistant artists: Andy Bellomo, Kamila Krusiva, Max Sansing; apprentice artists: Barahh Alaribe, Rhokym Alleyne, Ijeoma Arinze, Oneshia Collier, Kalvin Collins, Ramon Cruel, Dushawn Darling, Ikeyla Glover, Krystle Grayer, Luke Heikkler, Kevin Herron, Crystal Jackson, Zach Julian, Jade Lomax, Briana McCorkle, Samantha McCorkle, Lashawnda McCracken, Malik McCray, Dekiar McGee, Ziadelle McKeose, Alaysia Nelson, Ayana Peterson, Stephanie Posey, Darren Richardson, Kianna Richardson, Michael Schneider, Charie Toney, Ashley Weaver, Crystal Willis, Liah White, Lisa White; steering committee: Jolene Aleck, Richard Archambeau, Ruth Briccaman, Francis Hagemann, John Joe, Gerry Lang, Pascha Nihenhausen, Chris Pappan, Christine Redcloud, Sharon Skolnick, Cindy Starr, Doreen Weiss, Ernest Whiteman III, Debra Yepa-Pappan, J. Hae Yepa-Pappan.

20 The concept for the *Indian Land Dancing* bricolage mural is loosely based on the poem "Indian Land Dancing," by E. Donald "Eddie" Two-Rivers (Ojibwe), which was painted into the mural. For more on Eddie Two-Rivers, see Anne Terry Straus's chapter in this volume [pp. 69–70].

21 Clare Lane, "Vast Mural Will Depict Chicago's Indian Roots," *Chicago Tribune*, June 5, 2009, web.

22 Lane, "Vast Mural Will Depict Chicago's Indian Roots."

23 Nora Moore Lloyd, interview by the author, February 2, 2024.

24 Chadd Scott, "Center for Native Futures Gallery Opening in Chicago," *Forbes*, September 14, 2023, web.

25 "Chicago's Only Native Artist–Led Fine Art Gallery Opens in the Loop," Chicago Loop Alliance, September 2023, web.

Kathleen Bickford Berzock, Janet
Dees, and Marisa Cruz Branco
(Isleta Pueblo/Portuguese)

Plates

Woven Being: Art for Zhegagoynak/ Chicagoland at The Block

The curatorial approach to *Woven Being: Art for Zhegagoynak/ Chicagoland* was guided by the vision and preferences of four collaborating artists: Andrea Carlson (Grand Portage Ojibwe/European descent, born 1979), Kelly Church (Match-E-Be-Nash-She-Wish Band of Pottawatomi/Ottawa, born 1967), Nora Moore Lloyd (Lac Courte Oreilles Band of Lake Superior Ojibwe, born 1947), and Jason Wesaw (Pokagon Band of Potawatomi, born 1974). They conveyed their desire for an exhibition process in which they maintained control of the contextualization of their work. Supported by the project's curatorial team, they developed constellations that brought their own work into resonance with works by other artists, centering their perspectives without centering themselves. Over time, these individual constellations became interwoven, revealing complex entanglements of aesthetic, material, familial, communal, and thematic connections.

The oldest work in *Woven Being* is the painting *Deer and the Moon*, made by Woodrow Wilson "Woody" Crumbo in 1945. The installation also includes a number of works created especially for the exhibition. This selection of images is organized to capture the experience of moving through the installation, allowing readers to reflect on the rapport that developed among the works.

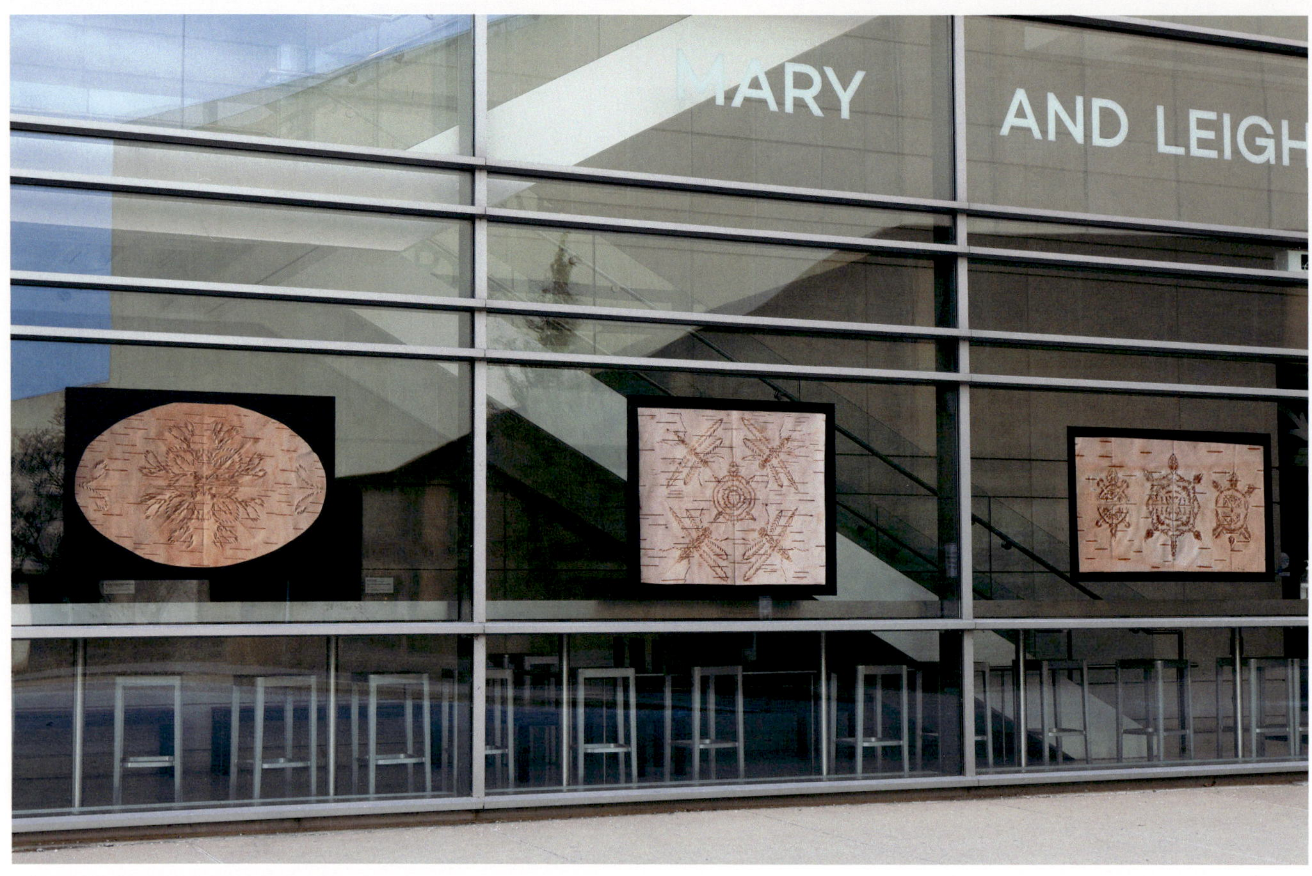

Plate 1 Exterior of The Block with reproductions of birch bark bitings
Enlarged digital reproductions of three birch bark bitings, from left: Denise Lajimodiere (Turtle Mountain Band of Ojibwe, born 1951), *Flower*, 2024; Kelly Church (Match-E-Be-Nash-She-Wish Band of Pottawatomi/Ottawa, born 1967), *Dragonflies and Turtle*, 2024; Wanesia Misquadace (Minnesota Lake Superior Chippewa Tribe, Fond du Lac Band, born 1971), *Three Turtles*, 2024. Collection of Kelly Church.

We wanted *Woven Being* to fully occupy The Block Museum of Art. As part of this effort, we reproduced enlargements of three birch bark bitings on the building's windows, so that the exhibition would face outward as well as inward. The original bitings, each no more than six inches square, are on view as part of the exhibition. The enlargements make visible the incredible delicacy of this unique art form.

On entering the museum, visitors are greeted by the sounds of black ash pounding and *manoomin* (wild rice) harvesting, which carry up the stairs to the second-floor landing. As noted in the accompanying label, "Sound is integral to the materials that shape art and culture, and the sounds you hear now are ones of artistic and cultural labor. These traditions produce food, materials for weaving baskets, and the sounds that Anishinaabe people have been making for generations and continue to make today."

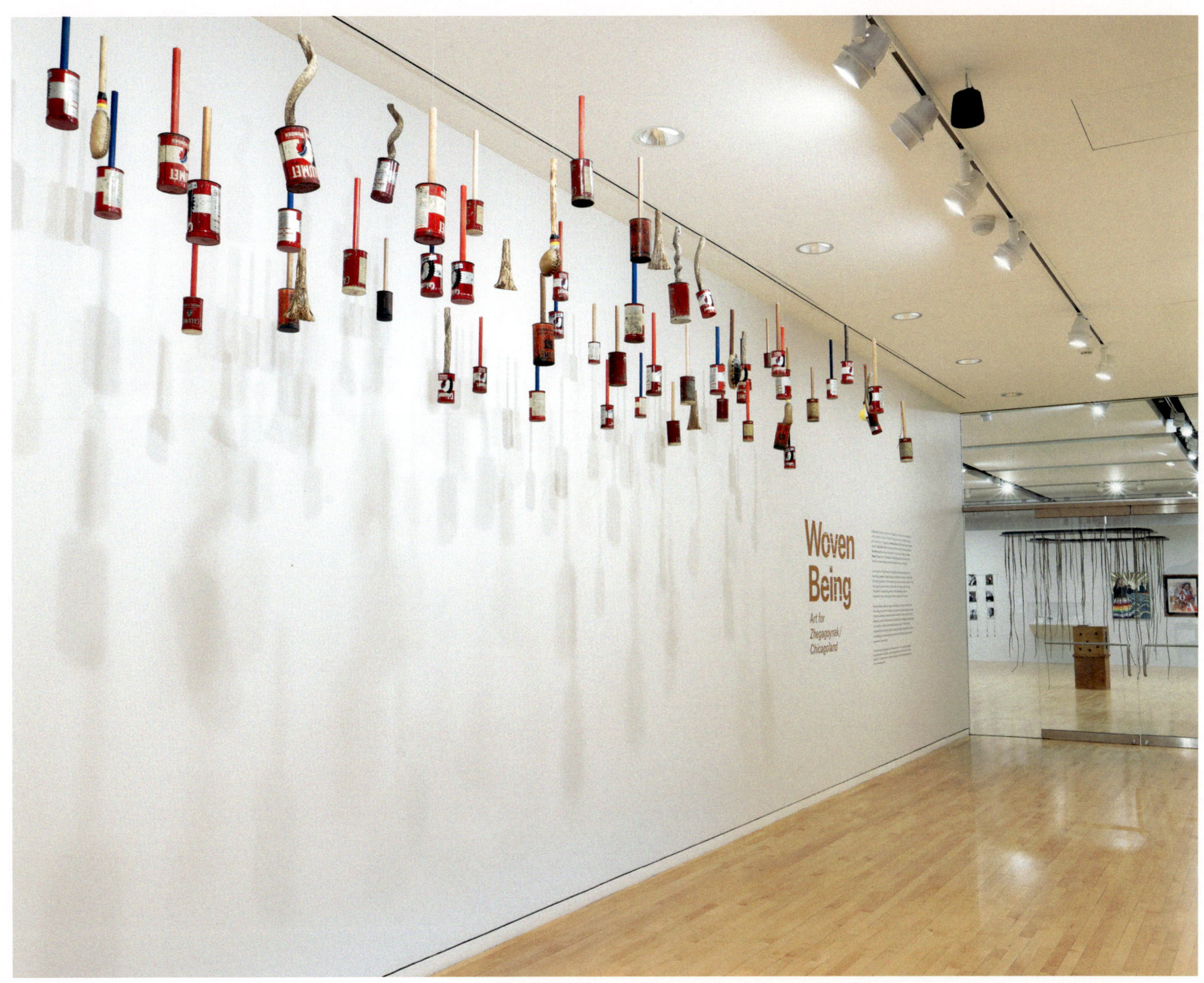

Plate 2 *Breath of Life* and exhibition title wall
Jason Wesaw (Pokagon Band of Potawatomi, born 1974), *Breath of Life . . . The First Song*, 2023; sound component, 2024, vintage Calumet cans, elm bark, elk hide, turtle shell, poplar and oak dowels, harvested wood (cherry, Osage orange, sassafras, and twisted), copper BBs, pebbles, paint, and sound, 132 × 192 × 48 inches, collection of the artist.

Jason Wesaw's *Breath of Life . . . The First Song* features shakers made from Calumet Baking Powder containers. The Chicago-based Calumet Baking Powder Company became known for the stereotyped logo of a man wearing a feathered headdress. Calumet is also the name of an Indiana township that is located on ancestral lands of the Potawatomi and Myaamia peoples, including the artist's family. *Breath of Life* was originally exhibited at the South Bend Museum of Art in the 2023 exhibition *On the Banks, Above by Jason Wesaw*. For *Woven Being*, Jason added a sound component, an original song with shakers and voice that he composed and recorded. The song plays softly on a directional speaker beside the work. In the accompanying label, Jason writes, "The sound of shakers reminds us that humans have a relationship to all other beings who also reside on this beautiful planet." This work welcomes visitors entering the upstairs galleries; its placement was conceived as an important transitional moment.

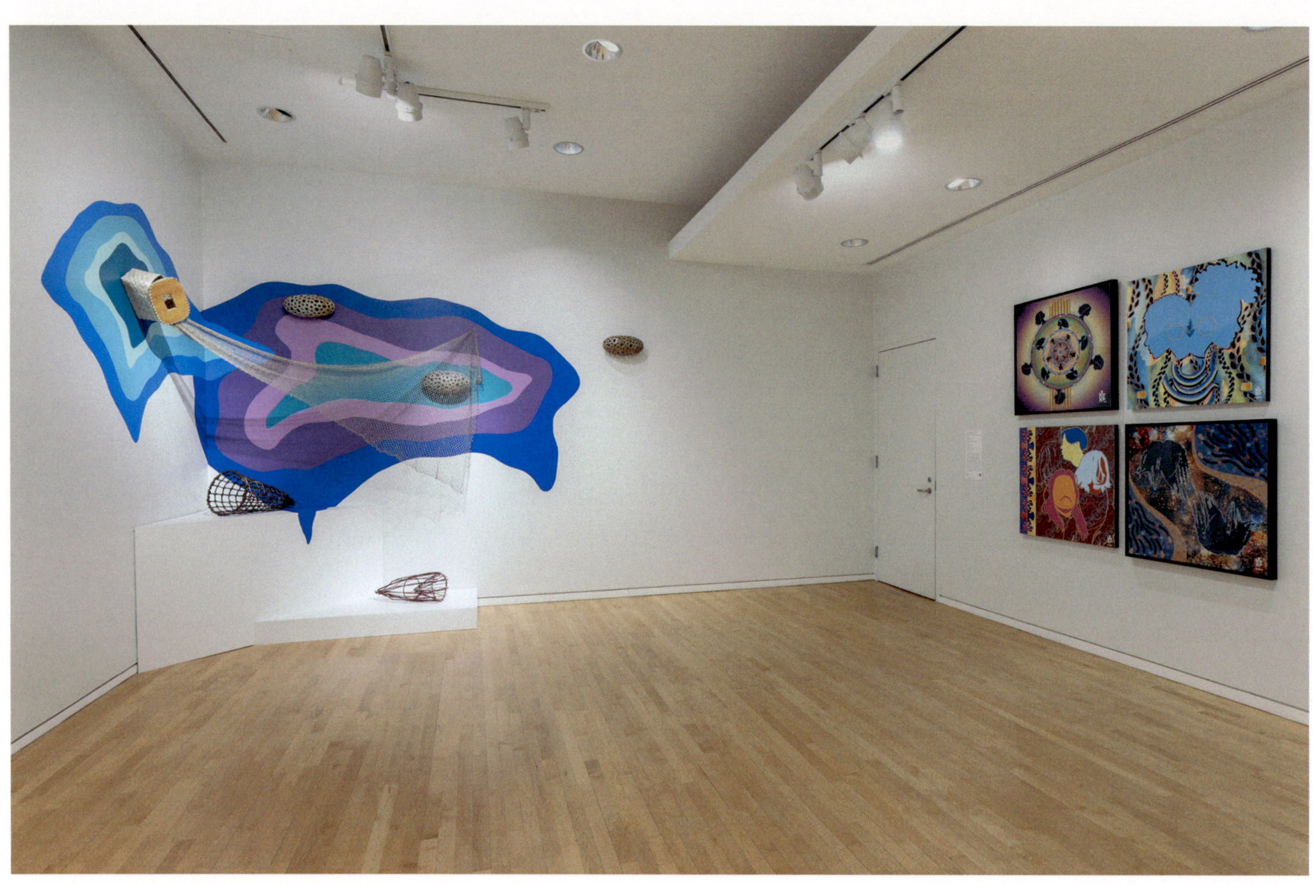

Plate 3 *Convergence and Continuity* and "Hair Stories"
From left: Kelly Church (Match-E-Be-Nash-She-Wish Band
of Pottawatomi/Ottawa, born 1967) and Courtney M. Leonard
(Shinnecock, born 1980), *Convergence and Continuity*, 2024,
acrylic, fired earthenware and stoneware, basswood, twine, black
ash, red willow, sweetgrass, and birch bark, approx. 114 × 132 ×
84 inches, collection of the artists; Monica Rickert-Bolter (Prairie
Band Potawatomi/Black, born 1986), *Mshike Kwe*, *The Big Chop*,
Perēhē: Black Girl Nebula, and *Zhenagwze'a: The Rocker*, from
the series "Hair Stories," 2021–24, digital paintings on aluminum,
31½ × 31½ inches, 30 × 30 inches, 31½ × 31½ inches, and 30 ×
30 inches, collection of the artist.

Collaborating artist Kelly Church partnered with Courtney M.
Leonard to create the installation *Convergence and Continuity*,
which speaks to their shared interest in the significance of water
and the need to protect it. This work merges Kelly's strong ties
to Lake Michigan with Courtney's ties to the Atlantic Ocean.
The painted shapes express the blending of freshwater and
saltwater and allude to the historic migration of Anishinaabe
people from the Eastern Seaboard to the Great Lakes region
over hundreds of years. The objects reference aquatic life, fishing,
and other relationships and movements between land and water.

Kelly also expresses an affinity for the work of Chicago-based
artist Monica Rickert-Bolter, whose series "Hair Stories" explores
her evolving relationship with her hair and stories others have
entrusted to her. Drawing from experiences growing up in
Potawatomi and Black communities, Monica considers common
traditions, such as braiding, and shared histories of repression and
forced assimilation, from the involuntary cutting of hair in Native
boarding schools to the ongoing stigmatization and banning of
Black hairstyles in US schools. Within this context, "Hair Stories"
offers a hopeful perspective on the path to bodily autonomy.

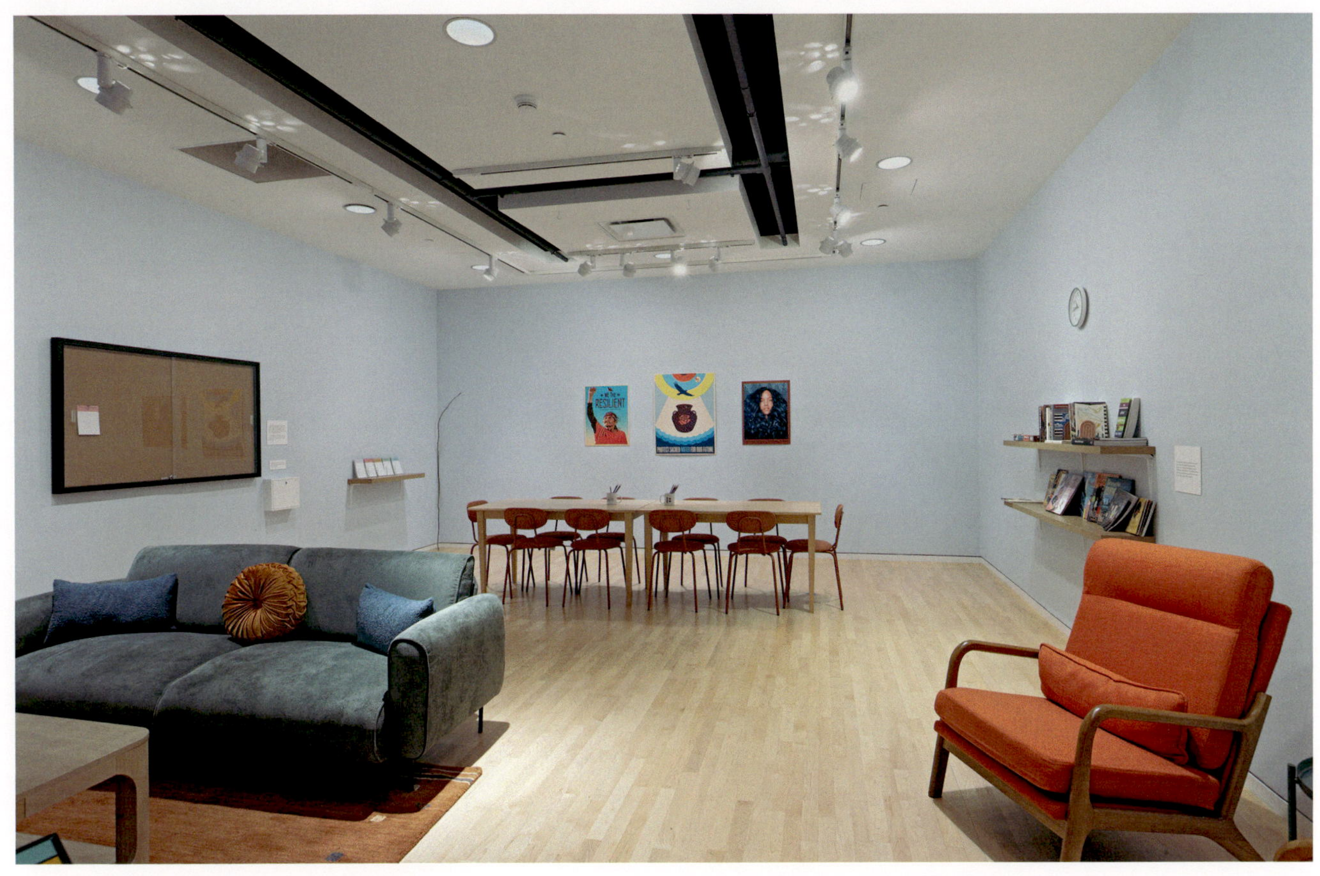

Plate 4 *Woven Being* Community Room

During the visioning sessions for *Woven Being*, making space for Indigenous community and connection emerged as one of the priorities of the exhibition. Though designed to center Indigenous community members, the Community Room is open to all, in the hope that conversation, reflection, laughter, and learning will flourish there. On the south wall (not pictured), a monitor plays an interview with the four collaborating artists concerning the themes of the exhibition. Some of the questions posed to the artists also appear as prompts on the Forum Wall to the left, inviting visitors to continue the conversation. Across from the Forum Wall, a reading nook is stocked with books by Indigenous authors that are important to the artists and project team, as well as texts that informed the creation of *Woven Being*. Offering comfortable furniture, games, puzzles, children's books, and more, the Community Room welcomes an intergenerational community for workshops, drop-in hours, and other events throughout the run of the exhibition.

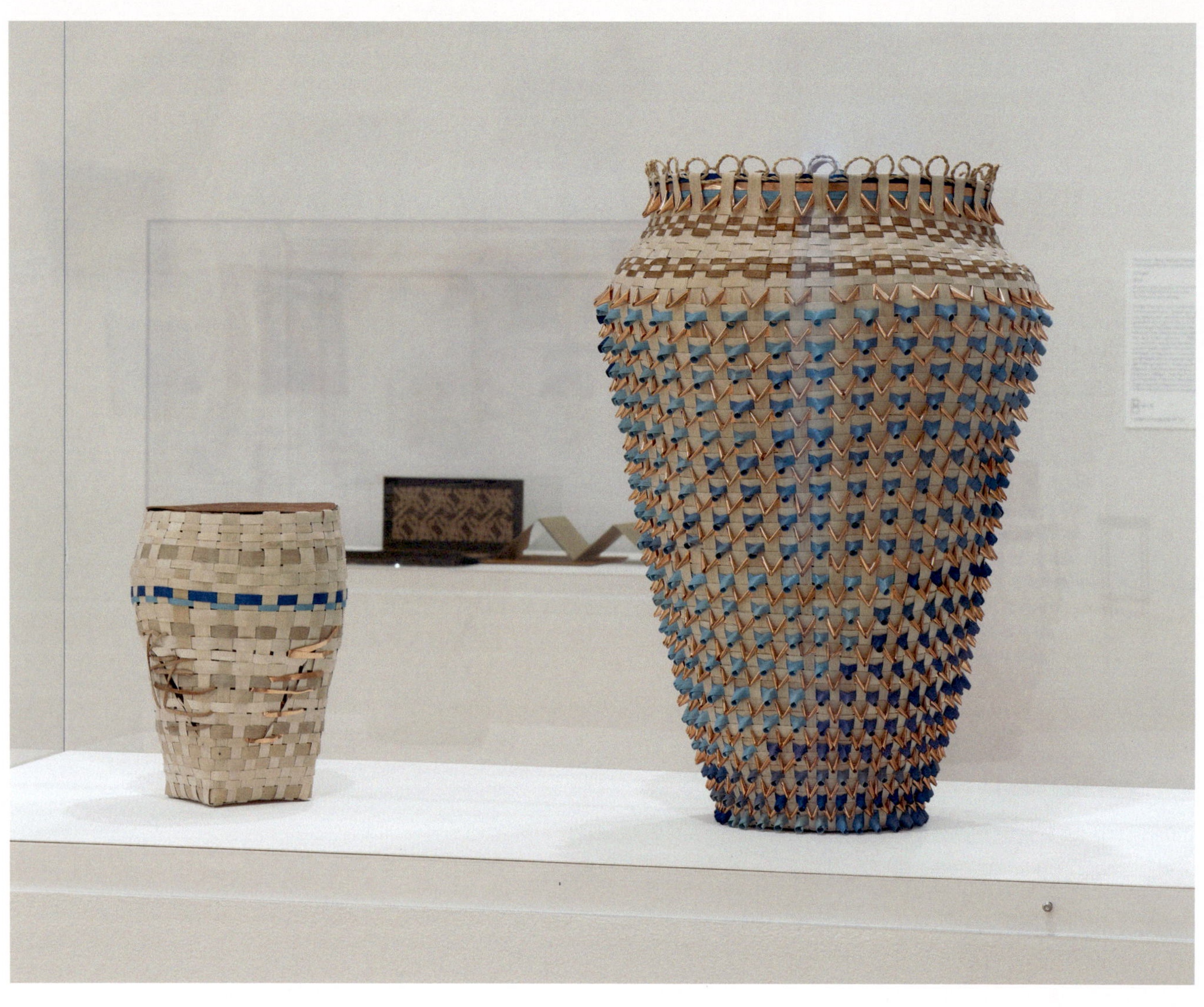

Plate 5 *Broken and Healing*
From left: Kelly Church (Match-E-Be-Nash-She-Wish Band of
Pottawatomi/Ottawa, born 1967), *Broken*, 2024, and *Healing*, 2024,
black ash, sweetgrass, basswood, white cedar bark, birch bark,
Rit dye, and copper, 10 × 8 × 8 inches and 23 × 14 × 14 inches,
collection of the artist.

Kelly Church made nine new works for *Woven Being*, including this
pair of baskets, which are placed at the main gallery's entrance.
Kelly conceived of the baskets in the face of a series of personal
losses, and she says that carrying forward her family's teachings
related to black ash weaving brought her comfort and a sense
of strength. The baskets also honor Indigenous strength and
resilience in the face of settler colonialism. Speaking of US federal
policies such as the forced removal of tribes from their lands,
boarding schools, and relocation, the artist says, "They have tried
to break us, and we have been broken in some aspects, but we are
healing in such big ways."

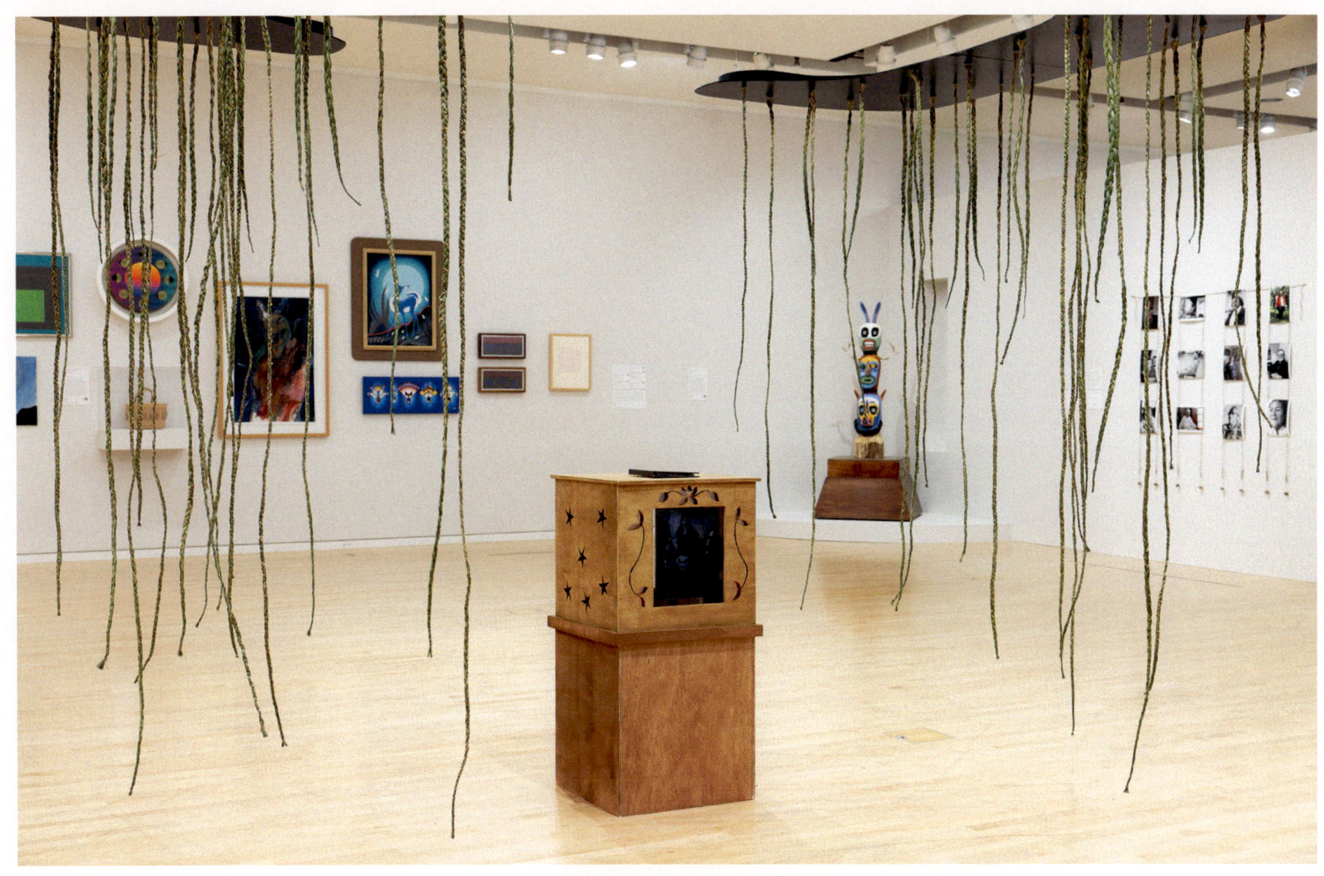

Plate 6 *Honoring Our Children*
Kelly Church (Match-E-Be-Nash-She-Wish Band of Pottawatomi/
Ottawa, born 1967), *Honoring Our Children: Never Forgotten*, 2024,
sweetgrass, copper, wood panel, photo transfer on plexiglass,
and laminated photo book, 102 × 96 × 144 inches, collection of
the artist.

For Kelly Church, braiding sweetgrass is about the strength that
comes from working together. Kelly calls on this unifying quality
of sweetgrass braiding in her installation *Honoring Our Children:
Never Forgotten*, which occupies the middle of the main gallery.
A podium stands in the center of two semicircles of sweetgrass
braids that hang from the ceiling. Adorned with copper wire
and beads, these braids of sweetgrass represent the strength of
Indigenous communities who survived America's repressive and at
times violent boarding school system; some braids have been cut
short, representing the children whose hair was cut at boarding
schools in order to sever their cultural ties. The work memorializes
the children lost to these institutions. Sheltered within the circle
of braids, a memory book sits on top of the podium. The smell
of sweetgrass suffuses the gallery, a testament to the survival
of Indigenous traditions, an expression of unity in the face of
suppression, and a comforting offering to visitors.

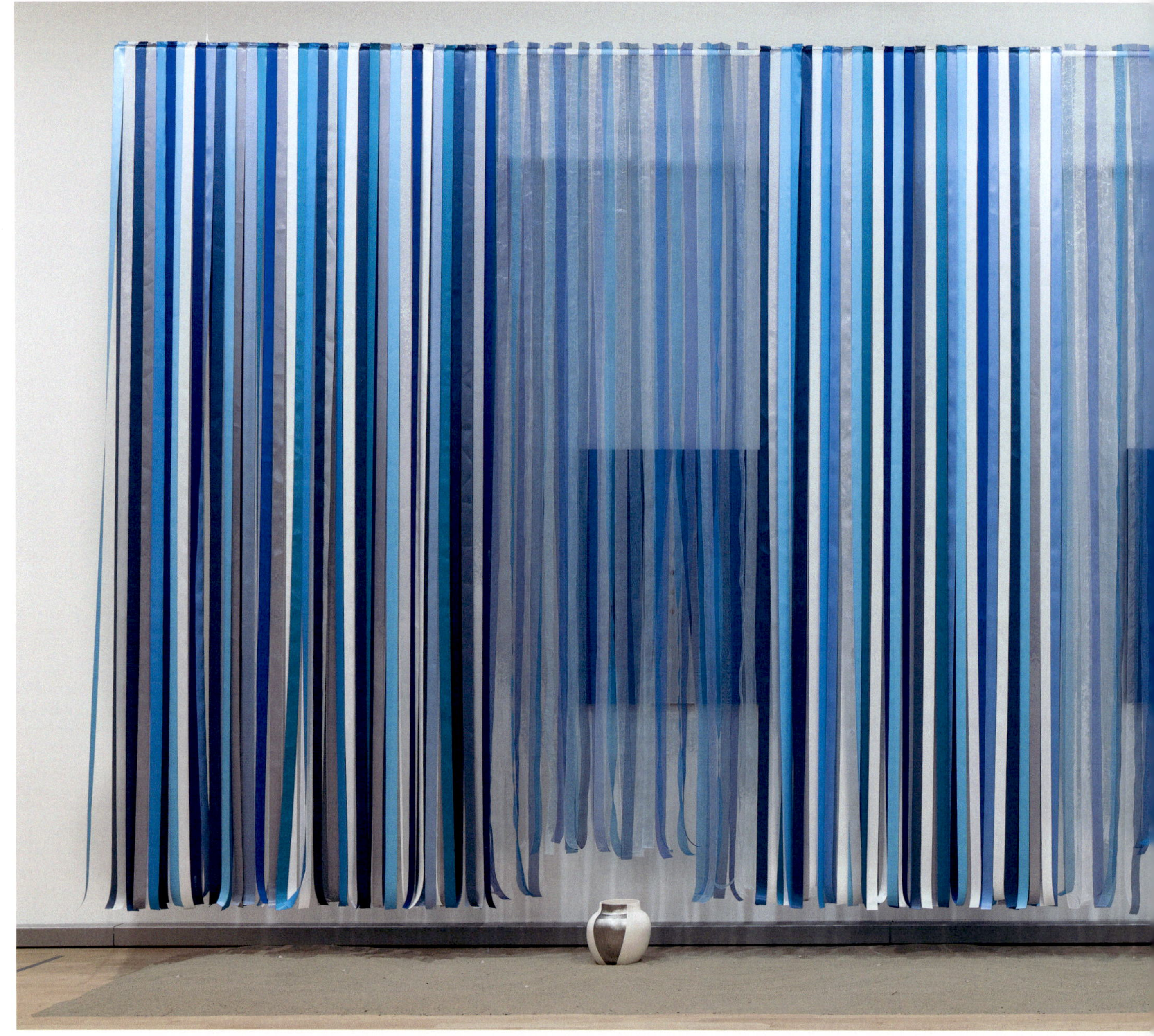

Plate 7 *Water Carries Memory*
Jason Wesaw (Pokagon Band of Potawatomi, born 1974), *Water Carries Memory*, 2024, satin and taffeta ribbon, hand-dyed canvas, acrylic, cowrie shells, ceramic, glaze, white gold luster, and sand from the shores of Lake Michigan, 132 × 312 × 48 inches, collection of the artist.

The Block is situated in close proximity to Lake Michigan, and while the lake can be seen from the museum's windowed facade, it is not visible from within the galleries. Jason Wesaw's installation *Water Carries Memory* extends more than twenty feet along the east wall of *Woven Being*'s large gallery, which faces the unseen lake. Satin and taffeta ribbons in shades of silver and blue form a dramatic veil, suggesting water and sky and gesturing toward the Anishinaabe use of ribbons to embellish clothing. At the base of the installation is a low dune formed with sand dug from the Clark Street Beach on the south side of Northwestern University's Evanston campus, which is in walking distance of the museum. This portion of the campus is built on landfill constructed in the 1960s using sand transported from the Indiana Dunes, land to which Jason has strong family and tribal ties. Chicagoland's landfills are unceded territory, as the 1833 Treaty of Chicago included only the land up to the lake. The work reminds us that the waters of Lake Michigan carry these memories and many others.

In his label for *Water Carries Memory*, Jason writes, "In spending a few moments with this installation of ribbon and sand, it's my intent that you may feel as if you were sitting on the lakeshore, mesmerized by the flow of the waves, coming to a calm, thoughtful awareness of your own place in society and the fragile, reciprocal relationships we have with the natural world."

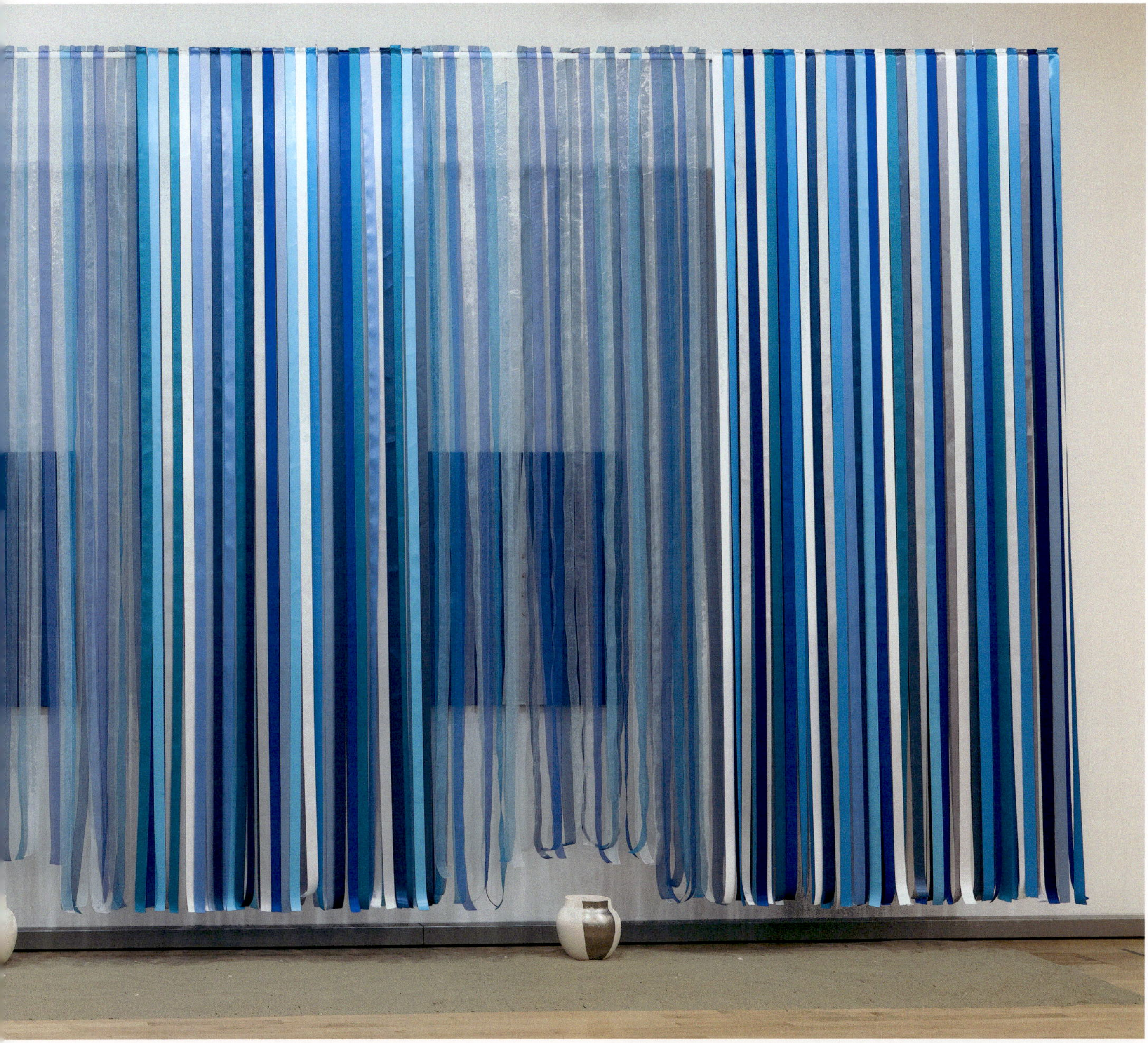

Plate 8 *Water Carries Memory* (detail)
Jason Wesaw (Pokagon Band of Potawatomi, born 1974), *Water Carries Memory* (detail), 2024.

The ribbon veil that dominates Jason Wesaw's *Water Carries Memory* alternates between satin and transparent taffeta, creating a scrim through which three textile panels can be glimpsed. Each symmetrical panel features a silver triangle at center, through which a line of cowrie shells descends. Below the panels, three ceramic vessels in the form of cooking jars, each decorated with a silvery metallic triangle, are set into a low sand dune that runs the length of the installation. Jason associates the shells with Anishinaabe origin and migration stories, while the jars point to the care and nurturing passed down through generations. Beyond the installation, visitors see Chris Pappan's large triptych, *Howageji Nizhuje Akipé (Where the Rivers Meet)*, through which ribbons of blue—the rivers referred to in the title—meander, creating a visual analogy between the two works.

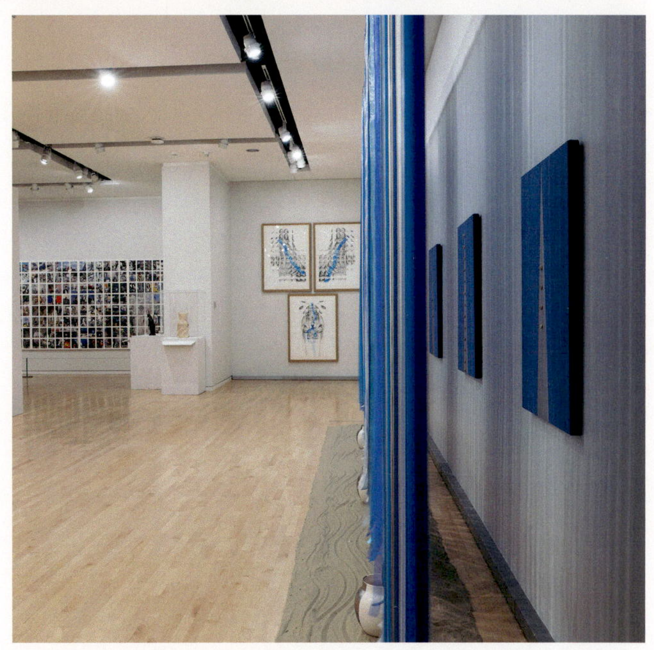

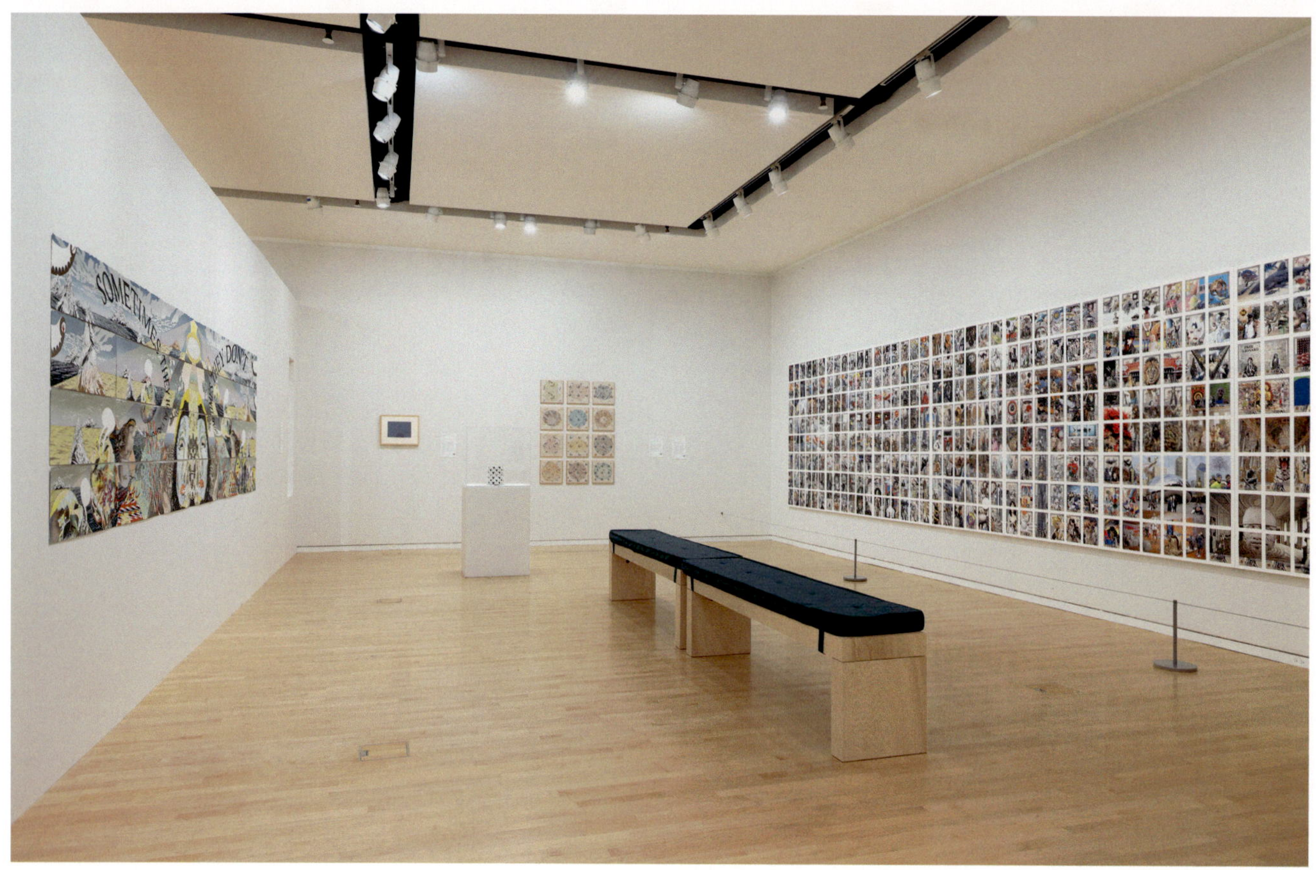

Plate 9 Artistic kinship and citation
From left: Andrea Carlson (Grand Portage Ojibwe/European descent, born 1979), *The Indifference of Fire*, 2023; George Morrison (Grand Portage Ojibwe, 1919–2000), *Untitled*, 1972; Kelly Church (Match-E-Be-Nash-She-Wish Band of Pottawatomi/Ottawa, born 1967), *Seventh Generation Black Ash Basket—Sustaining Traditions*, 2024; Debra Yepa-Pappan (Jemez Pueblo/Korean, born 1971), *Ancestors Speak (a visual repatriation)*, 2023; Frank Big Bear (White Earth Ojibwe, born 1953), *The Walker Collage, Multiverse #10*, 2016.

Artistic kinship and citation are currents that run through *Woven Being*, as evidenced in the works Andrea Carlson selected for her constellation. Andrea's *The Indifference of Fire* contains several references to artworks that have influenced her, including works by Kelly Church, whose *Seventh Generation Black Ash Basket* is seen in the case near the back of the gallery. On the far wall, George Morrison's untitled painting evokes the weaving and iterative processes fundamental to the work of artists like Kelly Church and Frank Big Bear, whose *Walker Collage, Multiverse #10*, much like *The Indifference of Fire*, is created from smaller parts joined together to form a unified composition. The monumental mixed-media work consists of 432 collages, each on an invitation card for an exhibition of work by Star Wallowing Bull (Ojibwe/Arapaho), Frank's son, and includes numerous personal, artistic, and cultural references.

Also on the far wall, Debra Yepa-Pappan's *Ancestors Speak* critiques the practice of displaying Pueblo pottery in isolated glass cases, in museum collections far from their ancestral homes. These ceramics were intended to pass on ancestral knowledge to future generations, but conventional collecting practices have silenced them. With this work, Debra helps these ancestors speak again, and compels viewers to listen.

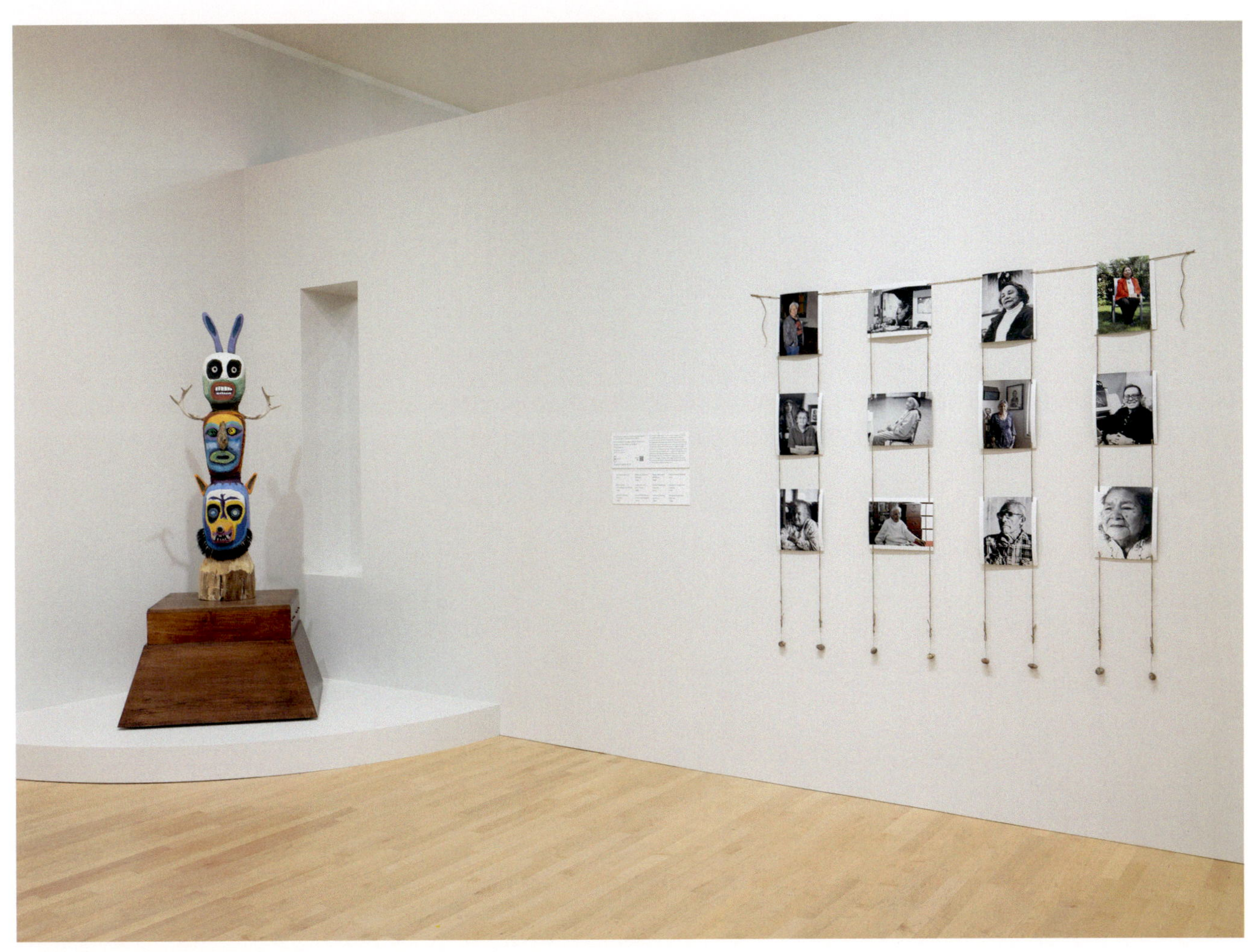

Plate 10 "Our Elders Look Back" and *Totem, Animal Spirits*
From left: Jim Denomie (Lac Courte Oreilles Band of Ojibwe,
1955–2022), *Totem, Animal Spirits*, 2021; Nora Moore Lloyd
(Lac Courte Oreilles Band of Lake Superior Ojibwe, born 1947),
"Chicago's Native American Community: Our Elders Look Back,"
1998–ongoing, photographs, twine, copper wire, and stones, 60 ×
66 × 1½ inches, collection of the artist.

The importance of honoring the influence of elders and ancestors
is a strong value shared by the collaborating artists in *Woven
Being*. Nora Moore Lloyd says, "A community's progress is based
on understanding its history . . . a reminder of how we arrived at
the present [from] those who brought us here." Her ongoing series
"Chicago's Native American Community: Our Elders Look Back"
features photographs of some of the elders who helped develop
Chicago's intertribal urban community, acknowledging how their
contributions connect to the present.

Jim Denomie was a prolific artist as well as a mentor to and
champion of numerous fellow artists. His work is an important
touchstone for collaborating artists Jason Wesaw and Andrea
Carlson. *Totem, Animal Spirits* is emblematic of Jim's view
of a spiritually connected natural world, a theme found
throughout his work.

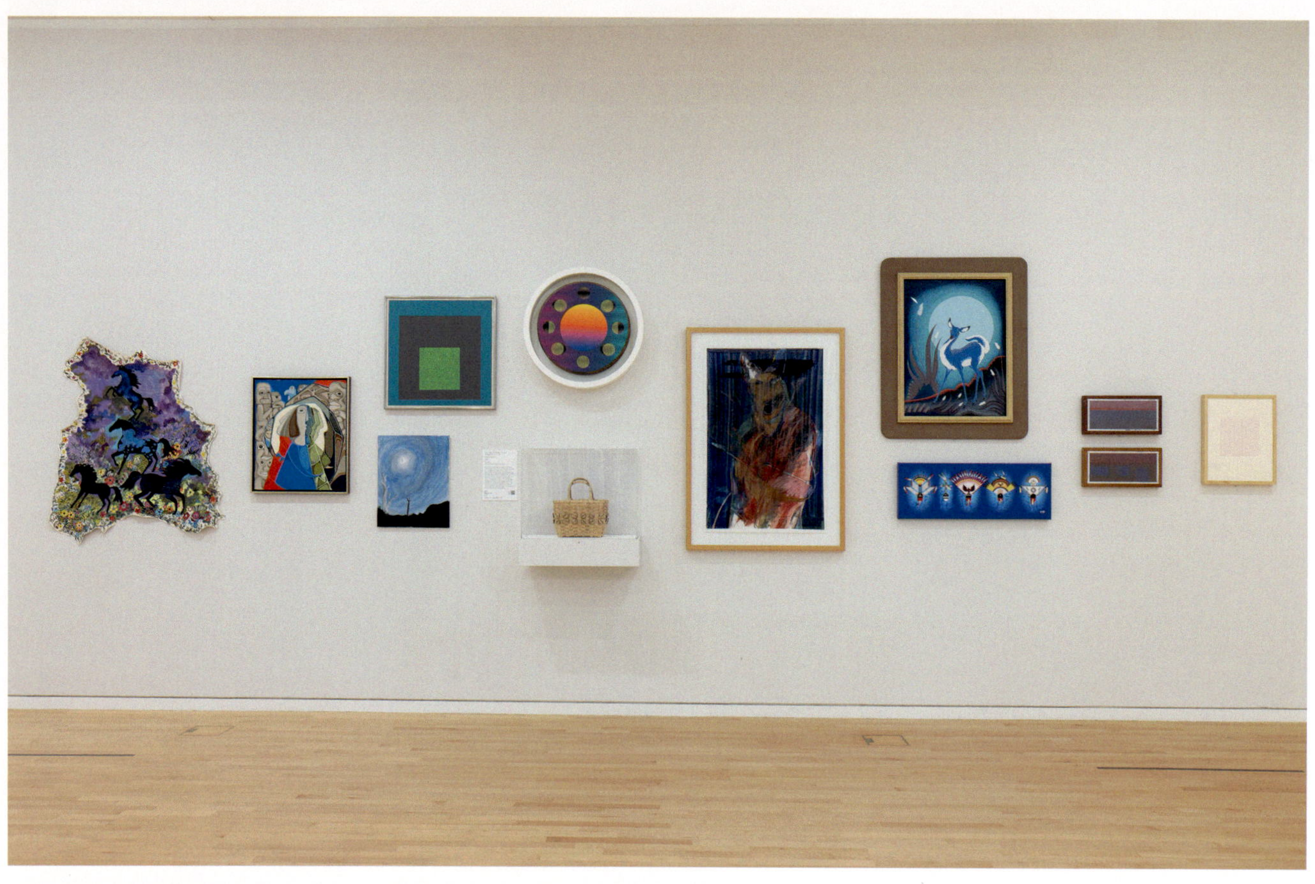

Plate 11 View of salon hang featuring diverse artists

From left and top: Sharon Skolnick (Fort Sill Apache/Lakota, born 1946), *Courage Is Like a Wild Horse*, 2002; Daphne Odjig (Odawa/Potawatomi, 1919–2016), *Entrance to the Lodge*, 1984; Josef Albers (American, born Germany, 1888–1976), *Homage to the Square: Green Myth*, 1954, oil on board in original polished metal frame, 24⅝ × 24⅝ inches, The David and Alfred Smart Museum of Art, The University of Chicago, gift of Jack Ringer, from the collection of Lotta Hess Ringer, Ph.B 1929; Mark LaRoque (White Earth Ojibwe, born 1948), *If*, 2022; Jeffrey Gibson (Mississippi Band of Choctaw Indians/Cherokee, born 1972), *A Time for Change*, 2020; John Pigeon (Pokagon Band of Potawatomi, born 1957), *Purse Basket*, 2005; Rick Bartow (Mad River Band of Wiyot Indians, 1946–2016), *Why He Sings*, 2004, pastel and aqueous medium on paper, 47¼ × 33¾ inches, Denver Art Museum, William and Dorothy Harmsen Collection, by exchange, 2005.61 © Rick Bartow; Woodrow Wilson Crumbo (Citizen Potawatomi, 1912–1989), *Deer and the Moon*, 1945; Joe Yazzie (Navajo, born 1942), *Apache Strong*, 2024; George Morrison (Grand Portage Ojibwe, 1919–2000), *Far Echo, Red Rock Variation: Lake Superior*, 1993; George Morrison (Grand Portage Ojibwe, 1919–2000), *Departure, Red Rock Variation: Lake Superior*, 1993, acrylic on canvas board, 8⁷⁄₁₆ × 16⅜ inches, Minneapolis Institute of Art, gift of Charlotte Karlen, 93.52.2; Agnes Martin (American, born Canada, 1912–2004), *Praise*, 1976, rubber stamp print, 15 × 19 × 1½ inches, Minneapolis Institute of Art, gift of funds from the Hersey Foundation, P.79.23.9.

The narratives that unfold within *Woven Being* are just some of the many that could be told about art in Zhegagoynak. Works selected by the four collaborating artists make visible the networks that inform their artistic perspectives. With works ranging in date from the 1940s to the present, the salon hang also honors elders who have paved the way for current and future generations of artists. The central position is occupied by a black ash basket, a foundational art form within Anishinaabe culture; this basket was made by John Pigeon, a relative of Kelly Church and her daughter, Cherish Parrish, who taught them basketmaking. Also pictured are works by Chicago-based elder artists Mark LaRoque, Sharon Skolnick, and Joe Yazzie. Works by George Morrison, Daphne Odjig, and Jeffrey Gibson utilize the visual language of abstraction, rooted in Indigenous aesthetics, to explore themes of land, spirituality, and music. The selection additionally includes works by Josef Albers and Agnes Martin, two of many white European and American artists of the twentieth century who drew inspiration from Indigenous abstraction. By presenting these artworks together, collaborating artist Jason Wesaw seeks to complicate mainstream Western art historical narratives that cast Indigenous art solely as source material for Euro-American abstraction.

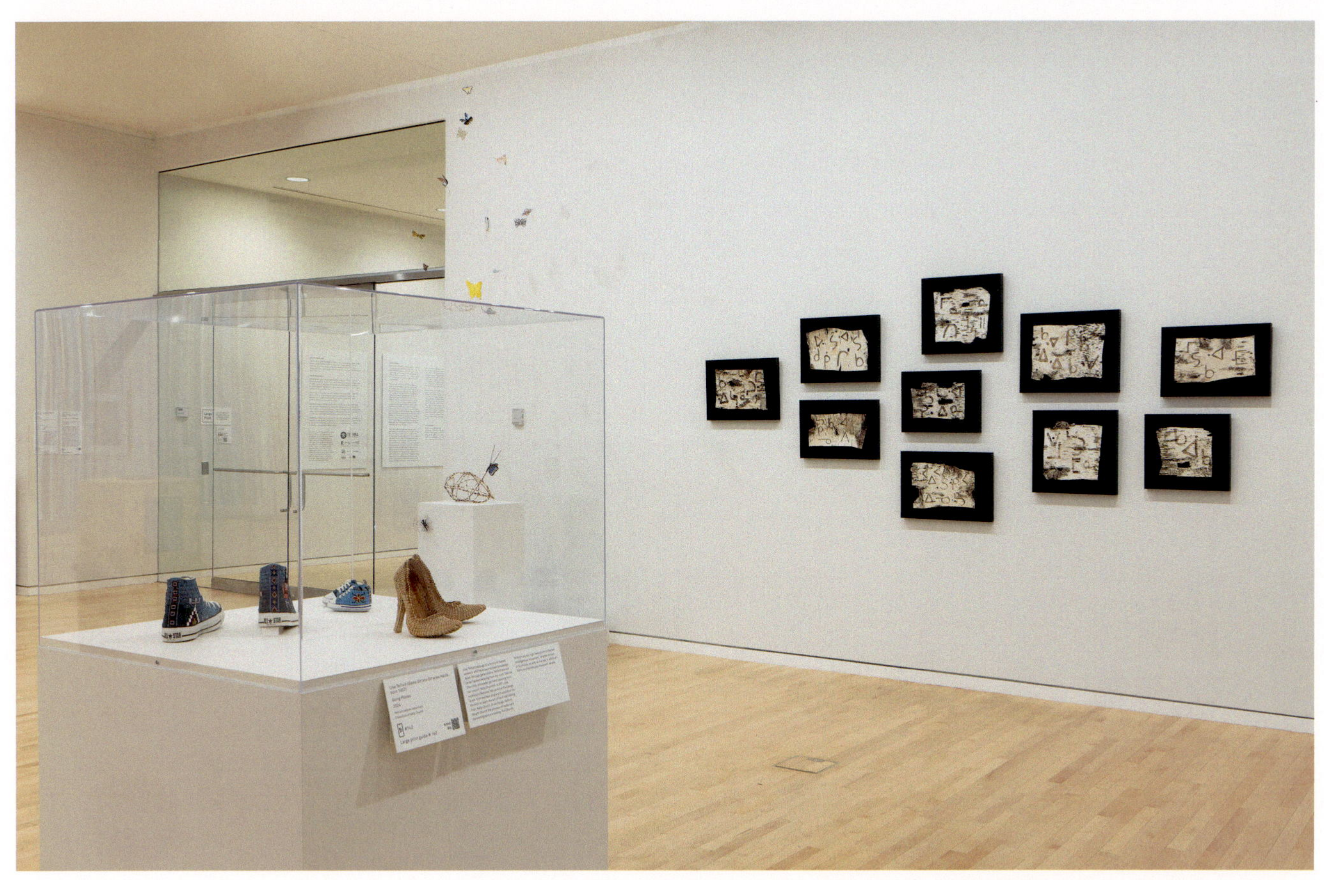

Plate 12 "Remembering Ancestors," *My Family's Tennis Shoes*, *Going Places*, **and** *Emergence*
In case: Teri Greeves (Kiowa, born 1970), *My Family's Tennis Shoes*, 2003; Lisa Telford (Haida, born 1957), *Going Places*, 2024; on wall: Nora Moore Lloyd (Lac Courte Oreilles Band of Lake Superior Ojibwe, born 1947), "Remembering Ancestors," 2024, acrylic on birch bark, 54 × 120 × 3½ inches; behind case: Kelly Church (Match-E-Be-Nash-She-Wish Band of Pottawatomi/Ottawa, born 1967), *Emergence*, 2024.

Kelly Church selected Teri Greeves's beaded tennis shoes and Lisa Telford's woven high heels for her *Woven Being* constellation. For Kelly, the shoes are emblematic of Indigenous movement, whether forced or by choice, as well as the way in which art forms and techniques move with people. Teri and Lisa expertly use long-practiced art forms to create artworks that address contemporary realities and experiences.

Nora Moore Lloyd's "Remembering Ancestors" series, installed on the wall beyond, also speaks to movement, in this case the generational impact of devastating US federal policies that separated Native children from their families. As a child, Nora's grandmother Anna was forcibly taken from her Ojibwe family, first made to attend a Presbyterian boarding school and later adopted by a white family in Warsaw, Indiana. In this series, Nora symbolically reunites her family, using Ojibwe syllabics to paint the names of relatives across six generations onto pieces of birch bark. The artist says, "What makes working with these particular birch bark pieces special is that they come from my home on the Lac Courte Oreilles reservation."

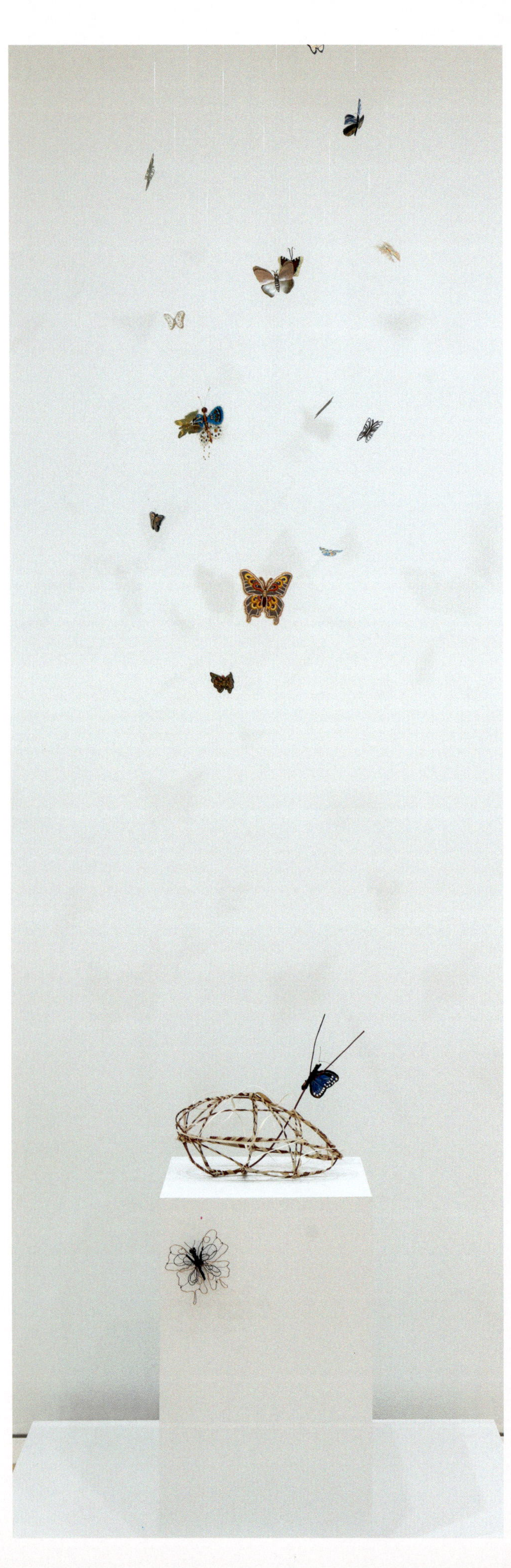

Plate 13 *Emergence*

Kelly Church (Match-E-Be-Nash-She-Wish Band of Pottawatomi/ Ottawa, born 1967), *Emergence*, 2024, beads, cloth, felt, velvet, leather, elk hide, watercolor, pen, oil pastels, acrylic, gloss medium, earthenware, glaze, resin, wire, silver, abalone, pink mussel shell, ribbon, thread, plastic, watercolor paper, canvas paper, titanium, buffalo horn, mother-of-pearl, orange sandstone, spruce roots, black ash, basswood, copper wire, and red willow, 150 × 30 × 30 inches, butterflies by Holly Alberts (Anishinaabe), Allen Aragon (Navajo), LeAna Asher (Anishinaabe), Keri Ataumbi (Kiowa), Karma Henry (Paiute), Karen Ann Hoffman (Oneida), Stephanie Jackson (Anishinaabe), Tom Jones (Ho-Chunk), Linda Lomahaftewa (Hopi), Kevin Pourier (Lakota), Pat Pruitt (Laguna Pueblo), and Joseph Sanchez (Apache), collection of Kelly Church.

The loose and open form of Kelly Church's *Emergence*, constructed out of materials harvested by the artist in Michigan's woods, evokes a cocoon. From it emerges a butterfly, woven by Kelly from black ash. The butterfly's two-tone coloring identifies it as one that manifests both female and male characteristics, honoring the important role of two-spirit individuals in Anishinaabe and many other Native American cultures. Thirteen unique butterflies float above the cocoon, and one rests on the pedestal beneath it. These were made by twelve Indigenous artists from across the country whom Kelly invited to contribute to the work, representing her extended community of makers. Kelly has built relationships with many of these artists through her participation in annual events such as the Eiteljorg Museum Indian Market and Festival, Santa Fe Indian Market, and Smithsonian Folklife Festival.

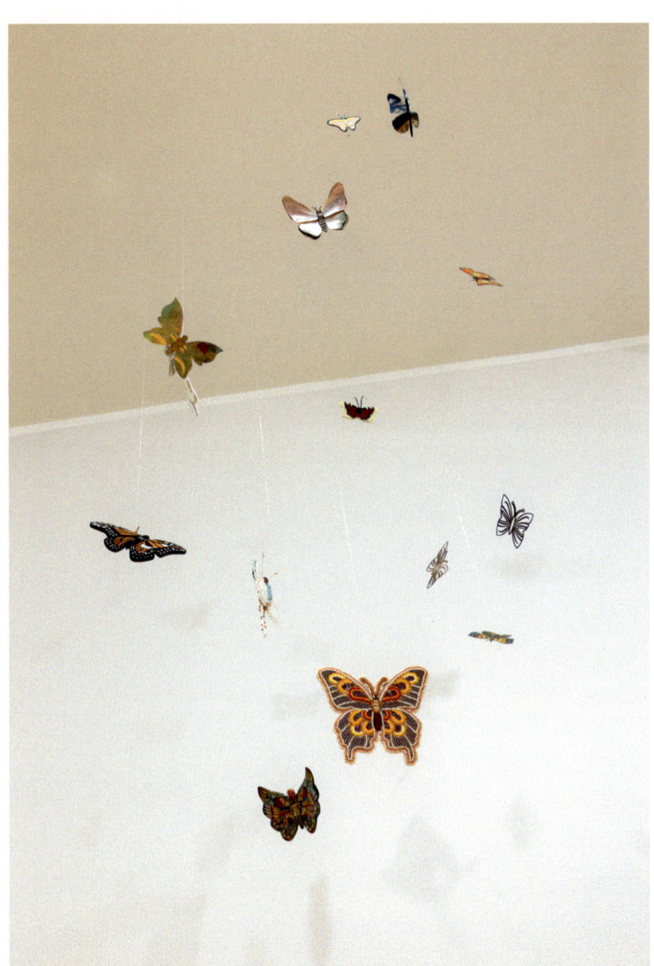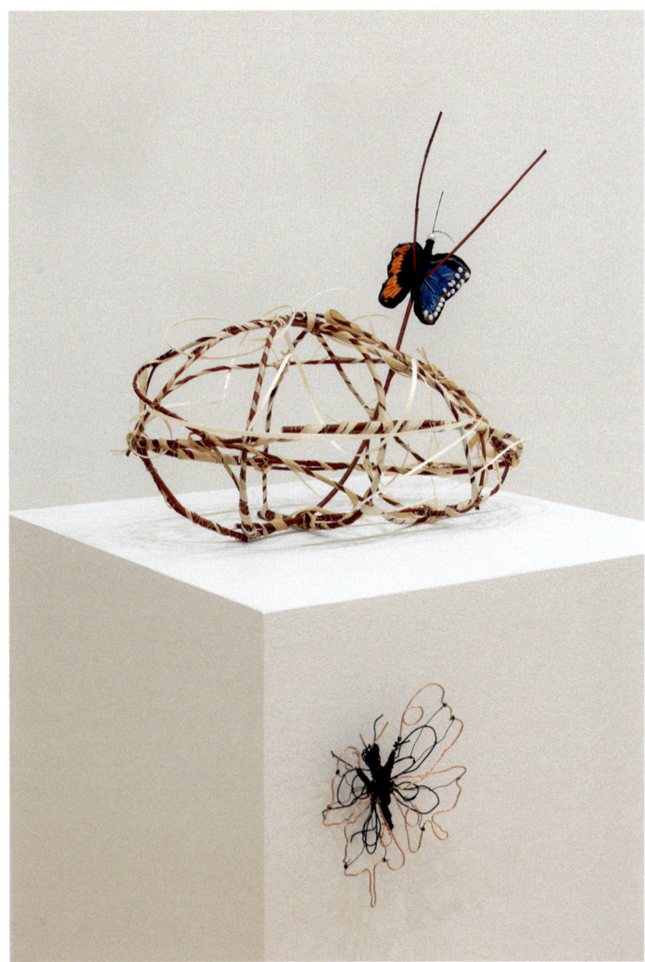

Plates 14 and 15 *Emergence* **(details)**
Kelly Church (Match-E-Be-Nash-She-Wish Band of Pottawatomi/
Ottawa, born 1967), *Emergence* (detail), 2024.

The butterflies, each unique, that populate Kelly Church's
Emergence represent the diverse techniques and styles of
twelve artists. Visible in this photograph, the wire butterfly on
the pedestal was made by LeAna Asher (Anishinaabe). Above, a
large butterfly with yellow, red, and brown-toned beads celebrates
traditional Anishinaabe beadwork; this was made by Holly Alberts
(Anishinaabe). Jeweler and ceramic artist Allen Aragon (Navajo)
contributed a painted ceramic butterfly with detailed Pueblo
and Navajo patterns. The monarch butterfly was made by Kevin
Pourier (Lakota) using buffalo horn with inlaid minerals, while the
butterfly above that was painted by Linda Lomahaftewa (Hopi).
The butterfly with iridescent wings was made by metalworker
and jeweler Keri Ataumbi (Kiowa) from abalone and pink
mussel shell set in silver, and Pat Pruitt (Laguna Pueblo) made
the metal openwork butterflies. The painted butterfly at top,
featuring a landscape of clouds and ground, was made by Karma
Henry (Paiute).

Works Cited

Adams, David W. *Education for Extinction: American Indians and the Boarding School Experience, 1875-1928*. Lawrence: University Press of Kansas, 1995.

Arndt, Grant. "'Contrary to Our Way of Thinking': The Struggle for an American Indian Center in Chicago, 1946-1953." *American Indian Culture and Research Journal* 22, no. 4 (January 1, 1998): 117-34. Web.

Arndt, Grant P. "Relocation's Imagined Landscape and the Rise of Chicago's Native American Community." In *Native Chicago*, edited by Terry Straus and Grant P. Arndt. Chicago: McNaughton & Gunn, 1998.

Bark, Lindsey. "Boney Creates Variant Cover for Marvel Voices: Heritage." *Cherokee Phoenix*, November 6, 2021. Web.

Brooks, Lisa. "The Primacy of the Present, the Primacy of Place: Navigating the Spiral of History in the Digital World." *PMLA* 127, no. 2 (2012): 308-16.

"Chicago's Only Native Artist-Led Fine Art Gallery Opens in the Loop." Chicago Loop Alliance, September 2023. Web.

Cocker, Jordan Poorman. *"Daum Yì:dop* (Touching the Earth): Researching Gilcrease Museum's Indigenous Paintings." Gilcrease Museum, June 14, 2022. Web.

Dawe, Amber. "Art Gallery's Sights Born in Sound: American Indian Show Has Its Roots in Music." *Chicago Tribune*, August 3, 2006.

Dees, Janet. "Home Is Where the Heart Is." In *C. Maxx Stevens: House of Memory*. New York: Smithsonian National Museum of the American Indian, 2012. Exhibition brochure.

Dees, Janet, and Ryan Rice. "A Questionnaire on Decolonization: 35 Responses." *October* 174 (Fall 2020): 31-38.

Dees, Janet, Irene Hofmann, Candice Hopkins, and Lucía Sanromán, eds. *Unsettled Landscapes*. Santa Fe: SITE Santa Fe, 2014.

Duarte, Marisa Elena. *Network Sovereignty: Building the Internet across Indian Country*. Seattle: University of Washington Press, 2017.

Fixico, Donald L. "The Federal Relocation Program of the 1950s and the Urbanization of Indian Identity." In *Removing Peoples: Forced Removal in the Modern World*, edited by Richard Bessel and Claudia B. Haake. Oxford: Oxford University Press, 2009. Web.

Gates, Paul W. "Indian Allotments Preceding the Dawes Act." In *The Frontier Challenge: Responses to the Trans-Mississippi West*, edited by John G. Clark. Lawrence: University Press of Kansas, 2021.

Hail, Barbara A., ed. *Gifts of Pride and Love: Kiowa and Comanche Cradles*. Norman: University of Oklahoma Press, 2001.

Hall, Lisa Kahaleole. "Navigating Our Own 'Sea of Islands': Remapping a Theoretical Space for Hawaiian Women and Indigenous Feminism." *Wicazo Sa Review* 24, no. 2 (2009): 15-38.

Hovens, Pieter, and Mette van der Hooft, eds. *Indian Detours: Tourism in Native North America*. Havertown, PA: Sidestone Press, 2016.

"Indian Entities Recognized by and Eligible to Receive Services from the United States Bureau of Indian Affairs." *Federal Register* 89, no. 5 (2024): 944-48.

Joachim, Joana. "'Embodiment and Subjectivity': Intersectional Black Feminist Curatorial Practices in Canada." *RACAR* 43 (2018): 34-47.

Johnson, Kate. *Radical Friendship: Seven Ways to Love Yourself and Find Your People in an Unjust World*. Boulder, CO: Shambhala, 2021.

Kaur, Harmeet. "Indigenous People across the US Want Their Land Back—and the Movement Is Gaining Momentum." CNN, November 26, 2020. Web.

Kimmerer, Robin Wall. *Braiding Sweetgrass*. Minneapolis: Milkweed Editions, 2012.

LaGrand, James B. *Indian Metropolis: Native Americans in Chicago, 1945-1975*. Champaign: University of Illinois Press, 2002.

Lajimodiere, Denise. *Stringing Rosaries: The History, the Unforgivable, and the Healing of Northern Plains American Indian Boarding School Survivors*. Fargo: North Dakota State University Press, 2019.

Landry, Alysa. "Diné Artist Appeals to All Ages." *Navajo Times*, December 6, 2012. Web.

Lane, Clare. "Vast Mural Will Depict Chicago's Indian Roots." *Chicago Tribune*, June 5, 2009. Web.

LaPier, Rosalyn, and David R. M. Beck. *City Indian: Native American Activism in Chicago, 1893-1934*. Lincoln: University of Nebraska Press, 2015.

Lauerman, Connie. "'What Do They Have to Prove?' Native American Artists Grapple with Questions of Culture, Identity and Seeing beyond Stereotypes." *Chicago Tribune*, December 24, 1995.

Lee, Robert. "Morrill Act of 1862 Indigenous Land Parcels Database." *High Country News*, March 2020. Web.

Lonetree, Amy. *Decolonizing Museums: Representing Native America in National and Tribal Museums*. Illustrated edition. Chapel Hill: University of North Carolina Press, 2012.

Low, John. "Chicago Is on the Lands of the Potawatomi: Why Land Acknowledgments for Chicago Should Acknowledge This Historical Fact." *Chicago History* 46, no. 2 (2023): 16-27.

Low, John. *Imprints: The Pokagon Band of Potawatomi Indians and the City of Chicago*. East Lansing: Michigan State University Press, 2016.

Malagón, Elvia. "As Chicago's Native American Population Grows, More Efforts Are Underway to Build Community." *Chicago Sun-Times*, April 8, 2022. Web.

Meadows, William C., and Kenny Harragarra. "The Kiowa Drawings of Gotebo (1847-1927): A Self-Portrait of Cultural and Religious Transition." *Plains Anthropologist* 52, no. 202 (2007): 229-44.

Momaday, N. Scott. "An American Land Ethic." In *The Man Made of Words*. New York: St. Martin's Press, 1997.

Native American Educational Services. American Indian Economic Development Association Records, 1869-2001. University of Chicago Library.

Neils, Elaine M. *Reservation to City: Indian Migration and Federal Relocation*. Chicago: University of Chicago Department of Geography, 1971.

Ortiz, Virgil. "Art Rooted in the Earth." Interview by Barron B. Bass, May 4, 2022. In *Frame of Mind*, podcast, produced by the Metropolitan Museum of Art and Goat Rodeo.

Poco, Loniel. "Interview with Loniel Poco, Director of the Chicago Indian Artists Guild, Chicago, Illinois." By Roberta Fiske-Rusciano and R. Hajnal. Chicago Ethnic Arts Project Collection, Library of Congress, May 19, 1977. Audio. Web.

Pokagon, Simon. *The Red Man's Rebuke*. Hartford, MI: C. H. Engle, 1893. Web.

Report of the John Evans Study Committee. Northwestern University, 2014. Web.

Report of the John Evans Study Committee. University of Denver, November 2014. Web.

Rifkin, Mark. *Beyond Settler Time: Temporal Sovereignty and Indigenous Self-Determination*. Durham, NC: Duke University Press, 2017.

Rudolph, Cameron. "MSU Researcher Shows Emerald Ash Borer Threatening Tree Species Vital to Indigenous Cultures." AgBioResearch, Michigan State University, September 19, 2023. Web.

Schilling, Vincent. "Watching over the Past: Virgil Ortiz's Futuristic Creations Are Perpetuating Cochiti Pueblo Pottery-Making Traditions." *American Indian* 23, no. 2 (2022). Web.

Scott, Chadd. "Center for Native Futures Gallery Opening in Chicago." *Forbes*, September 14, 2023. Web.

Silva, Kara. "Gallery Celebrates 5th Anniversary." *Chicago Tribune*, March 11, 2010.

Simmons, Dan. "Remembering Name, Tribe, Serial Number: Veterans Wall Honors American Indians' Military Service." *Chicago Tribune,* November 29, 2009.

Simpson, Leanne Betasamosake. *Dancing on Our Turtle's Back: Stories of Nishnaabeg Recreation, Resurgence and a New Emergence*. Winnipeg: Arbeiter Ring, 2011.

Skolnick, Sharon. "Interview with Sharon Skolnick, Artist and Coordinator of the Foster Care Program at the American Indian Health Service, Chicago, Illinois." By Roberta Fiske-Rusciano and R. Hajnal. Chicago Ethnic Arts Project Collection, Library of Congress, May 19, 1977. Audio. Web.

Skolnick, Sharon (Okee-Chee), and Manny Skolnick. *Where Courage Is Like a Wild Horse: The World of an Indian Orphanage*. Lincoln, NE: Bison Books, 2001.

Sleeper-Smith, Susan. *Indian Women and French Men: Rethinking Cultural Encounter in the Western Great Lakes*. Native Americans of the Northeast. Amherst: University of Massachusetts Press, 2001.

Smith, Linda Tuhiwai. "Decolonising Cultural Institutions: An Urgent, Necessary, Challenging yet Hopeful Journey beyond Colonialism." In *Uneven Bodies (Reader)*, edited by Ruth Buchanan, Aileen Burns, Johan Lundh, and Hanahiva Rose. Ngāmotu New Plymouth: Govett-Brewster Art Gallery, 2021.

Smith, Linda Tuhiwai. *Decolonizing Methodologies: Research and Indigenous Peoples*. London: Zed Books, 2021.

Straus, Terry, and Grant P. Arndt, eds. *Native Chicago*. 2nd edition. Chicago: Albatross Press, 2002.

Teaiwa, Teresia. "The Ancestors We Get to Choose: White Influences I Won't Deny." In *Theorizing Native Studies*, edited by Audra Simpson and Andrea Smith. Durham, NC: Duke University Press, 2014. Web.

This Is Indian Land: Okee-Chee's Vision. Directed by Sharon Okee-Chee Skolnick. Chicago: Shadow Bechtol Studio, 2017.

Two-Rivers, E. Donald. *A Dozen Cold Ones by Two Rivers: Native American Poetry in an Urban Setting*. Chicago: March Abrazo, 1992.

Vaioleti, Timote M. "Talanoa Research Methodology: A Developing Position on Pacific Research." *Waikato Journal of Education* 12 (2006): 21-34.

Whitaker, Kathleen. "Gifts of Pride and Love: The Cultural Significance of Kiowa and Comanche Lattice Cradles." *American Anthropologist* 103, no. 3 (2001): 803-12.

White, John K. "On the Revival of Printing in the Cherokee Language." *Current Anthropology* 3, no. 5 (December 1962): 511-14.

Whitepigeon, Monica. "Native in the Arts Spotlight: Visual Artist Andrea Carlson Talks about Her Chicago *You Are on Potawatomi Land* Mural." *Native News Online*, July 15, 2021. Web.

Yohe, Jill Ahlberg, and Teri Greeves, eds. *Hearts of Our People: Native Women Artists*. Minneapolis: Minneapolis Institute of Art; Seattle: University of Washington Press, 2019.

Contributors

Kathleen Bickford Berzock, PhD, is Associate Director of Curatorial Affairs at The Block Museum of Art, Northwestern University.

Jordan Poorman Cocker (Kiowa) is Curator of Indigenous Art at Crystal Bridges Museum of American Art and Terra Foundation Guest Co-Curator for Woven Being.

Marisa Cruz Branco (Isleta Pueblo/Portuguese) is the Terra Foundation Curatorial Research Fellow at The Block Museum of Art.

Janet Dees is the former Steven and Lisa Munster Tananbaum Curator of Modern and Contemporary Art at The Block Museum of Art.

Denise Lajimodiere, PhD (Turtle Mountain Band of Ojibwe), is an educator, a birch-bark-biting artist, a poet, and a dancer.

Jacqueline Lopez is a doctoral student in the Department of History at Northwestern University and The Block Museum of Art's 2024–25 Interdisciplinary Graduate Fellow.

John Low, PhD (Pokagon Band of Potawatomi), is Professor in the Department of Comparative Studies at the Ohio State University and Director of the Newark Earthworks Center.

Blaire Morseau, PhD (Pokagon Band of Potawatomi), is Assistant Professor in the Department of Religious Studies at Michigan State University.

Anne Terry Straus, PhD, is retired from the University of Chicago and the Native American Educational Services College.

Plates, pp. 138–51: Photographs by Clare Britt.

Front endpapers: Denise Lajimodiere (Turtle Mountain Band of Ojibwe, born 1951), *Flower*, 2024, birch bark, 6 × 3¼ inches, collection of Kelly Church; Wanesia Misquadace (Minnesota Lake Superior Chippewa Tribe, Fond du Lac Band, born 1971), *Three Turtles* (detail), 2024, birch bark, 4 × 2½ inches, collection of Kelly Church.

Back endpapers: Wanesia Misquadace (Minnesota Lake Superior Chippewa Tribe, Fond du Lac Band, born 1971), *Three Turtles* (detail), 2024; Kelly Church (Match-E-Be-Nash-She-Wish Band of Pottawatomi/Ottawa, born 1967), *Dragonflies and Turtle*, 2024, birch bark, 6 × 5 inches, collection of the artist.

This book is published in conjunction with the exhibition *Woven Being: Art for Zhegagoynak/ Chicagoland,* presented at the Mary and Leigh Block Museum of Art, Northwestern University, from January 25 through July 13, 2025.

Woven Being is part of Art Design Chicago, a citywide collaboration initiated by the Terra Foundation for American Art that highlights the city's artistic heritage and creative communities. Lead support for *Woven Being* is generously provided by the Terra Foundation for American Art. Major support is provided by the Andy Warhol Foundation for the Visual Arts. This project is supported in part by the National Endowment for the Arts, The Joyce Foundation, and a grant from the Illinois Arts Council. Additional generous support is provided by the Sandra L. Riggs Publication Fund and the Alumnae of Northwestern University.

Library of Congress Control Number: 2024950327
ISBN 978-1-7325684-4-0

Published by the Mary and Leigh Block Museum of Art
Northwestern University
40 Arts Circle Drive
Evanston, IL 60208
blockmuseum.northwestern.edu

Distributed by University of Washington Press
uwapress.uw.edu

Produced by Marquand Books, Seattle
marquandbooks.com

Edited by Kristin Kearns
Designed by OTAMI—
Typeset in Atlas by Brynn Warriner
Proofread by Carrie Wicks
Color management by I/O Color, Seattle
Printed and bound in China by Artron Art Group

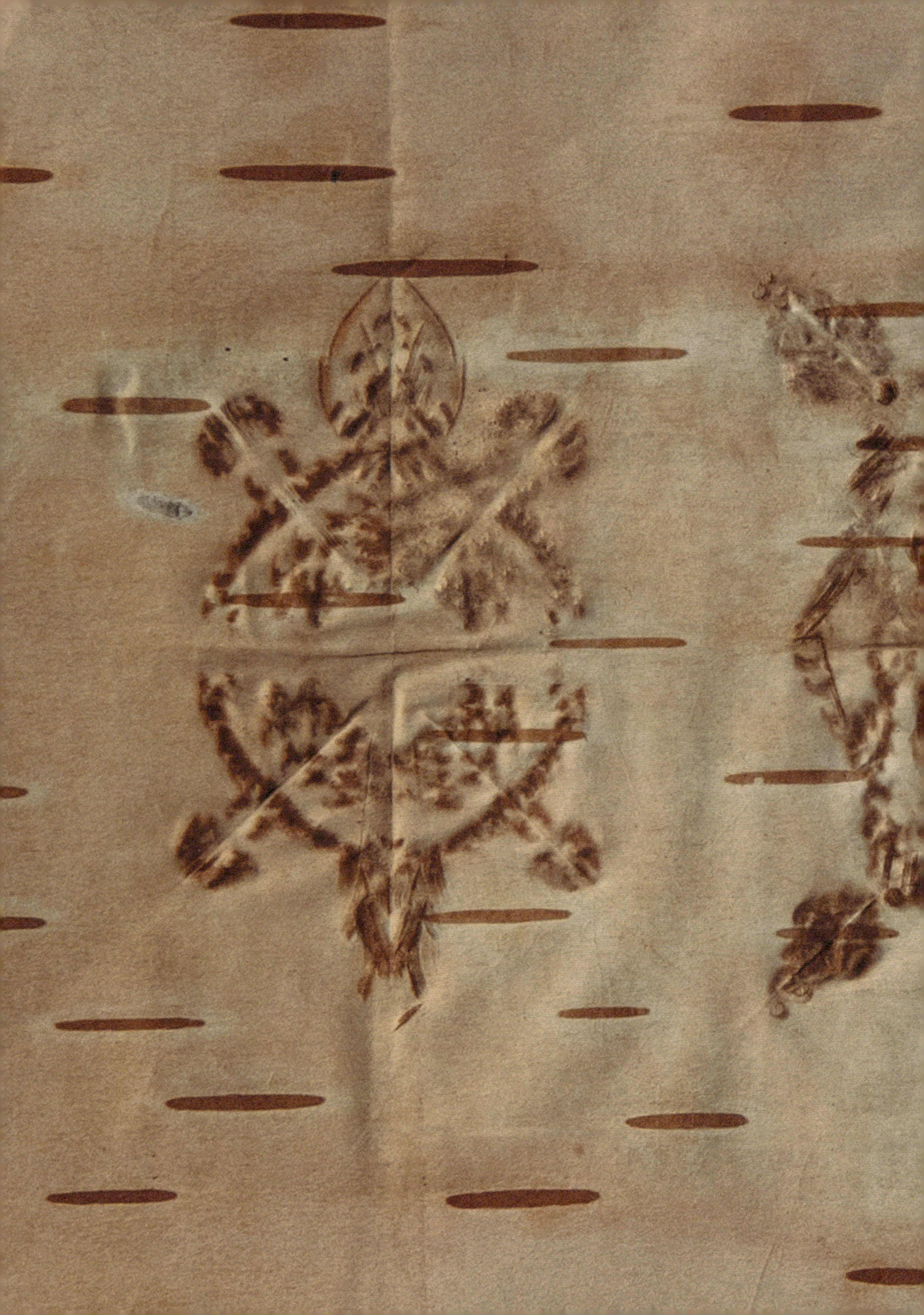

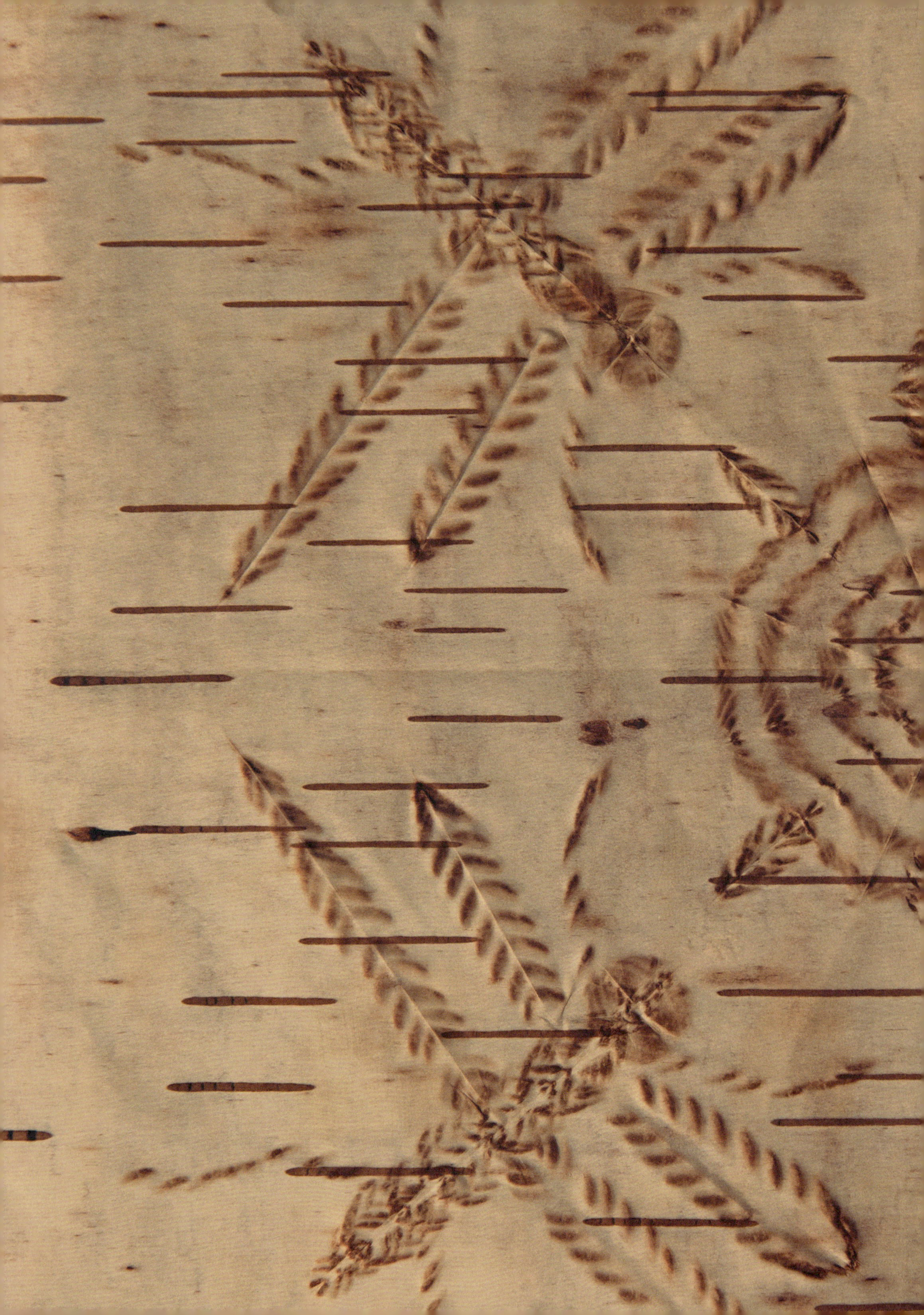